IN OUR INTEREST

ALEXANDER KUSTOV

IN OUR INTEREST

How Democracies Can Make
Immigration Popular

COLUMBIA UNIVERSITY PRESS

NEW YORK

Columbia University Press
Publishers Since 1893
New York   Chichester, West Sussex

Library of Congress Cataloging-in-Publication Data
Names: Kustov, Alexander, author.
Title: In our interest : how democracies can make
immigration popular / Alexander Kustov.
Description: New York : Columbia University Press, 2025. |
Includes bibliographical references and index.
Identifiers: LCCN 2024045092 | ISBN 9780231218108 (hardback) |
ISBN 9780231218115 (trade paperback) | ISBN 9780231562072 (ebook)
Subjects: LCSH: Western countries—Emigration and immigration—
Public opinion. | Western countries—Emigration and immigration—
Government policy. | National interest—Western countries. | Immigration
opponents—Western countries. | Skilled labor—Western countries. |
Foreign workers—Western countries.
Classification: LCC JV6255 .K87 2025 | DDC 325.4—dc23/eng/20250212

Cover design: Chang Jae Lee
Cover image: © Shutterstock

GPSR Authorized Representative: Easy Access System Europe,
Mustamäe tee 50, 10621 Tallinn, Estonia, gpsr.requests@easproject.com

For love of country and cost–benefit analysis.

CONTENTS

PREFACE

When it comes to policies that restrict emigration, there appear
to be trillion-dollar bills on the sidewalk.

Michael A. Clemens, "Economics and Emigration"

OVER THE PAST TWO CENTURIES, the United States has been the top destination for immigrants around the world, signifying its strength and desirability as an influential world power. But today the United States can no longer pride itself on being the most common destination for global workers or the ultimate refuge for people fleeing adversity. And it can no longer assume it is the first choice for "the best and the brightest." Other countries like Canada are now competing equally for top talent and other foreign workers. The increasingly convoluted U.S. immigration system has propelled prospective immigrants to apply their skills elsewhere. Unnecessarily restrictive legal immigration policies have gradually made the United States unable even to retain many of the foreign professionals educated at its own universities.[1]

From my experience, cosmopolitan-minded immigration advocates and academics like me are rarely moved by the plight of potential legal immigrants unable to migrate because of per-country caps or U.S. businesses that fail to recruit new employees because of visa quotas. While presenting some of the research in this book at conferences, I have often been asked why anyone should care about unrealized skilled immigration when so many less fortunate immigrants are demonized, deported, and denied entry at the border right now.

My hope is that this book and the evidence my colleagues and I have amassed over the years will convince skeptics on the more humanitarian side that a more popular, trusted immigration system could benefit everyone, including the most vulnerable populations, even if it would sometimes mean prioritizing some immigrants over others.

I also recognize that, for many on the more nationalistic side, the very idea of making immigration popular may be unappealing. After all, immigration can impose real costs on communities, including increased job competition, resource strain, ethnic and racial tensions, and security risks. Many also understandably feel uneasy witnessing cultural shifts in their communities and what seems to be regular border chaos. Despite my strong conviction that immigration can greatly benefit all parties, I myself gradually revised my views on the desirability of a free-for-all approach to immigration after learning more about the challenges faced by otherwise well-governed countries like Sweden.

But immigration and opposition to it will always be with us. Some people naturally want to improve their lives and reunite with their families whereas others prefer to avoid competition and social change when possible. Recognizing the enduring complexity and divisiveness of the issue, this book explores how relatively open immigration can be managed in a way that is *popular* and *in our interest*.

By "making immigration popular," I don't mean advocating for unchecked immigration or any other particular set of policies. Rather, I mean identifying responsive pro-immigration policies that can expand legal pathways *and* garner public support using the best available evidence. Importantly, this also means figuring out how democratic governments can consistently earn voters' trust to pursue responsible programmatic immigration policies even amid variably informed public opinion. This evidence could be informative regardless of moral disagreements. No matter your politics or convictions, it is also arguably in the interest of all citizens, their representatives, and potential immigrants alike to have a well-functioning, pragmatically open immigration system that commands broad support and legitimacy among citizens in a democracy.

Indeed, the continuous failure of the U.S. government to streamline its immigration admission system has arguably been a tragedy for all involved parties. It has been a tragedy for millions of potential economic immigrants trapped in poorly governed, authoritarian environments inconducive to achieving their fullest potential. It has also been a tragedy for the United States and its citizens, especially those unable to reunite with their families abroad, start businesses, or receive high-quality health care because of labor shortages. And it has been a tragedy for the most vulnerable people fleeing adversity who have been denied their legal asylum rights because politicians have either capitalized on voters' fears about or feared voter backlash to freer immigration.

Yet all attempts at comprehensive immigration reform over the last several decades have bitterly failed. Among the most promising efforts was the 2013 initiative by a bipartisan group of senators who introduced the "Gang of Eight" bill. The bill included sensible measures to strengthen border security, provide a path to citizenship for undocumented immigrants, and, most importantly, liberalize the legal immigration system. The bill passed in the Senate but was never voted on in the House of Representatives because of insufficient support on both sides of the aisle.

Several plausible factors contributed to this disappointing result, including congressional gridlock, competing interest groups, and extreme activists. Many rightly blamed the increasing influence of nativist groups among Republicans and the inability of pro-immigrant Democrats to compromise with more moderate members of their own party. Still, it is hard to deny that voters' general skepticism of immigration was itself a major factor.[2]

Democratic and Republican lawmakers have clearly failed to convince their constituents that increasing immigration is good for the country and to effectively communicate the benefits of the "Gang of Eight" bill. Immigration reform in 2013 faced strong opposition from conservative groups, who framed the bill as a grant of amnesty to unauthorized immigrants. Democrats failed to counter these arguments with clear and compelling reasons for supporting the bill, such as its potential to boost the economy and improve national security. Ultimately, the bill did not pass in the House of Representatives because of opposition from many congresspeople who feared that supporting the bill would be unpopular among their voters and thus harm their chances of being reelected. More than a decade later, as I write this paragraph in 2024, the latest bipartisan attempt at immigration reform has met the same fate.

The recent negative shift in U.S. immigration attitudes and the re-election of President Donald Trump further underscore the persistent challenges in building public support for more productive immigration policies. While some suspect that conservative politicians may benefit from a perpetually dysfunctional immigration system, all administrations, including Trump's second term, have a vested interest in securing public approval for their own immigration policies. Notably, some of Trump's earlier hardline measures, such as the family separation policy, proved deeply unpopular and politically damaging. As he and his allies push for even harsher measures that do not clearly benefit Americans, including mass deportations, they risk provoking significant public backlash.

Although the United States is notorious for its congressional gridlock and perpetual border crisis, it is not alone in its dysfunctional immigration politics. Many well-governed European countries have similarly failed to earn voters' trust on the issue and open up to even the most skilled foreign workers. Sweden, for instance, has managed to attract only a few thousand foreign professionals each year over the last few decades despite having the most generous—though increasingly unpopular—immigration policies among high-income democracies.[3] The struggle to balance openness with public trust has also paved the way for the rise of anti-immigration populists on both sides of the Atlantic, who capitalize on voter dissatisfaction with immigration policies to gain political ground.

In contrast, Canada's *more selective yet ultimately more open immigration policies* have allowed it to become the most desirable global destination, surpassing the U.S. immigration numbers in relative and sometimes in absolute terms. Perhaps even more remarkably, Canada has consistently accepted more refugees than any other affluent democracy while enjoying overwhelming support from its citizens.[4] Indeed, while much commentary focuses on how some right-wing politicians in the United States and elsewhere exploit anti-immigrant sentiments for votes, it is equally important to examine why such tactics find less traction in places like Canada and more traction in places like Sweden.

* * *

I know many researchers, myself included, who abandoned all their previous interests, having become obsessed with the idea of migration as a major form of economic development after seeing a table entitled "Efficiency Gain from Elimination of International Barriers (Percent of World GDP)" in Michael A. Clemens's famous 2011 paper, cited in the epigraph to this preface. This otherwise obscure technical paper radicalized numerous academics and practitioners on the premise of more open immigration because it strongly suggests that the economic benefits of liberalizing international migration absolutely trump those of any other possible international policy reforms.

I had a similar realization about how to make immigration popular when I first saw poll results showing how much more supportive people are of high-skilled immigration than they are of other types, and how much more the perceived national benefits of such immigration outweigh every other possible factor, including ethnic and racial prejudice. I encountered these results repeatedly in my own research and the research of my colleagues, and I saw them replicated in other countries, using various methods. I also saw such policies successfully tried out in the real world by a handful of governments. So, like the enormous efficiency gains of relaxing immigration barriers, the skills premium in the public opinion of immigration has not exactly been a secret. Scholars may still disagree about its causes, but I've always felt that the implications of these results for *making other types of immigration popular* are still not appreciated enough.

Over the past several decades, much ink has been spilled debating why voters oppose immigration. Social scientists and political commentators alike have identified a variety of possible factors at play, from people's "self-interest," "in-group favoritism," and "cultural anxiety" to the misinformation spread by opportunistic politicians exploiting these and other biases. My book takes stock of this research and distills it into a simple, coherent framework of voters' widespread altruistic nationalism and their responses to more or less demonstrably beneficial policies. This approach aims to clarify the confusion of myriad disparate findings, providing scholars and policymakers with a solid basis to more effectively understand and influence public opinion on immigration and beyond.

But I must admit that the subtitle of this book, "How Democracies Can Make Immigration Popular," is meant to serve as a lure. Based on my research over the past decade, I've come to realize that it is not easy, or even entirely possible, to make immigration popular by changing how we talk about it. Unfortunately, there's no simple information campaign or behavioral nudge that can suddenly enlighten voters about the benefits of immigration or win their support.

Instead, my research reveals that few voters are committed humanitarians or cosmopolitans, and even such individuals usually prefer immigration policies that prioritize their nation's interests over global ones. Commendable as they are, policies explicitly designed to aid foreigners are often unpopular, even among the most liberal voters. Notably, I am unaware of any democratic context in which principled cosmopolitanism and open-border policies can secure an electoral majority or even a plurality.

The successful experiences of countries like Canada, however, show that consistently high immigration *can* receive overwhelming public support under certain conditions. Perfecting immigration governance is challenging, as the experiences of most countries demonstrate. Yet doing so is essential, given the millions of lives and the billions, if not trillions, of dollars at stake.

This book is about how to make immigration popular slowly and gradually through the hard work of crafting better policies and meeting voters where they are, with all their imperfections. It's also about what it means for democratic governments to be responsive to their voters, who may have legitimate reservations about immigration, and to govern responsibly by realizing the economic opportunities of freer immigration.

Despite what you may think, this is not another book advocating for immigration, explaining why it is good, and urging everyone to be pro-immigration. Nor is it about what makes people so prejudiced against foreigners or what we can do to reduce prejudice. This is also not another exploration of how widespread prejudice makes people vote for right-wing populists against their own interests or how populists scapegoat immigrants to rally their vote.

Though this book is based on a comprehensive analysis of numerous cross-national surveys and original experimental studies, the essence of my argument is deeply intuitive. Voters care about their compatriots, so they prefer immigration and other policies that benefit their own countries. Democratic governments similarly try to enact immigration policies that advance national interests while being responsive to their voters. Pro-immigration policies that aim to attract skilled and other wanted workers are much more economically beneficial *and* much more popular among voters than any other types of pro-immigration policies. As a result, enacting pro-immigration reforms that demonstrably benefit receiving countries is the most effective way for responsible governments to durably persuade their citizens that freer immigration is a good thing.

There is no catch-22. As I show, when governments introduce new immigration policies that open new legal pathways for foreign workers *and* straightforwardly benefit their countries, voters do not lash out against them. On the contrary, relaxing immigration restrictions on skilled and other economically beneficial workers can only increase public support for immigration in general. When consistently high immigration flows of workers come to be viewed as legitimate in the electorate over time, room opens up for family, humanitarian, and other types of immigration.

Yet this argument could not be more controversial. On one hand, a number of right-wing, nativist, and populist political coalitions across the world are actively trying to reduce most of the existing immigration flows in their countries. They rightly understand the importance of government responsiveness to widespread nationalistic sentiments and legitimate concerns about certain types of immigration. But they generally exaggerate the potential threats from more open policies and ignore the vast unrealized benefits of greater human mobility. They claim to represent the people, yet they undermine even the most nationally beneficial forms of immigration that are popular among voters.

On the other hand, the existing left-wing, cosmopolitan, and liberal political coalitions—which are much more sympathetic to foreigners—often do not appear to have a realistic political vision of how to secure a more open immigration system in a democracy. They rightly focus on protecting the rights of existing immigrants, but they often fail to assuage the concerns of skeptical voters regarding growing numbers of new immgirants. They tend to dismiss the idea of prioritizing some immigrants over others, even when it is clear that doing so would be in the best interest of both citizens and immigrants. If no human is illegal and everyone has equal rights regardless of their citizenship status, then there would be no point in ensuring that a given immigration policy benefits the receiving country. The problem with this idealistic vision is that it is unlikely to ever be popular in a democracy in which few people prioritize their global humanitarian impulses over their nation. And the result is the same: even the most commonsense reforms to liberalize some immigration for substantial mutual benefit do not have enough votes to get passed.

My argument also goes against a large literature and conventional wisdom that documents various ethnic and racial biases and suggests that these biases prevent some people from ever supporting immigration. Indeed, when reading the vast academic literature and popular commentary on the topic, one can easily get the impression that opposition to immigration is predominantly—if not entirely—about racism, ethnocentrism, nativism, xenophobia, and ignorance. But, unfortunately, prejudice is a constant of the human condition that cannot be easily changed.

I do not dispute these findings about racism per se. But I question their implications and applicability. Trying to "fix" racism at scale within a few electoral cycles may not be the most pragmatic goal when millions are actively harmed by restrictive immigration policies every day.

What makes countries like Canada, which accept a large number of immigrants, unique is not that they have somehow managed to remove the racist tendencies from their citizens or make them fully enlightened. Nor is it that these countries have been merely lucky not to have a large border region. What sets such countries apart is that their immigration policies demonstrably benefit their citizens, and voters across the political spectrum can understand this, regardless of their level of education or policy knowledge.

Consequently, this book focuses on how to make attracting more new immigrants popular, rather than on reducing prejudice against immigrants who are already here or on improving their treatment by native majorities. While reducing prejudice is undoubtedly important and has been extensively explored, the challenge of increasing durable popular support for more open immigration admission policies has received less attention. This oversight is unfortunate because immigration admission policies ultimately determine how many people can enter, how well they will be able to integrate, and how native-born citizens will respond to them socially and politically. Indeed, there is little point in improving how society treats immigrants if there are and can only be a few, if any, immigrants to begin with.

While I believe my book holds important implications for policymaking, it is fundamentally positive, not normative. It examines the factors influencing people's views on immigration without prescribing what governments and advocates should do about it. Hence, while some readers might concur that immigration can become popular only through more selective policies, they may not agree that governments should pursue such selectivity, or vice versa. Similarly, the evidence provided in this book neither supports nor justifies imposing immigration restrictions under the guise of "merit-based" national interest, a stance frequently taken by populist right-wing governments as though it were unquestionable.

Immigration is a difficult issue on which many reasonable people disagree both factually and morally. There is unlikely to be an ultimate policy solution that would satisfy all relevant parties, even among those already sympathetic to immigration. That is why promoting more demonstrably beneficial immigration admission policies is not meant to be the only way to legitimize free immigration in the electorate. Changing social norms and cultural narratives, running information campaigns, and appealing to humanitarianism may be as important in certain contexts and among certain groups. Making immigration popular is also not meant to be the only way to improve immigration policy.

Still, to make freer immigration possible and sustainable, this book suggests that governments need to first prioritize demonstrably beneficial immigration. They have to prioritize such immigration in terms of policy design and implementation, not just communication. Instead of trying to open borders to all immigration or rejecting enforcement of existing restrictions, it may be wise to tag sideways and start with the least controversial policies, those related to streamlining skilled immigration, family reunification, student mobility, and bilateral agreements for temporary workers to fill specific vacancies.

While such selective immigration policies may seem hard-hearted or even discriminatory to some, it is important to recognize that *all* immigration restrictions are discriminatory by definition since they treat people differently based on their citizenship status. In this sense, the most discriminatory immigration is closed immigration, not selective immigration. Disregarding voters' widespread and legitimate concerns about the benefits of existing policies, even for well-intentioned humanitarian reasons, may come at a cost for the world's most vulnerable migrants.

IN OUR INTEREST

INTRODUCTION

Is Freer Immigration in Our Interest?

WHEN ASKED ABOUT THE MOST IMPORTANT ISSUE facing their governments, many voters in European Union (EU) countries and in the United States are increasingly saying immigration. However, the political conflict over the right to human mobility is not new. The question of migration has sparked controversy since the inception of modern democratic institutions: both citizens and their representatives have often been divided over who gets to be a member of their community. A large literature on the topic notwithstanding, it is unclear what combination of factors motivates the migration conflict and whether any democratic policy compromises are preferable to the status quo.

While suspicion of foreigners has probably been a constant feature of human societies, the almost total state-imposed regulation of human mobility as we see it today is a rather novel development. With the decline of colonialism and the spread of nationalism across the world, the idea that democratically elected sovereign governments have a right to restrict immigration as they see fit—provided they respect basic human rights and other binding international obligations—has become a widely accepted legal principle. Over the past century, most governments in rich countries have exercised this right extensively by adopting highly restrictive immigration policies, effectively banning most of the world's population from moving and being employed in those countries.

According to most economic estimates, this new status quo is very inefficient and harmful to the global poor who are forced to live in unproductive environments, unable to meet their needs or aspirations. Further, immigration restrictions often come at a price to the national economy—and to the freedoms of citizens who are unable to reunite with their families abroad. However, public opinion surveys consistently report that most voters do not want to increase immigration. Accordingly, elected officials tend to dismiss any possibility of relaxing restrictions, even for the most beneficial immigration policies, as politically unfeasible. Many scholars and pundits also worry that any pro-immigration change could be counterproductive by leading to a populist surge such as that behind Trump or Brexit.

Such opposition among educated voters with little ethnic or racial (hereafter just "racial") prejudice is hard to explain using existing theories that attribute anti-immigration sentiments to deep-seated prejudice. The extent to which many people currently oppose immigration is especially puzzling given that political behaviors and preferences are often motivated by prosocial motivations rather than self-interest. Why do otherwise "good" people—who genuinely care about others—support policies that severely restrict individual freedoms and leave the world and even their country worse off? More practically, under what conditions might most voters accept freer immigration? Ultimately, can national governments realize the potential economic gains of freer international migration while still being responsive to the wishes of skeptical citizens?

To address these questions, this book looks beyond the common stereotype of inherently prejudiced voters to consider the role of genuine altruism toward compatriots as a central driver of both public support and opposition to immigration. Pooling insights from my published work over the last decade and the previously disparate literatures on the drivers of immigration opinion, I develop a theory of *nationalism as parochial altruism* in politics. The theory argues that many people are ready to bear personal costs to benefit others, but among those others, they prioritize fellow citizens. As a result, voters, and especially those who are more altruistic, tend to oppose freer immigration when they believe it threatens the well-being of their compatriots. But such opposition is *conditional*, not categorical. Since immigration can also be an enormous asset for receiving countries, I argue that the widespread nationalistic sentiments that currently make people wary of immigration can also lead them to embrace it when it is clearly in their nation's interest.

Building on original surveys involving the use of real-stake experiments from the United Kingdom and the United States, as well as a wealth of cross-national public opinion data, I first corroborate that most people are in fact "altruistic nationalists" who *conditionally* oppose immigration. That is, people oppose immigration because of their concern about national well-being, as well as common perceptions about immigration's negative national impacts. Based on my use of a novel incentivized measure of elicited preferences, I show that most altruists who donate to domestic rather than global charities are as or even more anti-immigration than egoists who do not donate at all. Using a hypothetical policy choice experiment, I then show that most voters—especially those who are altruistic—support increasing immigration even from non-European countries when these policies benefit their compatriots. Throughout the book, I also repeatedly demonstrate that people's humanitarian motivations by themselves are not sufficient to generate public support for pro-immigration reforms.

What are the practical implications of this new evidence for persuading voters of the benefits of immigration and designing successful pro-immigration reforms? To understand how voters react to various pro-immigration reforms, I created a cross-national dataset combining the best available historical public opinion, voting, and policy data from across Europe and the United States. Despite the common concerns of policymakers in the aftermath of Trump and Brexit, I show that meaningful pro-immigration reforms that open more legal pathways for foreign workers and their families are unlikely to backfire because of populist backlash.

I then show, however, that simply framing immigration policies in terms of national interest or correcting misperceptions is not enough. As indicated by my analysis of cross-national and historical data and an in-depth qualitative comparison of Canada and Sweden, the countries that respectively exemplify the opposing utilitarian and humanitarian approaches to immigration, successful persuasion is a long process that must be grounded in *demonstrably* (i.e., explicitly and straightforwardly) *beneficial* policies. In other words, making immigration popular is not just about telling a better story about why immigration is good but also about governments convincingly demonstrating it by adopting better policies that meet voters where they are.

Pro-immigration advocates have often branded and dismissed their anti-immigration counterparts as prejudiced, but this has been to little avail: most borders are still closed. This book offers a clear path forward: enacting gradual pro-immigration reforms that prioritize skilled and otherwise needed foreign workers. Importantly, such demonstrably beneficial policies go beyond attracting the best and the brightest to include efforts to fill labor shortages, boost regional development, and reunite families.

As the title *In Our Interest* optimistically suggests, adopting more open yet selective immigration regulations would not just be good policy; it could also be good politics since surprisingly few voters on either the left or the right dislike immigration for its own sake. At the same time, dismissing people's legitimate concerns about the drawbacks of overly generous immigration policies may come at a cost for the mobility of the world's most vulnerable populations. Only when voters are confident that their government is managing immigration in their interest can they support freer immigration in general, including that of those fleeing persecution and poverty.

THE POLITICAL TRAGEDY OF INTERNATIONAL MIGRATION

Although 280 million people today live outside of their country of birth, international migrants have steadily accounted for only 3 percent of the world's population over the last century.[1] Meanwhile, more than 10 percent, or seven hundred million people, say that they would like to permanently emigrate to another country.[2] Among those, most would like to move to the United States, followed by the United Kingdom, Canada, Australia, Germany, and France. However, despite recent increases in immigration numbers, these high-income countries admit only a small fraction of would-be migrants. As one of the best illustrations of the disconnect between people's revealed aspirations and opportunities, there are usually ten to twenty million qualified applicants for the U.S. diversity visa against a quota of only fifty thousand.[3] In sum, many people want to emigrate but cannot.

This book purposefully focuses on the high-income democracies that have sufficient capacity to absorb large immigration flows and where many immigrants actually want to go. The list of *countries where immigration policy matters globally* includes the United States, Canada, Australia, the United Kingdom, EU countries, Japan, and South Korea, among others. In these desirable destinations, there is no need to distinguish between consistently high immigration flows and relatively open immigration admission policies that would enable such flows.

By *relatively (more) open immigration admission policies* or *freer immigration*, as I use these comparative terms conservatively throughout the book, I mean accepting roughly 1 percent or more of a country's population from abroad for legal permanent residence annually. While 1 percent is an arbitrary number, it is in line with the average annual internal migration rates to desirable destinations within countries that place no restrictions on mobility.[4] It is a conservative figure because there are examples of much larger annual immigration flows being successfully absorbed by receiving countries, including the Soviet immigration to Israel, which exceeded 4 percent of the population for several years.[5]

Despite the many headlines about mass immigration, the list of desirable countries that have had *consistently* freer immigration defined this way in recent history is surprisingly small: Australia, Canada, New Zealand, and Switzerland. Importantly, the relatively open immigration in these countries is highly managed and controlled. Notably, this list excludes the United States (which admits only around 0.3 percent of its population per year), the United Kingdom (which admits only around 0.5 percent per year), and Sweden (which permanently accepted many refugees in recent years but has since restricted admissions).[6]

The political conflict over international migration has many sides, including disagreements over whom to admit, how best to integrate new arrivals, and how to deal with unauthorized migrants—as well as the often-contentious asylum and refugee determinations. Despite this complexity, however, most immigration policies, as I will show, can be viewed as government laws that regulate the long-term admission of noncitizens to a country. In doing so, these regulations primarily restrict the rights of people to work in a particular jurisdiction based on their country of origin, parentage, and other demographic characteristics.[7] I thus use the term *immigration policy* primarily as a shorthand for any government restriction on long-term international human mobility. Accordingly, this book also considers attitudes toward policies that regulate (the "flows" of) *future immigrant population* as opposed to citizens' opinions about (the "stocks" of) *existing immigrant population*. While important, most other migration-related policies and attitudes are arguably contingent on the number of legal immigrants allowed into a country and their right to stay permanently.[8]

Similar to other policies implemented by democratic governments, the commonly stated purpose of immigration control is to advance the national interest of immigrant-receiving countries (subject to minimal international constraints). Although this message is rarely articulated clearly, such policies usually involve protecting domestic workers from economic competition, protecting public resources from overcrowding, and ensuring general public safety. Somewhat more controversially, such policies may also include the goals of preserving the racial demographic composition, cultural values, and political orientations of the population.[9]

Of course, government policy is only one factor affecting international human movement. For instance, opportunities in receiving countries or the lack thereof in sending countries may also be influential. But migration barriers play the most significant role since they prevent large international flows of people that would occur were those barriers not in place.[10]

Starting at the end of the nineteenth century, the wealthiest nations have increasingly adopted severe government regulations on immigration and thus prohibited the majority of the global population from moving to those countries. The consequences of essentially incentivizing or forcing people to stay where they were born have been profound. Though ordinarily nonviolent, the existing interventions to prevent human migration have substantial economic and human costs.[11]

Just as forcing U.S. citizens to remain in the state where they were born would clearly be counterproductive to the well-being of most Americans, international migration restrictions significantly reduce economic efficiency by misallocating labor to less productive regions, creating what has been described as "the greatest single class of distortions in the global economy."[12] For example, workers moving from an average middle-income country like the Phillipines to the United States can almost quadruple their earnings: a gain of more than $13,600 per year after adjusting for purchasing power.[13] Importantly, while this number highlights the enormous economic costs of U.S. immigration barriers per worker, such losses are not just about immigrants earning less—they are about everyone, including U.S. citizens, missing out on opportunities for mutual benefit. As a result, even the strongest arguments against immigration—such as those highlighting concerns about overcrowding and the potential impact of immigrants' cultures on productivity—do not justify the severity of the current restrictions.[14]

From an ethical standpoint, today's harsh restrictions also conflict with the foundational values of liberal democracies that champion individual freedoms, affecting both immigrants and citizens alike. For instance, controlling immigrants and monitoring their legal status inherently involves controlling citizens and monitoring their legal status, too. Protecting some citizens from perceived negative effects of immigration may also inadvertently harm other citizens who wish to engage with them. All citizens who are unable to reunite with partners or families abroad but who hire immigrants to work for their businesses or benefit from better services because of immigration are clearly not benefiting from immigration restrictions, however well intentioned these restrictions may be.

More practically, as with any other social process, immigration can be made more or less economically beneficial depending on the policy instruments at work. When managed effectively, immigration can present an enormous boon to receiving societies by creating businesses and jobs, increasing investment, and fostering innovation.[15] Further, considering that even a marginal relaxation of current restrictions may generate substantial economic gains, it should be possible to create policy solutions that benefit most parties, including potential "globalization losers" in both receiving and sending countries.[16] The desire of millions of people to emigrate to certain countries is a clear indicator of these countries' tremendous economic success in creating desirable living conditions, and their governments can harness this power to drive growth and prosperity by designing effective immigration policies.

But while domestic immigration policies affect the choices and well-being of everyone globally, they can and, as widely perceived, should be influenced only by citizens via applicable democratic procedures. Consequently, the conventional view is that national governments representing sovereign political communities have the right to control their borders and immigration flows as they see fit regardless of consequences.[17] What most voters in rich countries seem to want now is little, if any, immigration.

THE REALITY OF POPULAR OPPOSITION TO IMMIGRATION

This book examines the conditions under which most voters would support more open immigration admission policies. Nonetheless, it is important to acknowledge that immigration attitudes per se, as with public views on any issue, are only one possible determinant of the respective policy outcomes. In most representative democracies, elected officials are responsive to their constituents only to a limited extent, and this may be especially true in the case of immigration.[18] In fact, a significant amount of the variation in the global rise of immigration restrictions can be explained by changes in interest group composition rather than by public opinion.[19]

Still, even elite-driven accounts of politics usually acknowledge that robust public opposition to immigration remains one of the major barriers to enacting more open and economically efficient policies. Otherwise, it would be hard to explain why politicians rarely run pro-immigration campaigns or emphasize their pro-immigration commitments. When they do, it is usually to address the needs of existing immigrant constituencies rather than to welcome more new-comers.[20] At the same time, for those policymakers who are already in power, immigration is exactly the issue for which it is particularly hard to balance *responsible* governance, or managing mobility to better meet national economic needs, with *responsive* governance, or restricting mobility to meet public demand. As aptly put by Martin Ruhs, public views on immigration constitute an important but "soft" feasibility constraint on more effective policymaking.[21]

Although widespread public negativity toward immigration is well documented and widely understood, the sheer extent to which most voters across countries appear to dislike any kind of large-scale immigration is often overlooked in the academic literature. Of course, it is always possible to receive a seemingly positive pro-immigration response from most respondents by using certain suggestive or socially desirable wording. For instance, a common survey question about whether "immigrants are a strength" appears to elicit support from the majority in many immigrant-receiving countries. Similarly, very few people admit that they do not like having immigrants as neighbors.[22]

Agreeing with a pollster that "immigration is our strength," how-ever, does not imply that you would also support more open immigration admission policies. In fact, public responses to more concrete policy questions about immigration numbers are usually much more negative. From my years of experience working with immigration survey data, I have learned that there is simply no feasible way—no framing technique or particular wording—to make majorities state their support for freer immigration when they do not support it.

Figure 0.1 shows public preferences for immigration in a select group of immigrant-receiving high-income countries as reported in the 2013–2014 Gallup World Poll; these data represent most of the most desirable destinations for potential immigrants. As shown, plurali-ties or even majorities would like to decrease immigration in many of these countries. However, this is not to say that public preferences are more favorable toward immigration elsewhere. The poll also found that only 21 percent of people would like to increase immigration in their countries worldwide (for details on case selection, see chapter 1).

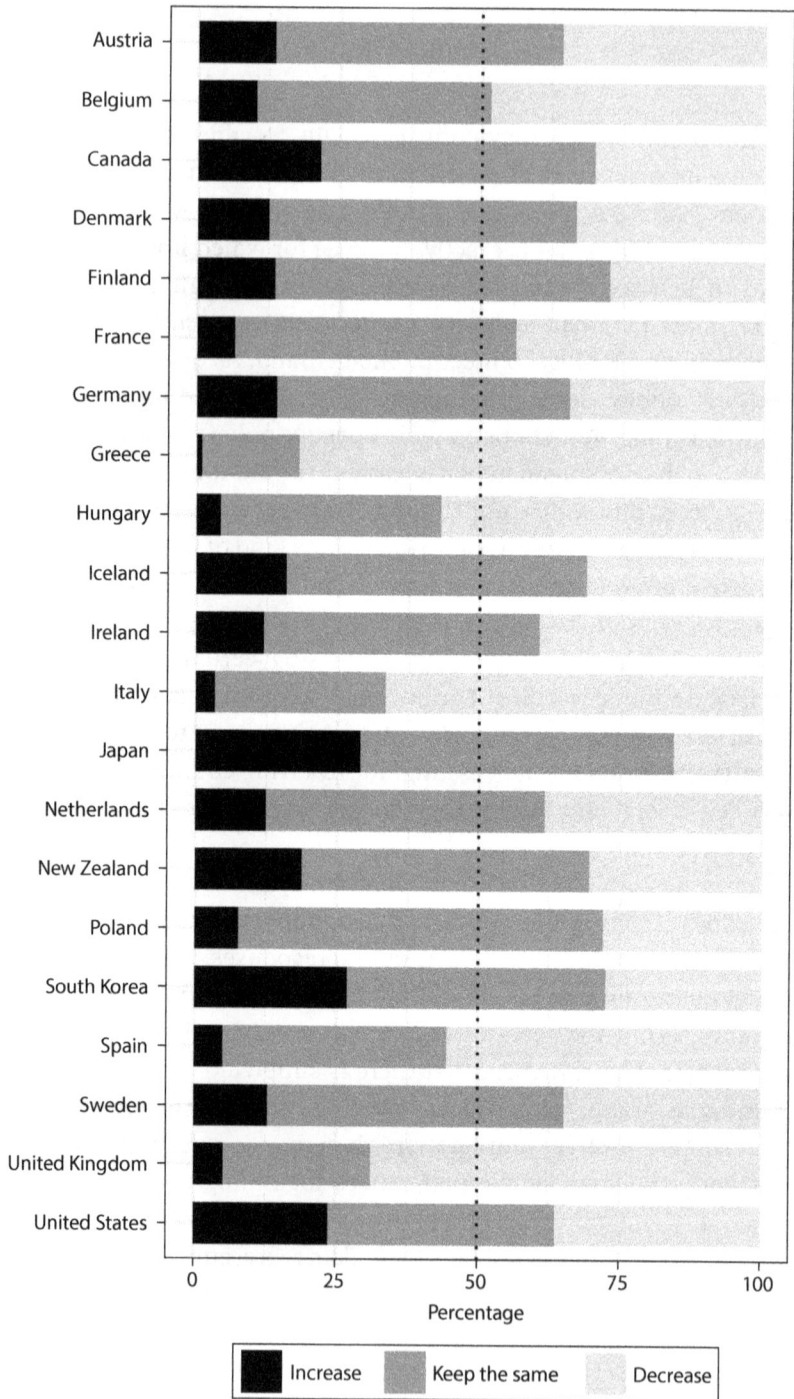

FIGURE 0.1 Immigration attitudes across countries. Immigration attitudes were measured as follows: "In your view, should immigration from this country be kept at its present level, increased, or decreased?"

Source: Gallup World Poll, 2013–14.

However, some long-running polls suggest a growing acceptance of immigration in both the United States and Europe over at least the past two decades.[23] In 2020, for the first time since Gallup started polling on the issue almost sixty years ago, more Americans (34 percent) said they supported increasing immigration rather than decreasing it (28 percent). This marked a significant change from 1965, when only 7 percent supported increasing immigration while 33 percent supported decreasing it. When politicians propose anti-immigration policies, pro-immigration advocates often cite these numbers to signal public support for their position.

I have occasionally been asked about the point of promoting immigration if there is already a secular trend toward greater support for it. The point is that U.S. and European immigration attitudes may not be as positive as these numbers suggest. For starters, even the highest-recorded support for increasing immigration (34 percent) in the United States means that a strong majority (66 percent) still do not support it. Further, as I will show, immigration opinion has more long-term stability than it may initially seem. The same U.S. Gallup poll shows that the 2024 numbers have reverted to pre-2010 levels, with more people supporting decreasing (55 percent) rather than increasing (16 percent) immigration. In fact, accounting for the inherent uncertainty of representative polling, current U.S. attitudes are not much different from those in 2001. That said, immigration attitudes are much more salient and polarized across partisan lines now than they were previously.[24]

In short, increasing immigration is decidedly unpopular among citizens. One of the main correlates and likely drivers behind the strong popular opposition to freer immigration is the widespread public perception of the negative impact of immigration on receiving countries, which I will discuss throughout this book. According to a comprehensive cross-national poll by Ipsos in 2017, for instance, in no immigrant-receiving democracy did a majority of respondents think that immigration was good for their country either economically or culturally. Related to these negative perceptions is widespread public distrust of how governments handle migration. With the possible exception of Canada, there are usually more people who do not trust their government on immigration issues than otherwise, and these numbers are usually worse than those for the public's trust in government more generally, which is already low.[25]

Of course, this general negativity toward immigration is often ascribed to misinformation and prejudice, but it is difficult to argue that millions of voters across so many countries are simply wrong to be skeptical about how immigration is managed in their respective nations. Indeed, while much is known about various factors that predict immigration attitudes—such as education level, racial attitudes, and political ideology—it is hard to find a single subgroup of voters who overwhelmingly support increasing immigration or believe it has positive impacts. Even among college-educated voters, the most pro-immigration group according to much research, those who support increased immigration are still in the minority. The same is true for racially egalitarian and left-wing voters, despite the significance of these factors and their prominence in the academic literature.

In the United Kingdom, for example, the vast majority of university-educated liberal voters with no explicit racial bias would like to maintain or decrease current levels of immigration. According to my calculations based on original survey data from the post-Brexit context, for instance, only 20 percent of such voters support increasing immigration (compared to 10 percent in the general population). Figure 0.2 shows public preferences toward immigration among several groups in the United Kingdom. As can be seen, most voters oppose increasing immigration regardless of education, racial prejudice, or ideology.

A common assumption notwithstanding, a relatively prevalent preference to keep immigration levels "the same as before" can hardly be considered a pro-immigration position given the severity of current restrictions in most countries. While many voters in high-income countries may be unaware of the exact amount of immigration in their countries, there is little evidence that misperceptions regarding such figures have a causal impact on restrictive preferences.[26] When people say that "immigration should be kept the same," they clearly do not embrace freer immigration even if they hold no prejudices against immigrants.

Of course, in modern representative democracies, majorities do not always get what they want. This may be especially true when it comes to immigration admission policies, which are often rather

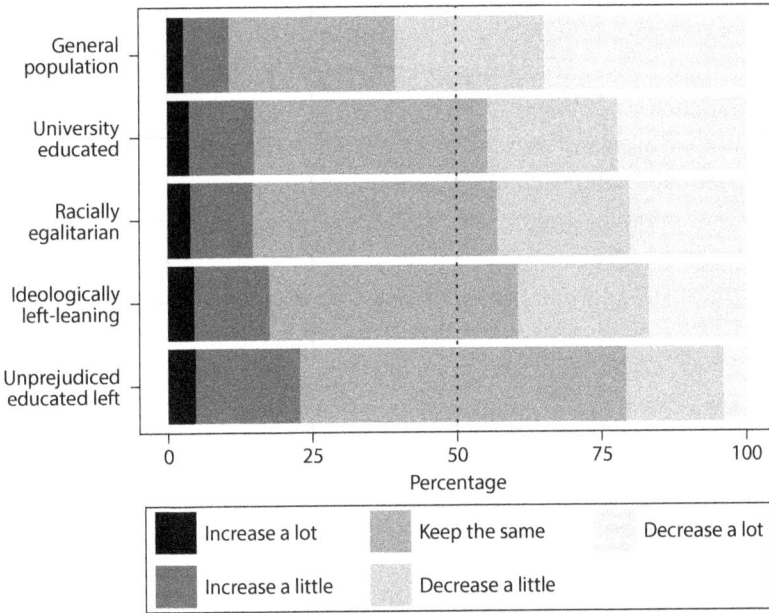

FIGURE 0.2 Immigration attitudes across various voter groups in England.

Source: Original England Qualtrics survey, 2018.

technical and isolated from people's everyday lives. Indeed, ever since Gary Freeman's seminal 1995 article, the disproportionate role of generally pro-immigration elite preferences in immigration policy-making has been widely and thoroughly discussed.[27] As evidenced by the success of anti-immigration politics and the rarity of forceful pro-immigration politics, however, immigration-skeptical public opinion is a major constraint on programmatic pro-immigration policymaking.[28] The fact that borders are now relatively closed for most willing global workers despite the wishes of the elites in immigrant-receiving countries is a testament to this idea.[29]

A recurring theme of this book is that policies can be successful and last only when they command broad support among voters. Considering the general public skepticism over freer immigration, what would it mean for democratic governments to be truly responsive to their citizens when it comes to immigration policy? The answer is not as straightforward as it may seem since democratic governments are also supposed to be responsible and advance the material interests of their citizens—which may often mean increasing immigration levels. Further, as I elaborate on later and document extensively, public preferences toward immigration are much more nuanced than usually assumed, and their apparent negativity is largely contingent on status quo policies and voters' (mis)perceptions about these policies.

Under what conditions, if any, might most voters support freer immigration? Despite the vast literature on the determinants of anti-immigration attitudes, there is still no understanding of how responsive these preferences are to various personal and social incentives. In other words, it is unclear whether people dislike freer immigration *categorically* or *conditionally* on its perceived effects as shaped by current policies and practices. Few people want to ban all immigration, and it is possible to imagine that even otherwise "principled restrictionists" may accept more open immigration admission policies if such policies clearly benefit their communities. Nonetheless, the examination of potential support for alternative policy solutions is suspiciously absent in the literature. In the end, it is hard to know whether some of these policies could be politically feasible without conclusive information about voters' individual preferences and their (un)conditionality.

As I argue, one of the main reasons that voters are hesitant to support freer immigration is simply that they do not believe immigration can be beneficial for them and their countries, and they do not necessarily trust the advocates who tell them otherwise. According to the latest comprehensive global poll from Ipsos mentioned earlier, only 21 percent of respondents across the world believe that "immigration has generally had a positive impact" on their country, and only 28 percent believe that "immigration is good for the economy." Negative beliefs almost always dominate such polls, and there are only a handful of countries where a plurality of respondents believe immigration is a positive force.[30]

Importantly, while people may misperceive the effects of immigration and use those negative misperceptions to rationalize their prejudice against immigrants, public perceptions about the impacts of immigration are grounded in objective policy reality. As I will demonstrate, countries with more utilitarian immigration policies that select immigrants based on their potential contribution have much more positive public perceptions of immigration than countries with a more humanitarian approach.

To understand why people currently support restrictions on human mobility and whether such attitudes can be changed, the study of immigration opinion must move beyond the traditional accounts of inherently "prejudiced" voters who hold biases against immigrants whose racial background differs from their own and who lack knowledge of the benefits of immigration. Instead, any successful and sustainable persuasion effort should consider the role of actual immigration policies on the ground and what people want from those policies based on their genuine altruistic preferences toward their compatriots.

THE ALTRUIST'S DILEMMA OF OPEN IMMIGRATION IN THE WORLD OF NATIONALISM

In his 2015 speech honoring Margaret Thatcher, the former Australian prime minister Tony Abbott equated support for immigration with genuine, albeit misplaced, altruistic intentions. He said that "no country or continent can open its borders to all comers without fundamentally weakening itself. This is the risk that the countries of Europe now run through misguided altruism."[31] Tony Abbott is not alone in relating immigration policy and public attitudes to altruism. For example, many pro-immigration and anti-immigration activists alike appeal to people's sense of charity in their arguments. But while the former group emphasizes the needs of vulnerable populations fleeing violence and poverty abroad, the latter group maintains that charity begins at home. Somewhat similarly, its sometimes prejudiced nature aside, the popular anti-immigration slogan of "America first" also taps into people's unselfish aspirations to help their country by preventing potential threats related to terrorism, increased job competition, and cultural change.

The notion that people's desire to help others drives their decision-making beyond considerations of self-interest is grounded in the growing academic literature in economics and psychology. Building on these advances, numerous behavioral and attitudinal outcomes in political science are increasingly seen as a function of altruistic preferences defined as one's willingness to help others at a personal cost. Most prominently, a genuine concern for the well-being of others may motivate political participation and support for redistribution of income or wealth to the poor among the rich.[32]

Nevertheless, political actors evidently disagree on whether their altruism leads (and should lead) to more pro-immigration or anti-immigration views. On one hand, altruistic people should be expected to resist harsh migration restrictions that harm the most impoverished people in the world. On the other hand, voters may feel especially compassionate toward fellow citizens and resist freer immigration because of the potential harm they believe it can do to their country. In line with these ideas, substantial evidence supports the idea that people base their immigration views on so-called sociotropic concerns: whether they think immigration has a positive or negative impact on others in their society.[33]

When respondents in rich democratic immigrant-receiving countries think of society, however, they almost always think specifically about their compatriots. We live in a world of nation-states where no other social category can command as much influence as nationality and national citizenship. Indeed, unlike most other ascribed identities like race, national citizenship is a circumstance of birth for which discrimination is legal and encouraged.[34]

At the same time, for all the talk about globalization and the demise of nationalism, legitimate democratic governments are universally assumed to act in the interest of their citizens. As a result, even the most cosmopolitan and socially egalitarian individuals who are sympathetic to the plight of foreigners understand that their compatriots should have priority in public policy. In one recent poll, for instance, U.S. respondents were told that "in many other countries, poverty is more extreme than it is in America" and asked whether they think "government should give money to the poorest people in those other countries, instead of giving it to the poorest Americans." Perhaps unsurprisingly, 78 percent of respondents, including people of a wide range of backgrounds, as well as the vast majority of those who identified as Democrats, said no.[35]

In chapter 1, I build on these insights and develop a theory of *nationalism as parochial altruism* in politics. In short, the theory argues that voters often face an altruist's dilemma: they are willing to help others, even at a personal cost, but they want to help their fellow citizens first. I thus hypothesize that, independent of their self-interest and various policy-specific concerns (e.g., those related to racial prejudice), people oppose or support freer immigration depending on whether they believe it hurts or helps their compatriots. As a result, conditional on some partiality toward their compatriots, more altruistic voters are expected to be *more* opposed to freer immigration and other globally efficient policies that pose a potential trade-off between greater national and global good.

Revealing that nationalists oppose immigration would hardly be surprising. But since freer immigration can also be an enormous asset for receiving countries, my theory predicts that even those who prioritize the well-being of their compatriots can still support more open immigration admission policies when the perceived national benefits of these policies clearly outweigh potential costs. After all, despite the prevalence of zero-sum thinking around the issue, "migration is what you make it," and policy solutions can always be improved to be beneficial to all parties.[36] In other words, an important practical implication of my theoretical argument is that the current public opposition to immigration across many rich countries is not categorical but conditional: widespread altruistic nationalism that generally makes people anti-immigration can also push them in a more pro-immigration direction.

I should note that the terms *parochial* and *nationalistic* frequently carry negative connotations in everyday language. However, I use these terms in a value-neutral manner to describe a distinct empirical pattern in alignment with usage in other scholarly works. Other terms in the literature, like *selective altruism*, *bounded altruism*, or even *patriotism*, may pertain to similar ideas but not be suitable for other reasons, as I will discuss.

MAKING IMMIGRATION POPULAR THROUGH DEMONSTRABLY BENEFICIAL POLICIES

The literature describes various factors that condition immigration preferences, from racial biases and group cues to negative emotions and misinformation. While interesting and important, however, many of these factors are arguably not very actionable in terms of persuasion or policy change. But even the ones that are actionable, such as those related to efforts to provide correct information or reduce prejudice against immigrants, often fail to change people's minds in a robust way.

According to the main argument advanced in this book, people's genuine desire to help their compatriots and their beliefs about whether immigration is actually good for them should be among the main factors conditioning immigration preferences. Put simply, people want policies that are good for them and their countries, and immigration is no exception. As of now, however, many voters are ambivalent about immigration because they are skeptical—and often rightly so—that it is something that can be in their national interest. But as I will show, it does not have to be this way. I argue that most voters would and do support more open immigration admission policies when these policies are *demonstrably beneficial* to their country.

So, what *could* make people durably change their minds to support freer immigration? The fact that people are much more likely to support policies that benefit their country implies that it is a good idea to inform people about those benefits and emphasize them in policy communication. But the real challenge is to ensure that people actually believe what they are being told. As I show throughout this book, it is not enough to just tell voters that immigration is good. Governments and other stakeholders must consistently demonstrate it through their policies, which can take years for people to observe and internalize.

In his book *The Price of Rights*, Martin Ruhs highlights that designing a good immigration policy is not just about having good intentions. In immigration, as in most of life, trade-offs are paramount. When pro-immigration advocates insist on granting rights to migrant workers that are costly to receiving countries, they effectively advocate for fewer migrant workers to begin with. This does not mean that rights are not important or that pro-immigration advocates should become complacent, but it does mean that it is always important to pragmatically consider the available policy compromises given a set of existing constraints.[37] In this sense, I emphasize the importance of prioritizing demonstrably beneficial immigration, even from the perspective of global justice, which is mindful of the needs of vulnerable migrants.

Immigration is a contentious political issue for a reason. It has economic winners and losers while also viscerally invoking people's social identities, moral convictions, and anxieties. That is why there is no silver-bullet solution. Any responsible immigration policymaking would necessarily involve making important trade-offs, such as between doing what is right and what is popular. I argue and show that these trade-offs are minimized most when a government enacts selective pro-immigration reforms that open legal pathways for skilled or otherwise needed foreign workers. Freer immigration can only be popular when most voters—including those who are relatively ethnocentric or not well informed—can intuitively understand the practical reasoning behind the policies enacted by their government.

Many U.S. observers have rightly lamented that the dysfunctional politics of illegal immigration across the southern border, driven by perceptions of constant chaos, takes significant energy away from the more productive debate on reforming legal immigration admission policies. Since the salience of border issues benefits some politicians and interest groups, they can always argue that the border is not secure enough no matter how much the government actually spends because it is in their interests to do so.[38] But while border security and unauthorized migration may never be fully resolved in a large country like the United States, it is still possible to minimize normative disagreements and make progress on these issues.[39] As the experiences of other countries show, the topic of immigration can become divisive and unpopular even in otherwise well-governed, cosmopolitan contexts without any border issues in sight.

Despite the many challenges, it is possible to make immigration popular, and, in a way, we already know it. For instance, it has been extensively documented that majorities support increases in skilled economic immigration across immigrant-receiving countries.[40] Importantly, however, such demonstrably beneficial policies are not just about attracting "the best and the brightest." They can also be about filling labor shortages, reuniting families, increasing population growth and diversity, revitalizing declining regions, or even improving national security. As I will document, most voters support policies bringing in needed workers, students, and immediate family members. Voters are also likely to support reciprocal policies like free movement agreements and bilateral labor mobility partnerships.

Policies that voters perceive to be beneficial to their country extend beyond those that promote the potential contributions of immigrants to the gross domestic product, productivity, job opportunities, or the economy at large. Although harder to quantify, the perceived social and cultural contributions of immigrants can be equally significant.[41] One does not have to be a rootless cosmopolitan to prefer living in a thriving community with a variety of recreational choices and activities. The popularity of vibrant neighborhoods, bustling ethnic restaurants, diverse cultural festivals, and innovative fusion experiences that immigrants bring to cities across the world are a testament to the vitality they add to the social fabric of their adopted homes.

Similarly, the perceived costs of immigration are often nonmaterial, such as the potential loss of social cohesion and concerns over lawlessness and border chaos, which many people strongly oppose.[42] Meanwhile, perceptions of rapid demographic and cultural change, such as the prospect of white majorities becoming minorities, can fuel anxieties about cultural displacement and lead to increased support for restrictive immigration policies.[43] Regardless of how national interest is defined, I argue that efforts to persuade people to support freer immigration can be successful only when they are reflected in objective political reality and grounded in people's own understandings of the national interest.

Several countries have clearly and extensively managed to realize this idea in practice. Canada is perhaps the best example of such an open, yet highly selective, immigration system that commands high legitimacy among voters. Since the elimination of racial quotas in the 1960s, Canada's immigration policies have been transparently designed to advance the national interest by boosting the economy through a targeted admission of skilled foreign workers. Importantly, most voters—regardless of their level of education or politics—understand that motivation and support such a system. Despite its economic focus, however, Canada also has the world's highest naturalization rate and admits a disproportionate number of humanitarian migrants. As a result, Canada has been able to maintain a consistently open immigration system without any of the mainstream anti-immigration politics so widespread among most of its peer countries.[44]

In stark contrast to the Canadian success, Sweden provides a cautionary tale of what happens when policymakers ignore or deliberately deprioritize considerations of national interest. Until recently, Sweden had one of the most generous humanitarian admissions programs among OECD countries. It was also the only country not to distinguish between workers of different skills in its economic immigration policies. Unfortunately, despite elite efforts to suppress anti-immigration politics, the Swedish government has not been able to maintain sufficient public legitimacy to sustain such an immigration system. As a result, after a few decades of relatively open immigration, the right-wing government coalition elected in 2022 is already reducing immigration numbers and is determined to continue doing so. This increasingly evident failure of managing immigration is particularly remarkable given that, according to many possible metrics, Sweden has been considered the most cosmopolitan society in the world.[45]

To the best of my knowledge, not a single developed democratic country in the world has been able to have relatively open immigration policies and sustain their legitimacy without also applying a number of selection criteria to its immigrant admissions. The divergent experiences of Canada and Sweden suggest that the explicit and straightforward prioritization of national interest in immigration policymaking is the best way for democratic governments to ensure the long-term success and legitimacy of the system among voters. Paradoxically, these experiences also suggest that such demonstrably beneficial policymaking may be the best way to ensure that governments have a sufficient public mandate to help the most vulnerable involuntary immigrants when a crisis hits.

PLAN OF THE BOOK AND HOW TO USE IT

The book is divided into two parts. The first part theorizes about and documents why people oppose immigration and when they would support it. I argue that people care about the national interest above

and beyond their self-interest and that they prefer immigration policies that reflect that view. When voters believe that certain immigration policies or immigrant groups are a threat to their country, they
oppose them. But when they believe that certain immigration policies or groups are beneficial to the nation, they are willing to accept
more immigration even if they are otherwise uncomfortable with
demographic change.

Readers who already agree with this perspective, or those wishing
to skip the theoretical nuances and empirical tests against alternative
perspectives, may wish to jump directly to part II. There, I explore
the practical implications of these insights for persuasion strategies
and policy design, providing actionable guidance for advocates and
policymakers.

After outlining my theory of nationalism as parochial altruism and
how it can help us to understand the immigration conflict, chapter 1
describes several testable hypotheses concerning immigration attitudes, including a few that address competing expectations based on
the predominant prejudice-based explanations. I also elaborate on
my argument regarding the conditionality of currently restrictive attitudes and how they could change under alternative policy conditions.

I then proceed with three empirical chapters, each of which tests a
part of my argument using different data and methods. In chapter 2,
I use existing cross-national survey data to provide initial empirical
evidence for my argument. First, using Gallup World Poll data, I document the surprising nonrelationship between self-reported altruism
and immigration attitudes in many immigrant-receiving countries.
Second, using data from a more detailed U.S. General Social Survey, I
show that altruistic voters can in fact be either more pro-immigration
or anti-immigration depending on how much they favor their compatriots over foreigners. Quite equivalently, these findings imply that
"nationalist" voters are much more opposed to immigration when
they are altruistic. To address social desirability and endogeneity
concerns, I then build on this evidence by reporting the results of an
original representative study using incentivized economic games and
choice experiments in the United Kingdom and the United States.

In chapter 3, based on the use of a novel incentivized measure of
revealed altruistic preferences, I show that almost one-third of English

and American voters are willing to contribute to domestic charities at a personal cost *and* at the expense of comparable global charities. I then show that altruists who choose to donate domestically ("parochial altruists") as opposed to globally ("humanitarian altruists") are as anti-immigration as those who choose not to donate to charity at all ("egoists"). Nonetheless, in line with my theoretical expectations, parochial altruists can be more supportive of policies to increase immigration than egoists when these policies explicitly aim to benefit their compatriots.

In chapter 4, I complement my survey findings with those of a policy choice experiment to test the causal implications of parochial altruism for immigration preferences against the two prominent explanations of self-interest and racial prejudice. To do this, I estimate the effect of perceived policy consequences for personal and various collective interests, as well as the number of immigrants and their countries of origin, on immigration policy preference. According to the experimental results, voters' policy preferences are highly responsive to collective interests *in addition* to self-interest. At the same time, however, voters are much more sensitive to national than global policy impacts. Further, conditional on these material consequences, preferences are only marginally responsive to the number of immigrants and their countries of origin. This finding implies that opposition to immigration is unlikely to be rooted primarily in the derogation of foreigners. Accordingly, most voters could support increasing immigration from non-European countries if they believe it is beneficial for them and their compatriots.

The second part of the book explores what the evidence on people's altruistic nationalism and their conditional immigration preferences implies for persuasion and policymaking efforts. Since national immigration policies can never be randomly assigned, causal inference is always inherently difficult at this level of analysis. As a result, part II is necessarily more speculative than part I.

In chapter 5, I consider the practical implications of widespread altruistic nationalism for successful persuasion and productive policy changes on immigration issues by setting out a framework of "persuasion by policy design." After discussing the requirements for successful and long-lasting persuasion on immigration, I discuss the premise and the limitations of existing efforts related to the positive reframing of the issue, providing information, and reducing prejudice. Since people's attitudes are grounded in their interests and political reality, I conclude that meeting voters where they are and enacting better, *demonstrably beneficial* immigration policies is the only way to robustly convince voters that freer immigration is good.

In chapter 6, I go beyond the hypothetical survey experiments to examine whether past legal pro-immigration reforms have, in fact, been historically productive. To that end, I estimate the impact of immigration policy on immigration attitudes and populist voting by exploiting the timing of major changes to immigration laws in a new dataset linking the best available public opinion and policy data from twenty-four European countries over the last forty years. I complement these estimates with the most recent fine-grained evidence on how voters responded to the Deferred Action for Childhood Arrivals (DACA) policy and other high-profile reforms in the United States. Overall, I show that the broad liberalization of labor and family immigration policies does not cause an increase in the populist vote and may even legitimize immigration under certain conditions.

Not all pro-immigration reforms are equally popular among voters. While various attempts to improve immigration attitudes by correcting misperceptions have generally been unsuccessful, chapter 7 empirically explores the alternative possibility of persuasion through policymaking. Using the best available public opinion, demographic, and policy data from across OECD countries, I show that voter perceptions of the economic benefits of immigration are systematically related to objective reality, including the skill selectivity of previous immigration policies and share of high-skilled immigrants. Overall, the evidence suggests that, while reducing prejudice and providing accurate information to voters are essential, only the adoption of selective pro-immigration policies can secure public support for consistently high immigration rates.

Chapter 8 illustrates this dynamic through a historical comparison of the divergent track records of Canada and Sweden in terms of designing their immigration policies and legitimizing these policies to the public. Since the 1960s, Canada has placed the most deliberate focus on national interest in its immigration policies, as indicated by its famed point-based system and a correspondingly high number of skilled economic immigrants. In sharp contrast to Canada, Sweden has adopted a much more universalist approach, admitting a high number of humanitarian immigrants and ensuring their equitable treatment. While both countries had long been deemed immigration success stories, only Canada was able to maintain its expansive policies—and its citizens' support for them. As the increasingly evident collapse of Sweden's notoriously generous humanitarian regime shows, voters can accept more open immigration admission policies only when they see that such policies have worked for them and their country over time.

Finally, in the conclusion, I review my results and discuss their broader implications for understanding public opinion and policy-making. If restrictive preferences are largely driven by beliefs about national policy impacts rather than an unequivocal rejection of foreigners, a political compromise on immigration should be feasible. Given the apparent failure of efforts to change voters' negative perceptions of immigration, the results suggest that a more effective government strategy is to consider alternative policy solutions that demonstrably benefit average citizens alongside immigrants. I conclude the book by outlining practical suggestions for pro-immigration persuasion efforts and making selective immigration more inclusive.

Taken together, the theory and evidence presented in this book suggest that the currently widespread opposition to immigration is conditional rather than categorical. Voters genuinely care about their country, and they are willing to compromise their anti-immigration sentiments and support more open immigration policies when they are confident in the favorable national consequences of those policies. The adoption of demonstrably beneficial pro-immigration policies by responsible governments in *our* interest is the only way to make freer immigration popular and sustainable for the sake of everyone.

PART I

BORDERS OF COMPASSION

HOW NATIONALISTS CAN EMBRACE IMMIGRATION

1

NATIONALISM AS PAROCHIAL ALTRUISM

A Theory of Conditional Support for Immigration

W HY DO MOST VOTERS—EVEN EDUCATED AND UNPREJUDICED voters—oppose freer immigration admission policies? Under what conditions might they support them? To answer these questions, part I considers voters' fundamental motivations in politics, policy, and opinion formation.

While social scientists have traditionally explored the potential conflict between selfish and collective interests, many political issues clearly involve decisions that favor certain groups at the expense of general social welfare and even one's self-interest. Drawing on a wealth of existing research in political psychology and behavioral economics, this chapter develops a new theoretical framework of what I call *nationalism as parochial altruism* in politics. This framework aims to describe individual differences in political behavior, clarify why avoiding conflict is challenging even among prosocial individuals, and explore the possibility of more programmatic pro-immigration policymaking.

In short, I argue that when choosing which immigration or other policies to support, people tend to favor those that benefit their compatriots, even at the expense of foreigners' well-being and sometimes their own. I then outline the testable implications of my theory for understanding the *conditional* nature of opposition to immigration and the potential for its broader acceptance in high-income democracies. Last, I preview the design of my studies and the evidence I will examine in subsequent chapters.

A vast behavioral literature argues and documents that people's identities, prosocial motivations, and political decision-making are guided by nationalism. Nationalism is notoriously hard to define; it can mean anything from an official political ideology of national supremacy to an average person's understanding of their social identity as an Australian. Still, many scholars have fruitfully explored how people's sense of nationalism and their national identities can shape their immigration attitudes. I learned a lot from these accounts and will get back to some of them later, but it is simply impossible to recount all the excellent works that have been written on the topic.[1]

My humble theoretical contribution here is simply to take stock of the ideas about the psychology of nationalism and connect them to the modern understanding of altruism in behavioral economics. As I argue here and demonstrate throughout this book, reconsidering nationalism as a currently predominant form of "parochial altruism"—a stable psychological trait driving voters' choices in democratic politics—can be enormously fruitful. In particular, it can help gauge the impact of perceived national interest on people's observable attitudes and behaviors compared to other possible personal and social incentives.

Based on this new theoretical conceptualization, I will then provide a new way of measuring revealed (more or less altruistic) nationalism and (more or less nationalistic) altruism using an economic game with real money at stake, as well as a new way of estimating the effects of national interest incentives using a conjoint policy choice experiment. Most important still, I will demonstrate what widespread altruism and nationalism mean for people's conditional support for freer immigration, existing persuasion efforts on the issue, and effective immigration policymaking.

UNCONDITIONAL OPPOSITION TO IMMIGRATION AS PREJUDICE AND ITS LIMITS

First of all, let me briefly explain why there may be a need for yet another theory explaining immigration attitudes. It is now common to attribute widespread anti-immigration attitudes to voters' uncon-ditional racial prejudice. Such categorical prejudice can be conceptu-alized as rooted in negative stereotypes, implicit bias, ethnocentrism, national chauvinism, xenophobia, or simply racism, among other psychological constructs. According to accounts of categorical preju-dice, people form policy preferences based on their intrinsic moti-vation to derogate racial out-groups *regardless* of perceived material policy consequences for them personally.[2] After all, one of the most robust findings in the public opinion literature is that most voters generally prefer immigrants from particular (predominantly white European) groups and countries.

What can explain such differentiated anti-immigration attitudes other than prejudice? That is, why do immigrants of certain ori-gins systematically face more public opposition than others? Poli-ticians and their electorates around the world are often willing to express their worries regarding the potential negative impact of spe-cific immigrant groups on their countries. The scholarly literature on the topic has closely followed these popular discourses, but vari-ous critics question whether such lay perceptions of threat are what *causes* anti-immigration attitudes and whether such justifications of exclusion should be taken at face value and used as analytical catego-ries in research. Some even consider the very articulation of threat arguments to be a form of racial prejudice.[3]

While misperceptions about immigration are robustly linked to anti-immigration attitudes, recent studies find no consistent evi-dence that people exposed to accurate information about the bene-fits of immigration change their stance on the issue.[4] Moreover, it has been shown that even genuine agreement with a statement such as as "immigrants undermine our culture" or "immigrants take our jobs" may simply be a post hoc rationalization of a prejudicial gut feeling.

Indeed, a growing literature is looking at the attribution of inter-group difference or competition *as* an expression of prejudice and at the legitimizing role of perceived threat in general. For instance, some recent studies suggest that people may say that they see a group as threatening to explain their own prejudice, rather than the threat being the original cause of their prejudice. It has also been shown that if someone already has negative feelings about a certain immi-grant group, they are more likely to start believing that the group is threatening.[5] As aptly noted by Neil Malhotra, "Individuals who are antithetical to immigrants . . . are likely to describe immigration as harmful on any dimension on which they are asked to assess its merits."[6]

Finally, there is evidence that many people want to limit immigration to preserve the racially homogeneous demographics of their communities.[7] As indicated by research in political psychology, such diversity concerns may stem from certain (conservative) ideological predispositions related to "social dominance" and "authoritarianism."[8] It is possible that some voters may not be willing to trade off between changing racial demographics and the potential economic benefits of immigration.[9]

Overall, there is abundant evidence that opposition to freer immigration is motivated by racism or categorical prejudice of some form. I take these findings as a given, but I question their practical relevance to immigration policymaking. While my theory of nationalism as parochial altruism is not incompatible with the existence of intrinsic racial prejudice or preference for homogeneous communities, it implies that the currently observed opposition to immigration is significantly *conditional* on existing policies and their assumed consequences. It also suggests that many voters who currently oppose freer immigration because of bias can support it when alternative policies are implemented by their government.

HOW (UN)CONDITIONAL IS PUBLIC OPPOSITION TO IMMIGRATION?

Before I outline my theoretical account, it is worth describing what I mean by *conditional* and *unconditional* preference toward freer immigration in more detail. One problem with most of the existing survey questions about immigration numbers is that most are explicitly about a relative policy change compared to the status quo (which many people may not be fully aware of). As a result, we do not have much information about how many voters (un)conditionally support or oppose freer immigration. For example, people with an extreme preference for either completely open or completely closed borders are rarely able to report those preferences.

What we see from the more detailed but fragmented data available is that very few people unconditionally support fully open immigration or even relatively freer immigration (defined conservatively here as accepting about 1 percent or more of a country's population from abroad each year). Similarly, very few people support a full stop to all immigration to their country. One of the only studies I am aware of that explicitly asked a nationally representative U.S. sample about people's absolute preferences regarding open immigration is the Cato Institute 2021 Immigration and Identity National Survey. In this survey, respondents were told, "Each year, about one million immigrants are admitted to the U.S.," and then asked what number they would prefer to be admitted.

Interestingly, 8 percent of respondents said "as many as want to come," and 9 percent said "none," indicating rather low public support for either fully open or fully closed borders (the reported margin of error is 3 percent). At the same time, an additional 4 percent expressed their preference for five million or more immigrants per year (which is roughly equivalent to supporting freer immigration as defined here). In other words, in 2021 in the United States—one of the most pro-immigration survey contexts in modern history—only 12 percent of citizens were willing to support open immigration unconditionally. Somewhat similarly, a survey I conducted in the United Kingdom found that about 12 percent of respondents were willing to support immigration no matter what. Importantly, such unconditional preference for open (or closed) borders never exceeds 30 percent, even among the most (or least) educated, liberal, and cosmopolitan respondent groups.[10]

A somewhat less precise but much more widely available question about absolute immigration preference can be found in the World Values Survey (WVS). WVS respondents from all over the world are asked "about people from other countries coming here to work" and are offered an explicit choice of letting "anyone come who wants to" as an option for what "the government should do."[11] Comparing the estimates of U.S. attitudes from the WVS and the 2021 Cato Institute survey (13 percent vs. 12 percent) shows that both surveys yield roughly similar percentages of people who support fully open immigration. Importantly, although this number varies across countries, it has never exceeded 18 percent in any immigrant-receiving countries (as recorded in Sweden in 2005). At the same time, less than 10 percent of WVS respondents in these countries usually say that the government should "prohibit people coming here from other countries."

More generally, few people consistently support or oppose immigration across all possible questions and policies.[12] However, this does not mean that the public is confused. Rather, it means that many people may have a nuanced opinion about the merits of various policies. For instance, one recent in-depth experimental study of German immigration preferences shows that most people do not have categorical attitudes toward immigration and that they are willing to compromise those attitudes. Almost half the respondents who opposed freer immigration were willing to support increasing immigration levels if the selection criteria were more selective and if greater restrictions were placed on immigrants' rights. Perhaps even more strikingly, more than one-third of currently pro-immigration respondents supported reducing immigration levels if immigrants' rights were expanded.[13]

In sum, despite the relatively high levels of stated opposition to immigration, categorical opposition to any labor mobility from foreign countries is rare. However, very few people are also willing to embrace immigration of any kind or size. In other words, the fact that only a small number of people unconditionally support or oppose immigration implies conversely that most people's preferences are conditional on the details of the human movements and policies in question. This fact also suggests that the vast majority of voters should in principle be susceptible to persuasion and open to compromise regarding the issue despite their various biases.[14]

A THEORY OF NATIONALISM AS PAROCHIAL ALTRUISM IN POLITICS

I will now briefly review the vast literatures on altruism and nationalism, and I will outline my account of nationalism as parochial altruism. I will then elaborate on how this widespread individual psychological predisposition can help explain political behaviors and opinions, including the current public resistance to and the potential public support of more open immigration admission policies.

THE POWER OF ALTRUISM AND THE WEAKNESS OF MERE SELFISHNESS

People are inherently selfish, but it is hard to be selfish in politics unless you are a politician yourself. As Anthony Downs first explained, most voters—unlike consumers in the market—exert very little personal influence on the outcomes of elections or other political decisions. When you buy something in a store, you know what you are getting, and you benefit from it immediately. However, when you vote for a candidate, it is far less certain that your vote will lead to the result you hope for. This uncertainty means that self-interest rarely drives people to get involved in politics or thoroughly research candidates and policies.[15]

The prevalence of what psychologists call *prosocial motivations* or "personality types" and economists call "other-regarding preferences" or "social preferences" may help explain the paradox of considerable political participation. Although this is only one possible explanation for why people turn out to vote or engage with politics otherwise, the basic idea is that the expected social benefits of these activities can outweigh the personal costs.[16] Essentially, even if people are uncertain about how their vote will affect them personally, they have good reasons to believe their participation can have a much larger collective impact.

In fact, extensive cross-cultural experimental research in the fields of social psychology and behavioral economics over recent years strongly indicates that people genuinely care about others' well-being. The notion that such prosocial motivations can fruitfully complement the standard self-interest account in explaining people's political attitudes and behaviors is well supported in theoretical discussions and empirical findings.[17]

Of course, prosocial motivations may be of different kinds. While there is no consensus in the literature, one way to categorize these motivations is to consider whether they are outcome dependent (e.g., altruism, inequality aversion) or process dependent (e.g., fairness, reciprocity). Perhaps most crucially for the purposes of this book, however, people can be altruistic in the sense that their personal well-being or "utility" increases with utility gains to others. Put simply, altruism implies "a willingness to incur a cost to oneself in order to improve the well-being of others."[18]

In both everyday language and social science, it is common to think of altruistic motivations and related behaviors as an ideal type of indiscriminate self-sacrifice for the greater good that, if it exists at all, is extremely rare. One prominent example of such altruism is the rescuing of Jews by gentiles during the Holocaust, which was both personally costly and out-group oriented.[19] Another key example of modern-day "extraordinary" altruism is a living kidney donation made to a stranger without any expectation of future benefit. While insightful, this perspective disregards the fact that most people engage in ordinary activities that they believe may benefit others but undermine their own interests, from blood donation and charitable giving to civic engagement and volunteering.[20]

Many seemingly prosocial activities can arguably be selfish in nature and explained away as social signaling.[21] Nonetheless, it is also true that people often donate to charitable causes anonymously or help strangers with no expectation of anything in return. Although there is some variation across individuals and contexts, *people generally prefer others to be better off*, independent of their personal interests.

Further, even genuine altruistic intentions often fail to achieve desired outcomes. That is why most social science research on the topic, including this work, focuses on altruistic motivations—whether self-reported or revealed through behaviors—rather than the consequences of those motivations. Thus, it should not be surprising that, similar to the idea of *enlightened* self-interest, there is a movement for "*effective* altruism."[22]

Building on recent advances in behavioral economics and psychology, numerous behavioral and attitudinal outcomes in political science are also increasingly seen as a function of altruistic motivations. Most prominently, altruism may help overcome the collective action problem and contribute to widespread political participation and civic engagement. Genuine concern for others also seems to shape support for greater redistribution (the reallocation of resources through taxes or government programs to reduce inequality within society), even among those who will not benefit personally from such policies.[23]

Similarly, some scholars argue that altruism, if it exists at all, is what motivates people to support immigration, especially given the plight of many less fortunate immigrants. After all, many people do view policies to increase immigration as an act of charity (whether rightfully or not). In line with this argument, there is some evidence from self-report surveys that altruistic people are more accepting of immigration in general and humanitarian immigration in particular.[24]

THE POWER OF NATIONALISM AND THE WEAKNESS OF COSMOPOLITANISM

Until recently, economic research on social preferences had largely neglected to address the fact that altruism, and other prosocial motivations for that matter, are rarely impartial. Humans tend to belong to distinct group categories that, as shown by social identity theory, may by themselves lead to in-group favoritism. In other words, altruism is predominantly *parochial*: people are willing to sacrifice more for some than others based on the group membership or perceived deservingness of those others.[25]

It has been a truism that people belong to countless social categories, but it is not readily apparent which should be most important in the realm of politics until one considers the role of the state, or the *nation*-state to be precise. According to Deborah Schildkraut, "what makes national identities unique relative to other social identities is that they are associated with . . . institutional, coercive, and legal authority."[26] Relatedly, national identity is also one of the most influential, albeit often unquestioned, social self-concepts that guides and determines the whole life of an individual, providing "a way of seeing the world."[27]

As famously defined by Ernest Gellner, nationalism is a political ideology that holds that the political and the cultural unit should be congruent.[28] In simpler terms, it is the idea that nations should be governed by their citizens in their national interest as opposed to being governed by or in the interest of foreigners.[29] The principle of having and striving for a distinct sovereign people who rule themselves is not just *an* ideology; it is arguably the most powerful ideology of the modern age.[30]

While some may disagree with this idea or its particular implementation, nationalism in some form is endorsed as self-evident by most democratic governments and their citizens around the world. This is true regardless of whether one emphasizes their altruistic commitments to compatriots in the form of patriotism or succumbs to denigrating foreigners in the form of chauvinism.

Despite being largely taken for granted by the public and even within social science, nationality or citizenship can be viewed as the most consequential ascriptive social category for one's material well-being.[31] Specifically, 66 to 73 percent of global variation in household income in purchasing power parity (PPP) is determined by one's country of residence (or one's country of birth in 97 percent of all cases since very few people migrate). In this sense, nationality is more influential in determining one's life chances than all other ascriptive characteristics such as race, ethnicity, and gender.[32] Importantly, even so-called civic nations are effectively ethnoracial groups in the sense of being primarily based on ascriptive descent, that is, the inheritance of citizenship status through one's parents or place of birth.[33]

Importantly, as a social identity, national citizenship is also one of the only circumstances of birth for which discrimination is, albeit variably, legal and encouraged.[34] At the same time, strong norms against racial parochialism in developed countries may significantly constrain the expression of these motivations.[35] Indeed, unlike other types of in-group favoritism, it is widely considered socially acceptable and even desirable to favor one's compatriots when engaging in real or perceived international competition.[36]

Given its importance and its potential to incite discrimination and conflict, it is no wonder that nationalism, especially in its extreme forms among self-proclaimed "nationalists," is viewed negatively by many academics and political observers. This is especially true among pro-immigration advocates and liberals who rightly see nationalist ideology as an impediment to individual freedoms and more economically sound policies.[37]

Still, the general political principle of nationalism and its proliferation around the world have arguably contributed to the establishment of modern state bureaucracy, representative democracy, and the welfare state. Even critics of nationalism often acknowledge that the large-scale social solidarity that currently exists in most rich democracies where citizens willingly pay taxes and contribute to public goods is simply impossible without the "imagined communities" of modern nation-states. Put simply, there is currently no viable liberal alternative to the principle of national citizenship.[38]

Of course, nationalism is only one possible value among many, and it has always been in conflict with more universal or humanitarian altruistic commitments. People have used the idea of cosmopolitanism in particular to challenge the nationalist assumption that individuals and governments should prioritize national interest, both morally and factually. Cosmopolitans (or "citizens of the world") believe in the ultimate interconnectedness of all people around the globe while rejecting the existence of ascribed out-groups on the basis of national citizenship.[39] Relatedly, *humanitarianism* implies the promotion of the well-being of all human beings regardless of their country of origin or residence.[40]

While parochial motivations likely dominate our lives, humanitarian altruistic motivations clearly do exist.[41] There is substantial evidence for the existence of genuine cosmopolitan identities and truly impartial altruistic motivations among people across the world. Many people also exhibit a sense of belonging to the world or humanity as a whole, and this sense is increasingly prevalent among the educated urbanites who vote for left-wing parties across the Atlantic.[42]

As my account makes clear, however, altruism is exactly what gives motivational power to the divide between nationalists and cosmopolitans. Since most people today say they love their country and care about the world,[43] it may be more fruitful to ask whether and to what extent voters are actually willing to sacrifice their own well-being for the sake of national or global interest. Given the absence of political institutions with legitimate power over the entire globe, genuine cosmopolitanism or humanitarian altruism among voters is probably quite rare. After all, only 1 percent of U.S. private charitable giving is directed toward helping foreign organizations and individuals despite the fact that the American dollar goes much further in low-income countries.[44]

A THEORY OF NATIONALISM AS PAROCHIAL
ALTRUISM IN POLITICS

We are now ready to discuss what the power of altruism and nationalism implies for people's politics. As we have seen, there can be at least three distinct ultimate motives for cooperation or conflict, the last two of which are often confused by observers: self-regarding *egoism*, in-group-regarding *parochial altruism*, and universally other-regarding *humanitarian altruism*. These motives respectively lead to behaviors that promote and prioritize one's real or perceived *self-interest, group interest*, and *human* or *global interest*.[45] Although these motivations and their distinctions have been thoroughly examined in laboratory settings using multilevel social dilemma games, they are arguably more pertinent in real-world political behavior and decision-making.

My general theoretical framework is agnostic regarding the relative importance of various social groups and related group biases for individual decision-making. However, as elaborated earlier, in the *national* politics of today's advanced democracies, parochial altruism is more often directed toward compatriots than any other nonfamilial in-group members. Consequently, unless specified otherwise, I use the terms *parochial altruism* and *altruistic nationalism* interchangeably as shorthand for "a willingness to help fellow citizens at a personal or global cost."

Importantly, the definition of *parochial altruism*—which some refer to as "weak parochial altruism"—explicitly excludes the motivation to harm out-groups when there is no benefit to the in-group. While some scholars assume out-group hostility is an inherent part of parochial altruism, it may be more constructive to distinguish these phenomena and consider hostility under the category of prejudice.[46] This distinction is especially relevant outside zero-sum contexts like immigration, where most parties can ultimately benefit.

To capture how this dynamic plays out in politics, I propose a succinct decision-theoretic model with two major components in which (1) more or less "parochially altruistic" individuals choose among (2) various policies, basing their decisions on the perceived personal, national, and global consequences of the policies. For interested readers, the formalization of my argument is available in previously published works.[47] But the basic idea of nationalism as parochial altruism can be neatly visualized, as shown in the trilemma graph in figure 1.1.

Figure 1.1 shows the potential differences in stable psychological predispositions among individuals that determine their prosocial motivations when deciding which policies to support or which candidates to vote for in response to the perceived consequences of these choices. Reflecting their personality types, people are assumed to consistently show varying degrees of *altruism* and *national favoritism*. This means that when forming their opinion about policies involving competing interests like immigration, people weigh how much they care about others in general versus their compatriots in particular. In practice, most people likely have multiple motivations for their decisions and thus can be placed somewhere within the area defined in figure 1.1.

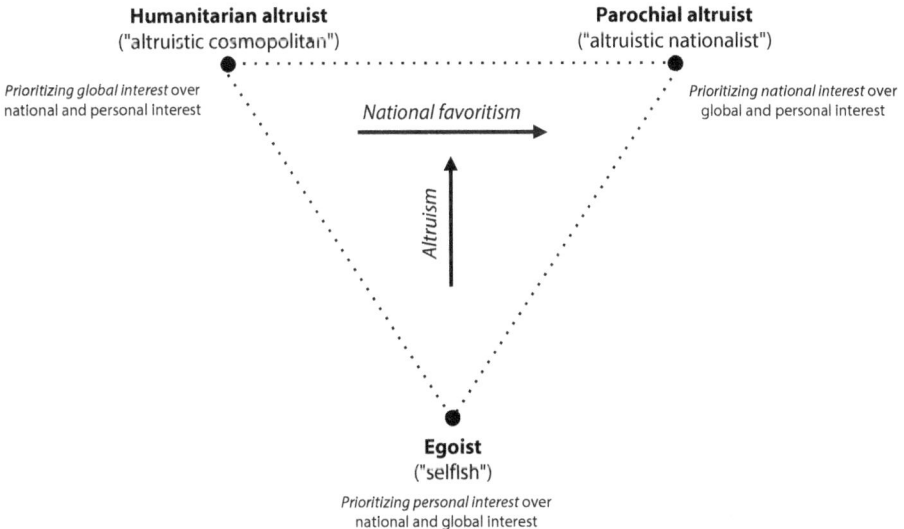

Humanitarian altruist
("altruistic cosmopolitan")

Prioritizing global interest over national and personal interest

National favoritism

Parochial altruist
("altruistic nationalist")

Prioritizing national interest over global and personal interest

Altruism

Egoist
("selfish")

Prioritizing personal interest over national and global interest

FIGURE 1.1 Possible individual differences in prosocial motivations. The figure shows the theorized variation in people's stable personality types that determines their prosocial motivations from egoism to more or less humanitarian or parochial altruism. Most people are expected to be consistently somewhat selfish and nationalistic when forming their political views.

Still, it may be useful to consider the extreme manifestation of these motivations separately. In advancing one's overall goals, for instance, a pure egoist or conventional *homo economicus* would advance just their own well-being with no regard for the well-being of anyone else (the bottom of the triangle in figure 1.1). This means that if a certain policy alternative provides clear social benefits at one's personal expense (e.g., increasing public spending by raising taxes), a pure egoist would reject it. Meanwhile, a pure parochial altruist would advance the well-being of their in-group members with no regard for the well-being of anyone else or themselves (the top right corner of the triangle). Here, one can think of a soldier who selflessly volunteers to die for their country. Finally, a pure humanitarian altruist (akin to a benevolent social planner) would strive to advance the well-being of everyone with no regard for the well-being of their in-group or themselves (the top left corner of the triangle).

Fortunately, depending on the political choice, individuals may or may not face all (or even any) of these trade-offs at once. After all, the advancement of group interest may imply the advancement of self-interest, or the advancement of everyone's interest may also advance self-interest, group interest, or both. As a stylized example, one can think of independently funded scientists who, in producing their research, generally face no conflict between these otherwise distinct motivations. Or at least that is what I want to believe about my own motivations when writing this book.

Still, consistent with common sense and existing behavioral evidence, my framework assumes that the level of people's concern generally decreases from self-interest to national interest and then to global interest. As such, most people are expected to prefer a positive change in their own well-being to a similar change in their group's well-being and to prefer a positive change in their group's well-being to a similar change in humanity's well-being. However, in absolute terms, global changes are always much larger than personal and group changes.

My theory of parochial altruism acknowledges that, aside from self-interest and other concerns, people have mixed prosocial motivations that may conflict with one another. Consequently, altruistic actors who care sufficiently more about their in-group may "rationally" decide to harm others when there is a real or perceived trade-off between group and global interests, even in the absence of any intrinsic out-group hate in their motivations. My argument thus also implies that both positive and negative consequences of nationalism and other group biases can be amplified by genuine altruism.

In this respect, the term *patriotism* normally emphasizes the positive aspect and the term *nationalism* normally emphasizes the potentially negative aspect of the same motivation to advance the interests of one's national in-group over those of both the self and other groups. Conversely, the terms *cosmopolitanism* and *humanitarianism* de-emphasize the priority of one's in-group in prosocial motivations. Although both nationalist and cosmopolitan voters can be selfish, most uses of these labels generally suggest at least some willingness to incur a personal cost to benefit others.

PAROCHIAL ALTRUISM AND CONDITIONAL IMMIGRATION PREFERENCES

What do people's altruistic and nationalistic motivations, as conceptualized here, imply for the way voters approach immigration issues? Despite the common assumption that altruism always makes people supportive of immigration, the current contentious debate over the issue provides a quintessential example of how ambiguous perceptions of social good can be in national and international politics. On one hand, harsh immigration restrictions are inefficient and harm potential immigrants. On the other hand, people may feel especially compassionate toward their fellow citizens—who are often perceived to be harmed by immigration—and thus oppose international mobility despite their personal interests or the global benefits involved. While this logic is more apparent in the distributive consequences of immigration as an economic phenomenon, it applies similarly to nonmaterial factors of well-being that are related to differences in norms and values.

The available evidence notwithstanding, the effects of immigration on receiving countries and their citizens are predominantly portrayed as negative in the media and correspondingly perceived as negative among voters.[48] Although voters are probably more optimistic about the effects of immigration on (potential) immigrants themselves and the world as a whole, these beliefs should matter only to those who care sufficiently about the well-being of foreigners. As a result, given widespread beliefs about the negative national impacts of immigration in advanced democracies, I formulate the following observational hypothesis:

> **Hypothesis 1: The altruist's dilemma** *Compared to egoists, people of higher parochial (humanitarian) altruism are less (more) likely to prefer freer immigration.*

While the model assumes that egoistic voters cannot be *intrinsically* biased toward their in-groups, a fruitful way to interpret this hypothesis is to expect an interaction effect between national favoritism and altruism. Somewhat counterintuitively, my argument thus implies that altruistic people may be more, rather than less, opposed to freer immigration since they find it incompatible with their partiality toward compatriots. After all, they are motivated by their in-group preference much more than are their nonaltruistic counterparts.

However, I also expect both parochial and humanitarian altruists to be supportive of more open immigration admission policies when such policies explicitly benefit their country. At the same time, I expect all altruists to be more supportive of domestic redistribution and engage more in politics than egoists. These conventional social dilemmas pit self-interest against the collective good but do not have to pose a conflict between national and global interests.[49] Similarly, my argument does not imply that parochial altruists necessarily have more negative attitudes toward the existing immigrant population, which may be considered by some native-born citizens to be part of their national in-group.[50]

Does the relative prevalence of parochial, rather than humanitarian, altruism imply that most electorates would never support freer immigration? Although parochial altruism likely has various (relatively immutable) genetic and environmental determinants, its consequences may still depend on available policies and beliefs.[51] My framework thus also implies that, independent of their self-interest and other concerns, in principle, most voters can be supportive of freer immigration as long as it is believed to help others, but especially their compatriots. Consequently, I will also experimentally explore the following counterfactual implications of my theory:

> **Hypothesis 2a: Altruism** *Independent of an immigration policy's personal impacts, the more positive voters' beliefs are about the social impacts of the policy, the more supportive voters are of it.*
>
> **Hypothesis 2b: Parochial altruism** *Independent of an immigration policy's personal impacts, voters' beliefs about the group impacts of the policy are more predictive of their support for it than are voters' beliefs about the global impacts of the policy.*
>
> **Hypothesis 2c: National parochial altruism** *Independent of an immigration policy's personal and global impacts, voters' beliefs about the national impacts of the policy are more predictive of their support for it than are voters' beliefs about other group impacts.*

If my theoretical account of nationalism as parochial altruism is correct, one should also expect to see systematic individual differences in how voters evaluate various counterfactual policies based on voters' personal characteristics. Most importantly, if sensitivity to collective interests (independent of personal interests) is indeed indicative of genuine altruism, we would expect it to be more pronounced among those who are independently revealed to be more altruistic in their behaviors.

SCOPE CONDITIONS AND CASE SELECTION

Of course, the posited relationships must be contingent on a particular political environment that connects (immigration) policy and related (mis)perceptions about its effects to voters' motivation to help their (national) in-group members at the potential expense of others. Consequently, although parochial altruism as a distinct individual predisposition is assumed to be universal, it can still be affected by change in institutional settings. Accordingly, while there is some evidence that the individual variation of altruistic and parochial motivations is comparable across contexts, the way these motivations translate into politics can vary substantially.[52]

Therefore, I specify the following two major scope conditions of my argument. First, the dominance of national parochial altruism relative to other types of racial and regional loyalties as a social norm is clearly limited to states with long-established national institutions and civic national identities among their citizens.[53] Second, the relationship between national parochial altruism as a predisposition and particular policy preferences (on immigration) assumes that voters have some awareness and knowledge about the issue. This relationship also implies that there are at least some immigration flows and discussion of them in the national political discourse.[54] To that end, I primarily focus on democracies that have (a) at least one hundred years of nation-state history, (b) a foreign-born population of at least 5 percent, and (c) currently positive net migration. While somewhat arbitrary, these thresholds approximate global averages for national history, immigrant population, and current migration trends among world countries.

These criteria produce the following list of countries: Australia, Austria, Belgium, Canada, Denmark, Finland, France, Germany, Greece, Iceland, Ireland, Italy, the Netherlands, New Zealand, Norway, Spain, Sweden, Switzerland, the United Kingdom, and the United States. Importantly, this list includes most of the most desirable destinations of potential immigrants.[55] In some analyses, I also include other European countries like Poland, as well as Japan, South Korea, and Mexico as potential immigrant-receiving destinations.

DATA AND RESEARCH DESIGN

How can one examine the relationship between parochial altruism and political preferences? The most straightforward way is to identify appropriate existing survey data and compare people's political views and behaviors by their levels of altruism and favoritism toward compatriots. To do that, I used representative cross-national data from the Gallup World Poll, the U.S. General Social Survey, and the International Social Survey Programme.

The procedure of correlating various endogenous survey responses—where respondents do not have an incentive to reveal their preferences—has well-known downsides. The problems of social desirability bias and "cheap talk" may be especially pertinent in the study of altruism and nationalism. To alleviate these concerns, scholars have increasingly incorporated various incentivized economic games in their political surveys. There is ample evidence that the individual acts of giving revealed in such tasks with real money at stake are internally valid and rather stable across time, as well as externally valid in terms of predicting various prosocial behaviors outside the lab.[56] Finally, since even revealed altruistic motivations can be endogenous to a variety of other predispositions, it is also important to consider experimental evidence for my argument. To test my theory of parochial altruism against existing accounts in a compelling way, I thus also conducted an original population-based survey with embedded incentivized economic games and choice experiments.

I concentrated my original data collection and empirical analysis on the United Kingdom and the United States: high-income, immigrant-receiving democracies with a long-established nation-state history. Given that these are also the top destinations for most aspiring immigrants in the world, their migration policies are extremely consequential both domestically and internationally.

While the British public has long been divided on immigration, public attitudes on the issue have become increasingly salient since the opening of the country's labor market to Eastern Europe in 2004. This widespread opposition to immigration has been further linked to the relative success of the Eurosceptic UK Independence Party (UKIP) and the "Leave" campaign in the 2016 referendum regarding the United Kingdom's withdrawal from the European Union.[57] Similarly, negative immigration attitudes have significantly contributed to partisan vote switching and Donald Trump's victory in the 2016 U.S. presidential election.[58] Despite various differences in electoral politics and institutions, however, the political conflict over immigration in the United Kingdom and the United States is arguably representative of those of other affluent democracies, at least in terms of the way it is perceived by voters.

The main analysis and hypothesis tests presented in the part I are based on my original survey of 1,973 English citizens administered in May 2018 by Qualtrics, a reputable online survey platform. The panel was largely representative of the overall population across most important demographic and political characteristics (see appendix B, table B.1, for summary statistics). The survey was focused on England rather than the United Kingdom as a whole to avoid potentially confounding British and other strong national identities in the state.[59] To ensure cross-national generalizability, I complemented the analysis with a U.S. pilot study of 604 citizen respondents recruited in January 2017 via Amazon Mechanical Turk (MTurk), a popular online crowdsourcing platform.[60]

Both surveys contained five consecutive sections, tapping into people's motivations, empirical beliefs, policy preferences, and demographic characteristics. I first asked multiple questions about immigration attitudes in which I had embedded a conjoint survey experiment of immigration policy choice. Next, I asked multiple questions about nonimmigration political attitudes for comparison and measured respondents' sociodemographic characteristics and political affiliations. Finally, I administered an incentivized charity game to reveal people's prosocial motivations. In the U.S. survey, participants were informed about the game either at the beginning or end of the survey, without any differences in relevant predictors and outcomes.

Over the next few chapters, I first provide observational evidence for my argument using existing survey data. I then reveal (parochial) altruistic motivations via a novel incentivized charity game with various recipients and then relate these motivations to people's political participation and attitudes toward immigration policy. Finally, I test the broader counterfactual implications of my theory by estimating the effect of perceived immigration consequences in a conjoint choice experiment of policy alternatives.

Part II then explores the practical implication of the results for pro-immigration policymaking and persuasion efforts. Unlike part I, which is focused on hypothetical survey experiments, part II draws on the wealth of historical public opinion, voting, and immigration policy data from European and OECD countries. In part II, I also provide a more qualitative, in-depth comparison of immigration politics in Canada and Sweden, the countries that respectively exemplify the nationalist–utilitarian and cosmopolitan–humanitarian approaches to freer immigration. Table 1.1 provides an overview of the data and research strategies used throughout the book.

TABLE 1.1 Data and research strategy overview

CHAPTER AND QUESTION	DATA TYPE	DATA SOURCE	CONTEXT	RESEARCH DESIGN
PART I				
2. Why don't altruists support immigration?	Self-reported survey data (individual level)	• Gallup World Poll • U.S. General Social Survey, International Social Survey Programme	• 21 OECD countries (2013) • United States (2014)	Between-individual comparisons with statistical controls
3. Why do most voters oppose immigration?	Revealed survey data (individual level)	Original surveys and experiments	England (2018), United States (2017)	Between-individual comparisons with statistical controls
4. When would most voters support immigration?	Experimental survey data (individual level)	Original surveys and experiments	England (2018), United States (2017)	Conjoint choice experiment
PART II				
6. Do programmatic pro-immigration reforms backfire?	• Policy data, aggregate survey data, voting data • Individual survey data	• IMPIC, PopuList, Timbro, other • U.S. Gallup Poll, other	• 24 European countries (1980–2016) • United States (2012)	• Between-country and across-time comparisons with statistical controls • "Unexpected event during survey design" (natural experiment)
7. Why does immigration have to be demonstrably beneficial to be popular?	Policy data, aggregate survey data	Ipsos, OECD, other	14 OECD countries (2000–2017)	Between-country comparisons
8. How (not) to design popular immigration policies	Aggregate data, historical data, qualitative data	Administrative data, academic literature, news media, think tanks	Canada, Sweden (1951–2022)	Qualitative between-country and across-time comparisons

Abbreviations: IMPIC, Immigration Policies in Comparison; OECD, Organisation for Economic Co-operation and Development.

WHY EXISTING EXPLANATIONS ARE NOT ENOUGH

Before I thoroughly analyze the evidence on national parochial altruism and conditional immigration preferences, I need to say a few words about the related and complementary frameworks that have informed my thinking on the issue. There is a large literature in social science suggesting that people's concerns about the well-being of their nation and other social groups may be a significant factor in determining their political behavior and immigration preferences. Next, I briefly review several alternative frameworks that attempt to explain what motivates people in politics and why they have particular views on immigration in light of the idea of nationalism as parochial altruism. While some of the empirical implications of my theory may seem straightforward, they qualify or otherwise inform these established theories. My hope is that, regardless of one's preferred theoretical framework, my readers can benefit from this discussion and the evidence provided throughout this book.[61]

NATIONALISM, SOCIAL IDENTITY, AND WELFARE CHAUVINISM

Many psychologists assert that people are often motivated in politics by their sense of social identity. According to some interpretations of social identity theory, for instance, a strong "social self" makes people intrinsically align their self- and group interests. In this sense, strong social identification is what enables both altruistic and discriminatory behaviors.[62]

As a growing part of this scholarship, various aspects of national identity are increasingly recognized to be an important predictor of political behavior.[63] Although there is no consensus in the literature, most scholars differentiate between the affective dimension of national identity and its cognitive dimension. With regard to the former, it is common to distinguish between more benevolent patriotism related to in-group love and more malevolent nationalism related to a sense of in-group superiority and out-group derogation. With regard to the latter, it is common to distinguish between (more inclusive) civic and (more exclusive) ethnic conceptions of national identity. These empirical constructs are then used to study a majority's attitudes toward various policies and social groups.[64]

Accordingly, there is also a large literature exploring the relationship between national identity and immigration attitudes.[65] With the recent rise of populist and anti-immigration movements in Western democracies, it may seem a truism to suggest that those who identify as nationalists oppose immigration. But what are so-called nationalists exactly? Ultimately, if nationalism is just about the derogation of those who are defined as foreign or about the exclusive descent-based definition of one's national in-group, its connection to restrictive immigration attitudes amounts to nothing more than a tautology. At the same time, the evidence on the link between strong national identity and anti-immigration attitudes is mixed.

One possible reason for these inconclusive findings is that most people in rich countries report feeling a strong attachment to their nation and endorse at least some ascriptive criteria for its membership.[66] In turn, this widespread national attachment naturally limits the amount of variation in those explanatory factors. Additionally, unlike in the study of other social categories, the existing research on national identity suspiciously lacks a direct interpersonal measure of intergroup bias distinct from a mere in-group identification or its strength.[67]

In other words, the term *nationalism* and its variations can be used to describe at least two psychological dimensions: (1) preference for one's national group relative to other national groups (i.e., a form of in-group favoritism), and (2) preference for one's national group relative to oneself (i.e., a form of altruism). As the parochial altruism account makes clear, these two dimensions are distinct, and they interact with each other such that those who favor their compatriots over foreigners are expected to be especially anti-immigration when being altruistic.

Of course, such in-group love per se does not imply the derogation of out-groups. In fact, there is substantial evidence that strong national identities may help overcome various racial and ideological divisions within countries.[68] Nonetheless, strong identity may eventually lead to substantial out-group discrimination, especially under the conditions or widespread perceptions of intergroup competition. The latter seems to be the rule rather than the exception in international relations.[69]

Accordingly, some studies show that citizens willingly perceive a duty to support policies that benefit their nation even when doing so is inconsistent with the interest of everyone else. While few people would intentionally want to harm foreigners, people tend to significantly discount the value of foreigners' lives. Similarly, other studies indicate that most people fail to realize socially efficient outcomes by devaluing the well-being of people who are deemed less deserving for being born abroad and not being a part of their national community.[70]

While insightful, social identity theory and its empirical applications do not account for people's selfish motivations. Starting with the famous minimal-group paradigm, social identity has been devoid of the question of self-interest, which is arguably one of the most important behavioral drivers. Therefore, it is unclear how people make trade-offs between their selfish and social identity motivations. As my account makes clear, altruistic predisposition is exactly what gives identity its power over self-interest. As a result, the ambivalent consequences of nationalism can be as much about greater altruism toward the in-group as about a sense of superiority or hostility to out-groups. As opposed to existing accounts of national identity, however, my theory predicts that even seemingly prosocial motivations (e.g., related to what people usually call "patriotism") can be linked to anti-immigration attitudes. After all, genuine altruistic decisions to help some people at a personal cost also come at the explicit or implicit expense of not helping some others.

I should also mention *welfare chauvinism*, a concept that has been increasingly used by academics to describe voters and politicians who support redistribution policies that exclude immigrants.[71] While this idea highlights one possible consequence of national parochial altruism among voters for their welfare attitudes in the context of international migration, it is consistent with a variety of other theories of human behavior, including alternative explanations I will describe later. This notion is also not directly applicable to explaining or even describing people's preferences regarding immigration admissions (e.g., by the standard definition of *welfare chauvinism*, welfare chauvinists may support fully open borders as long as immigrants do not get access to welfare).

SELF-INTEREST, GROUP HEURISTIC, AND
STATISTICAL DISCRIMINATION

One may argue that the seemingly prosocial and antisocial concerns in public opinion may be a function of one's self-regarding motivations in disguise.[72] As some scholars rightly point out, people may decide to advance their perceived collective interests as a proxy for their self-interest without being at all altruistic.[73] For example, people of similar identity categories like race or ethnicity can be expected to share a "linked fate" and thus use their perceived group interests rationally as a "group utility heuristic" for their self-interest. Similarly, the phenomenon of in-group favoritism can be a mental shortcut for an expectation of generalized reciprocity.[74]

Numerous studies have argued for a purely selfish account of opposition to immigration.[75] From this perspective, when people say that they would prefer to reduce immigration because of concerns about its negative impact on the national economy, what they actually care about is their own well-being. It is difficult, if not impossible, to accurately calculate the long-term implications of national immigration policy changes for any particular individual, so using average effects makes sense as a heuristic. Nonetheless, since advancing one's group interests frequently fails as an effective heuristic for self-interest, some skeptics consider it a form of cognitive bias.[76]

While my account similarly assumes that self-interest may be the single most influential motivation, it also specifies that it does not have to explain most of the variation in people's policy preferences. In other words, while important, group heuristic is only one possible reason that people respond to social incentives and discriminate against outsiders. All in all, genuine prosocial motivations cannot be neglected in economic or political analysis.

The consideration of genuine prosocial motivations also has an important implication for the prevalent idea in labor economics that discrimination can be either "statistical" or "taste-based."[77] Unlike the theory proposed here, most existing accounts simply assume that people discriminate statistically based on selfish incentives only. Instead, at least in the political realm, my theory posits that voters might support discriminatory policies like immigration restrictions based on their sincere beliefs about the positive impacts of these policies on others, even without any inherent dislike for immigrants.

SOCIOTROPIC POLITICS, GROUP THREAT, AND SOCIETAL LOCUS OF CONTROL

Theories of sociotropic politics explain voting and other political behavior by asserting that people act on what they think is good, not necessarily for themselves but for society in general.[78] Accordingly, these theories suggest that people oppose immigration because they think it is bad for others in their country. Consistent with this idea, extensive public opinion literature finds that self-regarding motivations rarely shape policy attitudes, including those related to immigration.[79] For instance, contrary to much of the political economy scholarship, most native-born citizens prefer high-skilled to low-skilled immigration regardless of their own individual characteristics because high-skilled immigration is perceived to be more socially beneficial.[80]

Related to these ideas, many scholars have conceptualized popular negative perceptions of immigration and its impact as a group threat. Although there are many ways to categorize potential threats, the growing consensus points to either economic or realistic threats and cultural or symbolic threats. The underlying assumption of most sociotropic and group threat accounts of immigration attitudes—regardless of the particular mechanism at work—is that people favor or oppose a certain policy if they *think* it poses an opportunity or threat to their *national* in-group. Accordingly, there is substantial literature suggesting that, with regard to immigration, people's subjective perceptions of their group threat could be grounded in the contextually heterogeneous objective conditions of immigrant numbers, scarce resources, and cultural distance.[81]

One particularly important manifestation of sociotropic concerns relates to the idea of "societal locus of control": the perception of whether one's country has control over immigration. According to the control hypothesis of immigration opinion, when people believe that their national borders are more secure and that the immigration process is more orderly, they feel safer and thus support freer immigration. Conversely, the chaos theory posits that perceptions of uncontrolled borders make individuals less welcoming of immigration.[82] In essence, akin to other sociotropic threat theories, people naturally resist efforts to increase immigration if they perceive it as a threat to their compatriots' well-being owing to border chaos or bureaucratic mismanagement.

While it might have been important to establish that political preferences are not just self-regarding, conventional sociotropic explanations are limited since they do not adequately reflect the distinction between various group interests and more general prosocial motivations. In fact, there is a wide variety of public policy instances in which the pursuit of national and other group interests unavoidably comes at the expense of social efficiency. Besides, people belong to multiple social categories whose perceived collective interests may not align with the nation's interest.[83]

Moreover, although sociotropic accounts are generally consistent with the parochial altruism thesis, they do not distinguish between self-interest and (more or less parochial) altruism as competing motivations to advance national interest both theoretically and empirically.[84] Thus, they assume that all people care about (various) others equally despite the overwhelming evidence showing individual variation in both altruistic and ethnocentric tendencies. Unfortunately, many authors avoid addressing these limitations by also assuming that all people are (as if naturally) self-interested in advancing the national interest. Among international relations theorists, it is also common to assume that countries—when viewed as independent actors—are expected to follow their "national self-interest." While this perspective may be in line with my account in terms of highlighting the role of national interest in policymaking, it is not particularly useful in explaining individual variation in public opinion since it makes no distinction between the various motivations of voters and their representative governments domestically.

According to the framework proposed here, however, voters are expected to oppose a policy in the national interest if its personal (global) consequences are sufficiently worse or if they are sufficiently self-interested (humanitarian). After all, the literature indicates that voters are never completely parochial with respect to immigration and other policy choices, and there is room for both selfish concerns and impartial benevolence in their political decision-making.

In sum, existing sociotropic accounts are insightful because they establish the fact that people tend to prefer policies that they think are better—not necessarily for them but for their compatriots. The theory of nationalism as parochial altruism goes further to specify when this would or would not be the case as testable hypotheses. Put differently, the theory proposed here provides microfoundations to the overwhelming evidence of sociotropic politics. In doing so, it clarifies (a) why sociotropic perceptions matter, (b) who is more susceptible to their influence, and (c) toward whom they are directed.

2

THE ALTRUIST'S DILEMMA IN THE DATA

Why Don't Altruists Support Immigration?

INITIAL DESCRIPTIVE DESIGN: SELF-REPORT SURVEYS

In the previous chapter, I outlined a general account of nationalism as parochial altruism that described the role of prosocial and parochial motivations in political behavior. I then argued that genuinely altruistic voters may perceive immigration—but not domestic social welfare programs or redistribution of resources—to be incompatible with their concern for their compatriots, regardless or even in spite of their personal interests. Contrary to conventional wisdom, my argument implies that—because of the high prevalence of national favoritism and beliefs about the negative national impact of current immigration policies—especially altruistic people may be more likely—not less—to oppose freer immigration.

While many studies have explored the link between altruistic preferences and behavior via small-sample economic games or psychological experiments, their external validity and generalizability to various policy-relevant issues and contexts may be limited. To address these concerns and provide an initial test for my argument, this chapter builds on existing cross-national surveys with a unique set of relevant items on altruism and political preferences.

First, using the 2013–2014 Gallup World Poll data from twenty-one high-income democracies, I document the relationship between altruism and political participation or immigration attitudes around the world. Second, using data from the 2014 wave of the U.S. General Social Survey (GSS) and the International Social Survey Programme, I provide more detailed evidence for the connection between more or less parochial types of altruism and public opinion.

Overall, the evidence in this chapter confirms that many people do seem to have an intrinsic concern for others that translates into greater political participation and support for redistributive and social welfare policies for various vulnerable populations in their home countries. Strikingly, while this support encompasses support for racial minorities, it does not seem to transcend national boundaries. Specifically, while people who exhibit greater altruistic motivations are substantially more likely to support policies in favor of welfare spending and helping the poor than are those who are less altruistic, they are not more or even less likely to support policies in favor of foreign aid and freer immigration. I then demonstrate that, in the case of immigration but *not* redistribution, this result is contingent on the stength of national favoritism among respondents. Namely, respondents high in both altruism and national favoritism are the most opposed to immigration, and respondents high in altruism but low in national favoritism are the most supportive of immigration regardless of racial prejudice, ideology, religiosity, and other possible confounding factors.

GLOBAL PATTERNS OF ALTRUISM IN POLITICS

To provide a global picture of anti-immigration sentiments, I rely on Gallup World Poll data. While the survey addresses a variety of social and economic issues, it also uniquely provides the most comprehensive global coverage of people's altruistic behaviors and views on immigration. As described earlier, the Gallup data convincingly show that most voters across major affluent democracies oppose more open immigration admission policies. As further demonstrated by my 2018 UK data, the same applies to those who are educated, racially egalitarian, and ideologically left-leaning (see figure 0.2). The fact that even most cosmopolitan voters oppose freer immigration generally runs against accounts that prioritize the role of personal material considerations and racial prejudice in people's attitudes toward immigration.

To explain this puzzle, I argue that people may resist mass immigration *because* of—not despite—their genuine motivation to help others. The Gallup World Poll data provide an initial test of my argument by comparing those who are more altruistic with those who are less altruistic. In particular, the poll includes questions about three types of (self-reported) altruistic behaviors, including donating money, volunteering one's time, and helping a stranger: "Have you done any of the following in the past month? (1) Donated money to a charity? (2) Volunteered your time to an organization? (3) Helped a stranger or someone you didn't know who needed help?" I used these three binary variables to create an altruism index based on the average of the responses to each question.

I restricted my analysis to the following twenty-one OECD countries with available data for altruism and immigration admission attitudes from 2013–2014 surveys: Austria, Belgium, Canada, Denmark, Finland, France, Germany, Greece, Hungary, Iceland, Ireland, Italy, Japan, the Netherlands, New Zealand, Poland, South Korea, Spain, Sweden, the United Kingdom, and the United States. In some of my specifications, I also employed statistical controls for standard sociodemographic factors, including gender, age, nativity, income, employment status, and religiosity. This technique helps isolate the specific effect of the main (altruism) variable I'm interested in, by accounting for the potential influence of these other factors that might also be related to the relevant (policy preference) outcomes.

First, to corroborate the importance of altruism in politics, I looked at its relationship to political participation (figure 2.1). Though Gallup does not ask about voter turnout, it does ask about people's efforts to contact politicians ("Have you done any of the following in the past month? How about voiced your opinion to a public official?"). Consistent with previous single-country research based on convenience samples, I confirmed that those who report helping others are more likely to contact politicians to voice concerns. Despite the potential

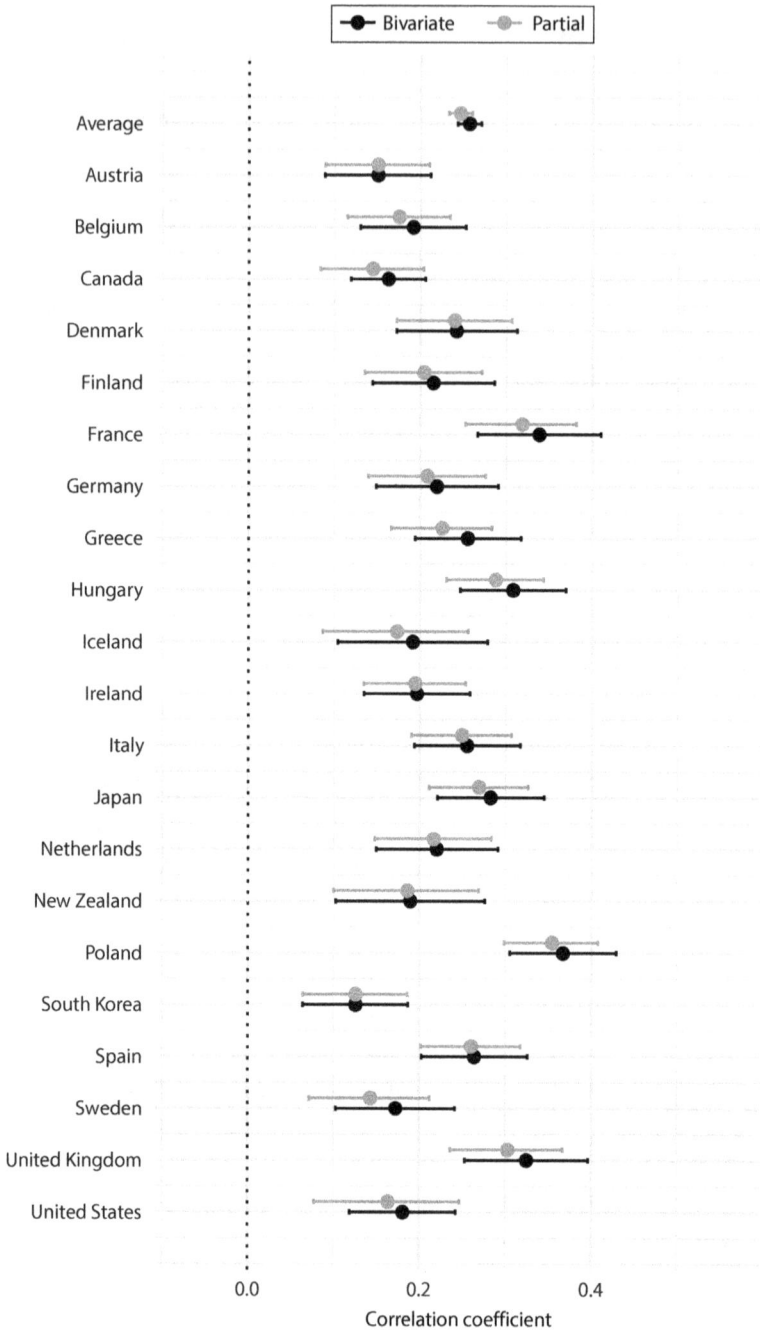

FIGURE 2.1 Altruism and political participation across countries. Black estimates are based on bivariate correlations of altruism and contact with politicians. Gray estimates show partial correlations after controlling for sociodemographic factors.

Source: Gallup World Poll, 2013–2014.

limitations of using this single measure of participation, it is remarkable that political participation positively correlates with altruism across representative samples of all selected countries (with an average bivariate correlation coefficient of 0.25). This relationship remains the same even after controlling for major demographic covariates, including age, gender, education, income, and religion (the gray bars in figure 2.1), and when using alternative model specifications such as multilevel logistic regression.

I then looked at the relationship between altruism and pro-immigration attitudes using responses to the following question I examined previously in the introduction: "In your view, should immigration from this country be kept at its present level, increased, or decreased?" To simplify the analysis, I recoded this variable so that "increased" equaled 1, "present level" equaled 0.5, and "decreased" equaled 0.

According to conventional wisdom, people who genuinely care about others should be more open to people's freedom to immigrate than those who are less altruistic. However, as shown in figure 2.2, altruism is largely unrelated to support for increased immigration across most countries. The average coefficient is more than twice as small as that for contacting politicians, which indicates that altruism has a much weaker influence on immigration attitudes compared to political participation. In fact, in only a handful of countries, such as Sweden and Denmark, is the relationship for both outcomes is comparable (see figure 2.1). Conversely, no relationship between altruism and immigration attitudes was found among respondents from the most popular immigration destinations, including the United States, Canada, Germany, and the United Kingdom. In other words, in most cases, people who claim to be altruistic are as opposed to immigration as are those who do not claim to be altruistic.

However, this finding does not imply that voters' altruistic motivations are not connected to their views on immigration. According to the framework proposed in chapter 1, the observed nonrelationship may be an artifact of conflating more or less parochial types of altruism in samples of the general population. In other words, while some altruistic voters may be very pro-immigration, others may actually be more anti-immigration than are nonaltruists.

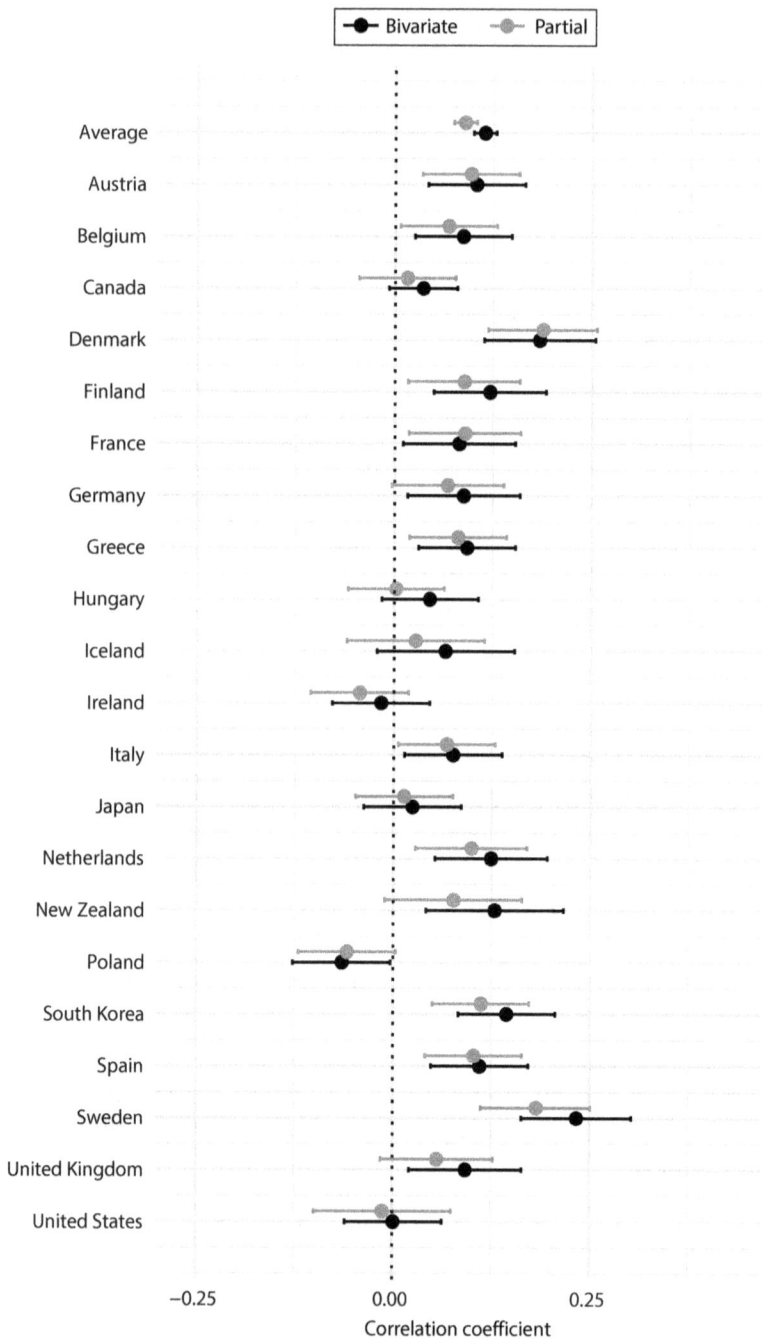

FIGURE 2.2 Altruism and pro-immigration attitudes across countries. Black estimates are based on bivariate correlations of altruism and pro-immigration attitudes. Gray estimates show partial correlations after controlling for sociodemographic factors.

Source: World Gallup Poll, 2013.

SELF-REPORTED ALTRUISTIC NATIONALISM AND IMMIGRATION ATTITUDES

To explore the relationship between immigration attitudes and altruism in more detail, I used a representative sample from the 2014 GSS. This survey is valued in public opinion research for its extensive range of social and political attitudes. The 2014 wave of the GSS is particularly notable for its integration of a module examining self-reported *altruistic values*. This previously validated index of altruism is based on people's average agreement with seven relevant statements such as "People should be willing to help others who are less fortunate." It is worth noting that, perhaps because of social desirability bias, only about 20 percent of respondents admitted to being more selfish than altruistic.

Equally important, the 2014 GSS incorporated a module on national identity from the International Social Survey Programme that included several relevant measures pitting the interests of one's national in-group against those of people in general. To create an index of *national favoritism*, I looked at people's average agreement with the following two statements: "People should support their country even if it is in the wrong" and "America should follow its own interests, even if this leads to conflicts with other nations." These items pose a clear trade-off between national and global interests and thus are preferable to other commonly used national identity items that indicate mere attachment to one's country. I recoded both indices so that the lowest and highest possible levels of altruism or national favoritism were equal to 0 and 1, respectively.

As before, I thought it would be instructive to compare immigration preferences to choices between political alternatives in which the conflict between national and global interests is minimized. Most prominently, such choices involve domestic redistribution, social spending, and political participation. Overall, in line with expectations from the literature, my analysis of the 2014 GSS data confirms that "altruistic values are higher among those backing more government spending for health care, [Black people], children, social security, and welfare/the poor, [as well as] among those in favor of more government efforts to help the elderly, the poor, the sick, and [Black people,] for reducing inequality in wealth, and for more government action in general."[1] Therefore, it appears that support for policy measures to help various vulnerable populations is at least partially driven by altruistic concerns.

But how impartial are these concerns? Remarkably, at least in the contemporary United States, this effect transcends racial boundaries. Indeed, after replicating the existing analysis with an additional set of controls, I confirmed the robustness of the relationship between one's altruistic values and one's preferences for various kinds of redistribution (figure 2.3; see also appendix B, table B.2).

One may reasonably expect that this relationship also translates to pro-immigration attitudes since support for immigration is often viewed as a selfless act of compassion toward less fortunate foreigners. Nonetheless, there is also reason to believe that many people may not apply as much altruistic concern to foreign others as to their predominantly ascribed and subjectively important citizenship-based in-group.

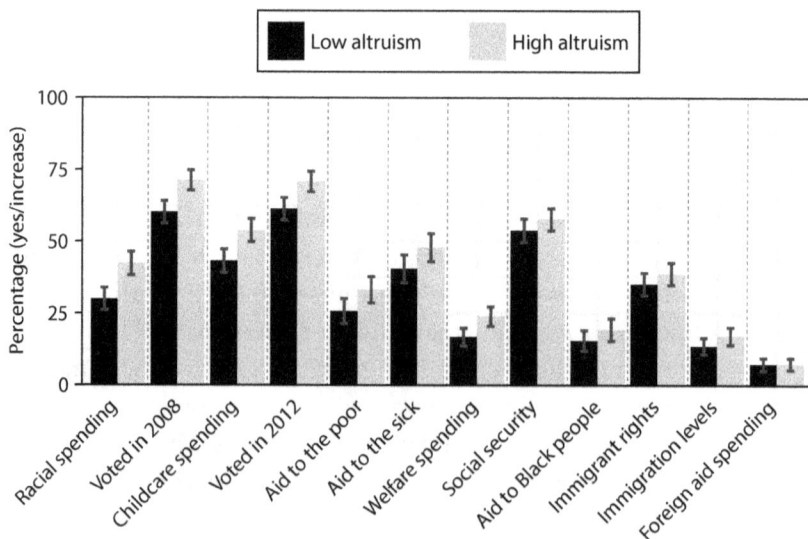

FIGURE 2.3 Differences in policy attitudes by self-reported altruism. The graph compares policy preferences between people below and above the median in altruistic values, respectively.

Source: U.S. General Social Survey, 2014.

To test this assertion, I added a number of available items on immigration policy to my analysis, and the results were quite striking. People who score higher on altruistic values are on average much more likely to vote for and support an increase in government spending on the poor and even racial minorities compared to those who score lower on altruism. However, highly altruistic people are *not* more likely than less altruistic people to favor an increase in immigration or equal rights for legal immigrants. To provide an additional check, I included a policy item on foreign aid—another issue for which national and global interests are not necessarily aligned— which appears to be the only government spending item unrelated to altruism. These results hold even after controlling for a number of major demographic covariates (see appendix B, table B.2).

These counterintuitive results do not appear to be driven by prejudice or ideology. The observed null effect for immigration (but not redistribution) items holds among both conservatives and liberals, as well as among people with either low or high levels of racial prejudice. In sum, despite the significant role of altruistic motivations in shaping people's opinions on redistribution and even race-targeted policies, there is no evidence that altruism extends to those who are not a part of one's national in-group.

The relationship (or lack thereof) between altruism and support for immigration likely depends on national favoritism or the extent to which people prioritize their compatriots over others. Interestingly, the correlations between national favoritism (as measured here) and other established predispositions, such as racial prejudice and conservatism, are very weak. While people reporting higher altruism are marginally less likely to be racially prejudiced, they also have an equally high relative preference for their country. This findings thus suggests that many people exhibit both altruism and national favoritism, though in varying degrees. In particular, the proportion of those who explicitly endorse both altruism and national favoritism (thus demonstrating *altruistic nationalism*) is 22 percent, while the proportion of those who endorse altruism but not national favoritism (thus demonstrating *altruistic cosmopolitanism*) is 29 percent.

Given that the national effects of immigration are popularly framed as negative and that most voters, regardless of their altruistic values, at least weakly favor their country, I argue that many people face an altruist's dilemma in deciding whether to support certain policies. Importantly, this tension between supporting the national in-group and out-groups should be more pronounced for some (immigration) policies than for others, depending on their perceived nation-regarding effects, while being less relevant or absent for most redistribution policies.

To test my hypothesis formally, I used linear regression to model various policy preferences as a function of altruistic values and national favoritism, as well as their interaction term. This analysis reveals how altruism and national favoritism, both independently and jointly, shape policy preferences. Strikingly, the interaction term seems to completely reverse the relationship between altruism and support for immigration, such that when national favoritism is considered, it dramatically changes how altruism relates to immigration support (see appendix B, table B.2, columns 1–3).

Specifically, *depending on whether they exhibit national favoritism, voters with high altruism can either be the most anti-immigration or most pro-immigration group in the United States* (figure 2.4). This pattern holds irrespective of voters' degree of ideology, racial prejudice, religiosity, and education. As may be expected, the interaction is significantly stronger for attitudes toward illegal versus legal immigration (see appendix B, table B.2, columns 4 and 5). At the same time, only altruism (but *not* national favoritism or the interaction effect between altruism and national favoritism) is predictive of preferences toward domestic redistribution (see appendix B, table B.2, columns 6 and 7). These differences are even greater when the sample is restricted to native-born non-Hispanic white people.

Overall, the joint effect of self-reported national favoritism and altruism trumps the explanatory power of other predictors that have been established in the literature (table 2.1). After all, the often overlooked fact is that most voters oppose freer immigration, even those who are liberal and college educated and who do not demonstrate explicit racial prejudice. At the same time, while altruism was found not to be related to immigration attitudes, the interaction of altruism with national favoritism explained four times more variation than education and twice more variation than partisanship (as well as twice more variation

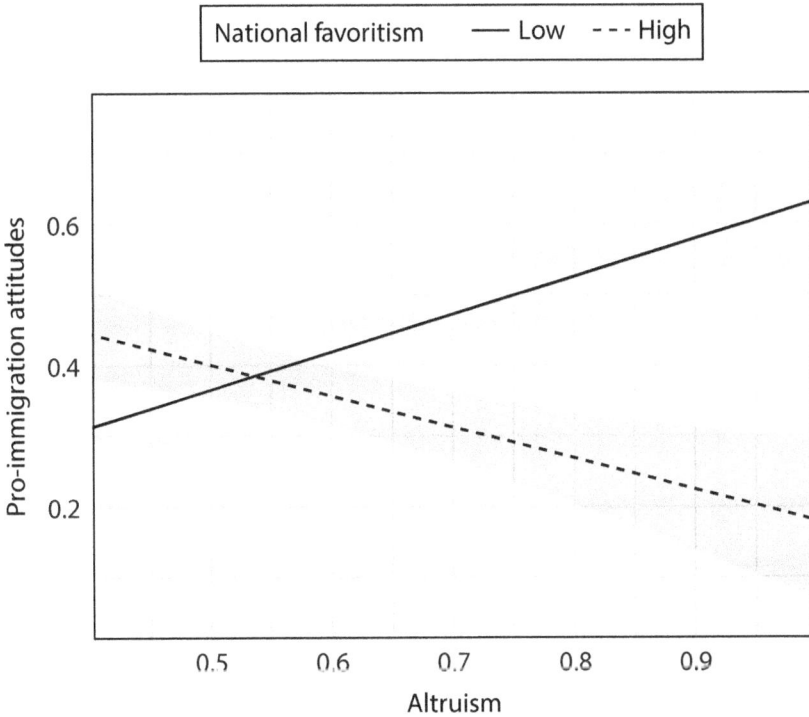

FIGURE 2.4 Pro-immigration attitudes by altruism and nationalism. The graph shows the predicted effect of altruistic values on immigration support by level of national favoritism. Estimates are based on the empirical model from table 2.1 (column 5).

Source: U.S. General Social Survey, 2014.

than national favoritism by itself). Even more important, the strength of the effect of parochial altruism was found to be largely unaffected by these prominent confounding variables. But it is worth mentioning that voters' social attitudes (e.g., views on gay marriage and abortion) are unrelated to parochial altruism, as would be expected.

* * *

The results from the Gallup World Poll and GSS surveys discussed in this chapter confirm that altruistic nationalism is a major determinant

TABLE 2.1 Relative predictive power of parochial altruism on immigration attitudes

	(1)	(2)	(3)	(4)	(5)	(6)	(7)
Education	0.020***					0.013**	
	(0.006)					(0.006)	
Partisanship (Republican)		−0.020***					−0.017***
		(0.004)					(0.004)
National favoritism			−0.177***		0.472***	0.475***	0.478***
			(0.035)		(0.145)	(0.145)	(0.144)
Altruism				0.073	0.587***	0.569***	0.570***
				(0.053)	(0.129)	(0.130)	(0.128)
National favoritism × Altruism					−1.065***	−1.047***	−1.039***
					(0.232)	(0.232)	(0.230)
Observations	1,081	1,081	1,081	1,081	1,081	1,081	1,081
Adjusted R^2	0.008	0.023	0.023	0.001	0.040	0.043	0.057

Source: U.S. General Social Survey data, 2014.
Note: All models were ordinary least squares (OLS) regressions, and all variables were coded to vary from 0 to 1. To allow for better comparison, the number of observations was made equal across all models. Standard errors are given in parentheses.
* $p < .05$, ** $p < .01$, *** $p < .001$

of political attitudes independent of other widely explored individual differences. According to Gallup World Poll data, many people worldwide perform altruistic acts (or report doing so), and those who do are more likely to be politically engaged than those who do not. However, most altruists appear to be as opposed to freer immigration as is the general population. Building on the GSS data, I further corroborated that highly altruistic people are much more likely to participate in politics and support domestic redistributive or race-targeted policies than nonaltruistic people, but they are not more likely to favor immigration or foreign aid.

Given the current prevalence of state-sanctioned national favoritism, nationality is often viewed as the most legitimate ethnic marker for discrimination and the assessment of deservingness in modern liberal states. Consequently, voters may often favor helping their (relatively) less fortunate compatriots over helping a greater number of immigrants. In line with this reasoning, I demonstrated that respondents high in both altruism and national favoritism (parochial altruists) are the most opposed to immigration and that respondents high in altruism but low in national favoritism (humanitarian altruists) are the most supportive of immigration. While I found that altruism was not related to immigration attitudes, its interaction with nationalism explained four times more individual variation in immigration attitudes than education and twice more variation than national favoritism alone.

In sum, the evidence provided in this chapter indicates that voters who favor their compatriots over foreigners are more—not less—opposed to immigration when they are altruistic. Put differently, altruism amplifies existing group biases, meaning that altruistic nationalists are much more anti-immigration than are selfish ones even after controlling for other major covariates such as education, partisanship, religiosity, and racial bias. In turn, this finding suggests that nationalism as parochial altruism constitutes a psychological predisposition distinct from ethnoracial prejudice, as well as from economic and social conservatism.

At present, people who say that they care about others but prioritize their compatriots over foreigners are generally *more* opposed to immigration than are those who say they mostly care about themselves. But can nationalists embrace immigration? The next two chapters propose a more discriminating measure of altruistic nationalism and consider the conditions under which it is positively related to support for immigration.

3

ALTRUISTIC NATIONALISM REVEALED

Why Do Most Voters Oppose Immigration?

A S CHAPTER 2 DOCUMENTED, many people around the world report prosocial attitudes that relate strongly to their political behaviors. Somewhat counterintuitively, however, I also showed that many self-proclaimed altruists oppose immigration because of their stated commitment to prioritizing their compatriots, who are often perceived to be harmed by it, over foreigners. Overall, these patterns are in line with my initial hypothesis that people who exhibit greater parochial altruism should be less likely to support freer immigration policies, whereas those who exhibit greater humanitarian altruism should be more likely to support such policies.

However, despite these insights, this evidence is so far solely based on people's self-reported motivations and policy attitudes. As rightfully argued by some economists, the major problem with such analysis is that respondents lack the incentive to reveal their actual motivations or preferences.[1] Instead, they may simply choose a random or what they believe is a socially desirable response. This issue is especially pertinent in the study of parochial altruism, in which most modern societies constantly incentivize people to signal their patriotism and prosociality regardless of their actual motivations.[2]

To provide a more compelling, "incentive-compatible" test of my theory, this chapter and the next rely on my May 2018 survey of about two thousand English citizens, conducted by Qualtrics using an online panel designed to represent the national population across key demographic and political characteristics. I also fully replicated this analysis using a survey of six hundred respondents in the United States. In this chapter, I focus on data about people's prosocial motivations and the relationship of those motivations to people's attitudes toward immigration.

PREFERENCE REVELATION DESIGN: AN ECONOMIC GAME

How can people's altruistic and nationalistic motivations be revealed simultaneously? To separate egoist from parochial and humanitarian altruist types of people, I incorporated an "altruist's dilemma" game with real stakes into my survey that asked respondents to consider whether they would allocate a potential cash prize to themselves, to a nationally or globally oriented charity, or some combination of the two. The prompt read as follows: "Independent of your compensation for the survey, we raffle off £100 among all respondents. If you are selected, you can decide to keep this money as a bonus or donate any or all of it to top charities that are committed to helping British citizens or people around the world. The winner will be contacted and the money will be distributed within five working days." For charitable donations, respondents could choose from a randomized list of six well-known national and global charities matched by specialization or identify a different charity.

For instance, respondents could choose to donate a share of their potential prize to the British Red Cross or the International Committee of the Red Cross and keep the rest (which many did). In other words, respondents were incentivized to make a difficult choice among advancing their self-, national, or global interests and thus reveal their prosocial motivations in the absence of any reputational or other confounding concerns. Those who chose to donate an amount to global rather than national charity that was equal to or greater than the amount they allocated to themselves were coded as humanitarian altruists, those who chose to donate less than they chose to keep were coded as parochial altruists, and those who chose not to donate anything were coded as egoists.

After the survey closed, the prize money was distributed according to the preference of a randomly selected respondent. The raffle prize was real and, according to my analysis of respondents' open-ended feedback explaining their decisions, most respondents perceived it this way, too. In fact, after running a few of these experiments in England and the United States, I donated a considerable amount of money to various domestic and international charities on behalf of my respondents. It is quite common for survey researchers to incentivize their participants with a raffle and for universities' research ethics boards to enforce those extra remunerations, so most respondents were accustomed to the idea. What was different about my raffle from those of other incentivized donation experiments was the requirement to choose between domestic and global charities, which provided a novel measure of people's revealed parochial altruism.

Given the contextual limitations of the revelation procedure, however, it may be reasonable to interpret the decision to donate most or all of the potential winnings as representing a *marginal* difference in prosocial motivations. For example, it is possible that many of those who decided to keep the winnings for themselves had significant parochial (and some perhaps even humanitarian) altruistic motivations that might have been revealed under a more elaborate repeated procedure. Consequently, while my analysis focuses on the differences between revealed voter *types* for the sake of simpler interpretation, it is possible that it captures only some of the underlying variation in altruism. In other words, choosing to donate all potential winnings to a national charity means that a person likely cares more about national interest than others do. But it does *not* mean that they do not care at all about their own interest or that of humanity.

THE PREVALENCE OF REVEALED ALTRUISTIC NATIONALISM

In line with my theoretical model (see figure 1.1), figure 3.1 illustrates the distribution of donation behavior from my May 2018 study, thus

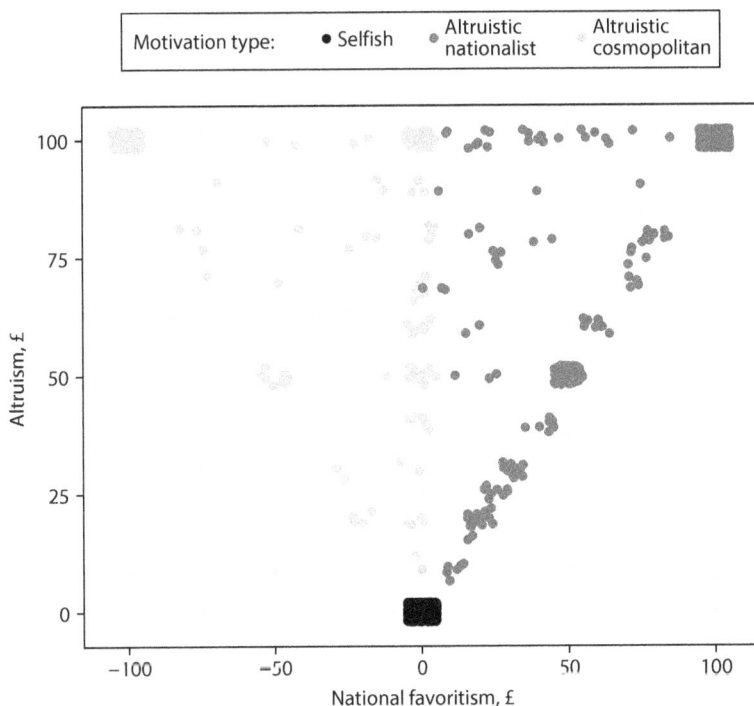

FIGURE 3.1 Revealed individual differences in prosocial motivations. The graph shows the distribution of donation behavior in the incentivized game based on the parochial altruism model (see figure 1.1).

Source: Original England Qualtrics survey, 2018.

revealing voters' altruistic and nationalistic motivations. While there are many ways to use these data, the most straightforward way to operationalize the main independent variable is to divide the sample into three types of altruists. However, the results remain consistent even when using a more nuanced measure of parochial altruism based on the specific amounts people choose to donate.

As may be expected from the literature, most respondents (57 percent) decided to keep the whole £100 prize and can thus be considered egoists. However, a whopping 30 percent chose to make a primary contribution to a nationally oriented charity; these respondents can be considered parochial altruists or altruistic nationalists. The remaining 13 percent chose to make a primary contribution to a globally oriented charity (9 percent) or to make equal contributions to globally oriented and nationally oriented charities (4 percent); these respondents can be considered humanitarian altruists or altruistic cosmopolitans.

Importantly, these differences cannot be explained by the greater credibility or familiarity of domestic charities since, for instance, more than twice as many respondents chose to commit to Red Cross projects at home (9 percent) rather than abroad (4 percent). Overall, while genuine altruism was abundant, many more respondents opted to advance their national rather than global interest.[3]

It is important to note that the actual share of individual charitable donations to organizations and causes abroad in the United Kingdom and other European countries has historically been much less than 10 percent, depending on the measure used.[4] Similarly, according to a 2021 report by the Giving USA Foundation, the share of international donations in the United States has been consistently below 6 percent.[5] The relatively greater prevalence of international donations in my incentivized task likely resulted from the availability of international charities among the possible options. It is also interesting to compare my incentivized task data and actual donation data with the data on people's self-reported motivations discussed in chapter 2; there, a much greater percentage of people claimed to be both altruistic and humanitarian than actually demonstrated these traits in my incentivized task or when making real donations.

Finally, among the most prominent subgroups differentiated by gender, age, income, education, ideology, religiosity, and racial prejudice, respondents chose approximately the same amount to donate. As may be expected, however, older or prejudiced respondents were slightly more likely to prioritize domestic rather than global charities, whereas those who were more educated or religious prioritized global charities (figure 3.2). In sum, consistent with my analysis of self-reported attitudes, this finding indicates that parochial altruism is largely independent of other major socioeconomic and political divisions.

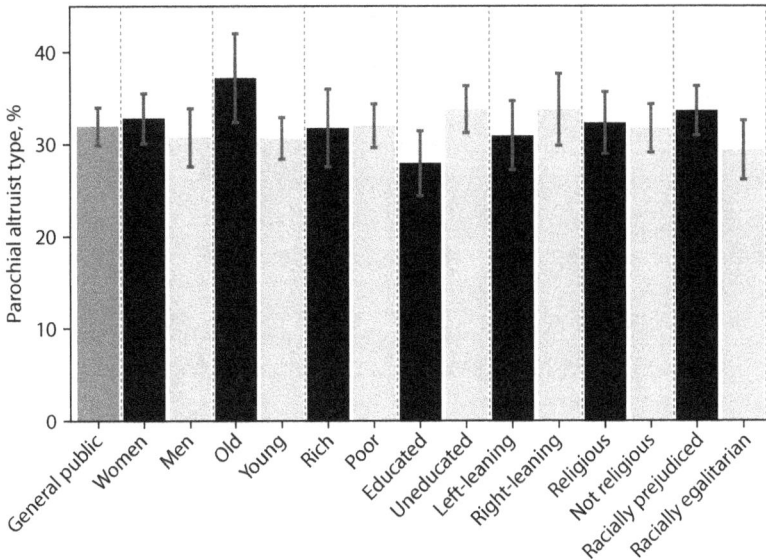

FIGURE 3.2 The prevalence of revealed parochial altruism across various demographic characteristics. The graph shows the (lack of) differences in nation-oriented donation behavior in the incentivized game across various voter subgroups.

Source: Original England Qualtrics survey, 2018.

REVEALED ALTRUISTIC NATIONALISM AND POLITICAL ATTITUDES

Does the joint variation of altruistic and parochial motivations relate to important political choices? To answer this question, as before, I first tested the "placebo" hypothesis by looking at the relationship between altruism and the conventional social dilemmas of political participation and redistribution (where the degree of national favoritism is not supposed to matter).

I measured attitudes toward political participation and redistribution as follows. The political participation index (ranging from 0 to 1) is an average of seven self-report items capturing whether respondents had engaged in various political and social actions, such as signing a petition, boycotting products, demonstrating, attending political meetings, contacting politicians, and voting in the last UK general election or the 2016 referendum regarding the United Kingdom's withdrawal from the European Union. The pro-redistribution index (also ranging from 0 to 1) averages two items measuring support for increasing government spending on housing for low-income families and aid to the poor on a five-point scale ranging from "significantly decrease" to "significantly increase."

As can be seen from figure 3.3 (as well as appendix B, table B.3), both parochial and humanitarian altruists are indeed more likely to participate in politics and to support welfare spending than are egoists, which is consistent with the previous findings overall.[6] At the

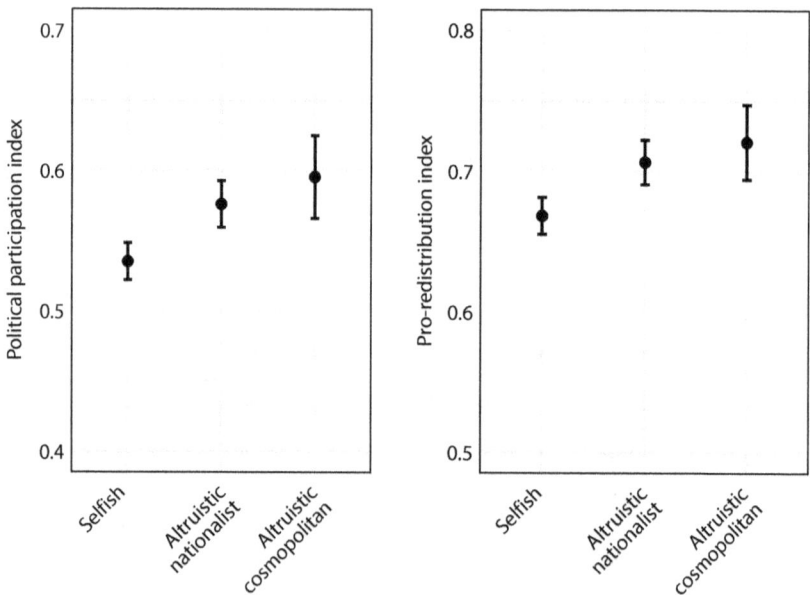

FIGURE 3.3 Political participation and redistribution attitudes by parochial altruism. The three revealed prosocial motivation types are based on respondents' contributions in the incentivized task. The bars represent 95 percent confidence intervals.

Source: Original England Qualtrics survey, 2018.

same time, similar to the self-reported results from the U.S. General Social Survey, revealed altruism is not at all linked to social attitudes, such as those related to gender or sexuality.

As I argued earlier, however, the distinction between altruist types should become crucial when policies pose a trade-off between national and global interests. Accordingly, altruism is not always related to support for increasing government spending. Similar to the results presented in chapter 2, for example, most parochial altruists are not more supportive of foreign aid than are egoists (figure 3.4). Yet while parochial altruists are more likely to support domestic military spending than are egoists, humanitarian altruists are much less likely to support it. In other words, altruism can also be related to the polarization of important political attitudes.

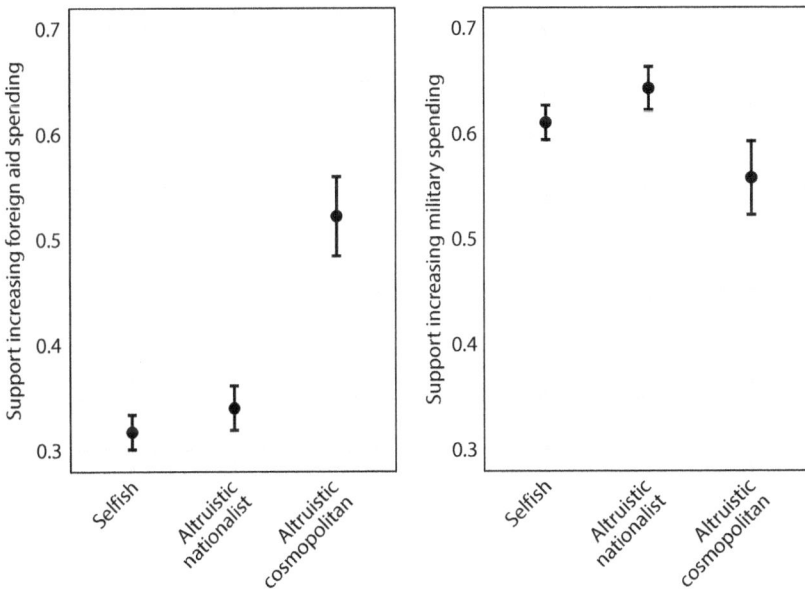

FIGURE 3.4 Foreign aid and military spending attitudes by parochial altruism. The three revealed prosocial motivation types are based on respondents' contributions in the incentivized task. The bars represent 95 percent confidence intervals.

Source: Original England Qualtrics survey, 2018.

REVEALED ALTRUISTIC NATIONALISM AND IMMIGRATION ATTITUDES

To measure people's immigration admission attitudes, I created a pro-immigration index (ranging from 0 to 1) as an average of the following two standard policy items. The first item asked respondents whether they thought immigration to Britain should be increased a lot, increased a little, left the same as it is now, decreased a little, or decreased a lot. The second item measured agreement with the statement, "Britain should make it much easier for people from other countries to come and live here regardless of their contribution to our economy," on a five-point scale ranging from "strongly disagree" to "strongly agree."

As can be seen from figure 3.5, parochial altruists—the majority of altruistic respondents—are as opposed to it as those who are not

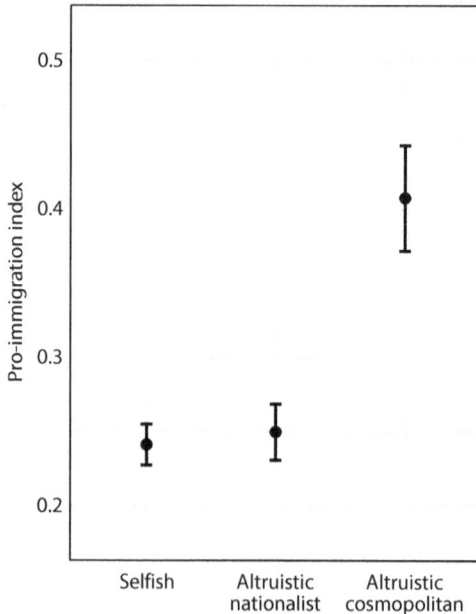

FIGURE 3.5 Immigration attitudes by parochial altruism. The three revealed prosocial motivation types are based on respondents' contributions in the incentivized task. The bars represent 95 percent confidence intervals.

Source: Original England Qualtrics survey, 2018.

altruistic. Only humanitarian altruists—the minority of prosocial respondents who also consider the global impacts of immigration—are substantially more pro-immigration than other groups (by at least 0.5–0.8 standard deviations). While people are often uncertain about the personal effects of immigration, their reliance on perceived social consequences clearly depends on their revealed altruistic motivations.

These differences in motivation persist and remain consistent after controlling for demographic and other major covariates (see appendix B, table B.3). Remarkably, the size of the coefficient for humanitarian altruism is comparable to or larger than that for education and racial prejudice, which are considered the strongest predictors of immigration attitudes in the literature. These results are even more pronounced when using a continuous measure of parochial altruism (in terms of money to be donated to charity). Moreover, the findings were strikingly similar in my U.S. survey, suggesting that the consequential altruistic divide among voters is a general phenomenon.[7]

As I have argued, an important reason for these results is people's general skepticism about the positive effects of current immigration policies. Their disagreements notwithstanding, for instance, voters are more pessimistic about national than global consequences of immigration. While many respondents in my 2018 UK survey acknowledged that increasing immigration is more positive than negative for the world (33 percent vs. 29 percent), most believed that it is more negative than positive for their country (47 percent vs. 32 percent). That said, many more respondents were uncertain about the personal effects, rather than the national and global effects, of increasing immigration (46 percent vs. 25 percent and 38 percent, respectively).

Nonetheless, under alternative conditions, parochial altruism can also be related to increased support for freer immigration. While only a small percentage (12 percent) of respondents reported being willing to relax existing restrictions in principle regardless of their national impacts, most (58 percent) also said that they were willing to do it at least for those immigrants who would contribute to the national economy. About the same number of respondents would also support a policy significantly increasing immigration if it were specifically designed to benefit average British citizens through greater selection and taxation of immigrants.

As can be seen from figure 3.6, such policies also yield relatively greater support from both parochial and humanitarian altruists. Importantly, the differences between parochial and humanitarian altruists in terms of endorsing nationally beneficial immigration policies are smaller than when it comes to immigration in general ($p < .02$). While the level of support for freer immigration among parochial altruists is not as high as among humanitarian altruists, it is substantively more significant given the much larger size of the former group.

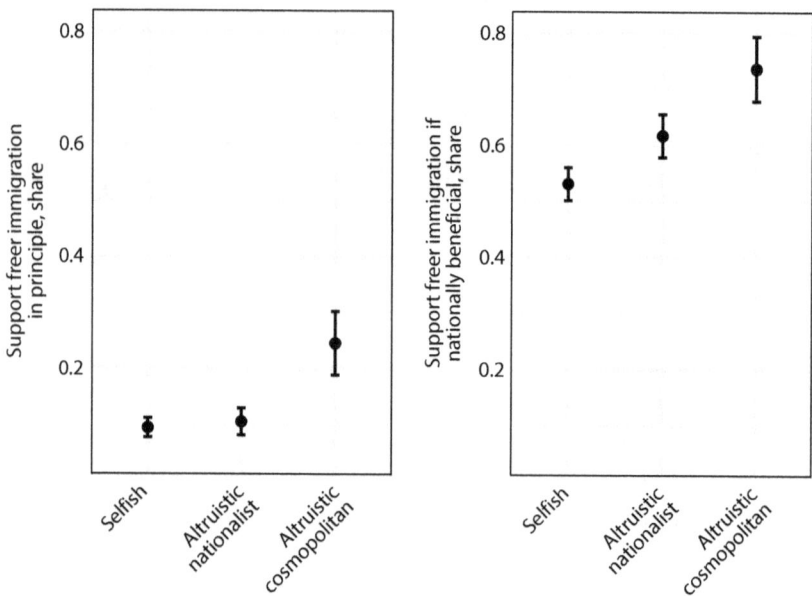

FIGURE 3.6 Immigration support by national impact and parochial altruism. The three revealed prosocial motivation types are based on respondents' contributions in the incentivized task. The bars represent 95 percent confidence intervals. The outcomes indicate the share of voters who support relaxing immigration restrictions regardless of national impact (left) or conditional on positive national impact (right).

Source: Original England Qualtrics survey, 2018.

* * *

Contrary to the conventional wisdom that altruism is inextricably linked to immigration support and that nationalism is linked to immigration opposition, my new revealed-preference evidence demonstrates systematic variation in these links that is related to the intended target of altruism and the perceived national impacts of immigration. Put differently, I have shown that compassionate individuals are rarely impartial in their compassion and that, when it comes to immigration policy, they are more likely to advance the perceived interest of their own country even at the expense of the well-being of foreigners or a more general collective good. However, I have also shown that those who are more nationalistic can actually be supportive of freer immigration policies when those policies clearly benefit their compatriots.

While people's humanitarian motivations are real, I have shown that such motivations on their own can never be sufficient to generate public support for freer immigration admission policies in a representative democracy. First, only a minority of voters prioritize global over national interest. Second, even such few committed humanitarians or cosmopolitans are much more likely to support freer immigration when it is clearly beneficial to their country.

While my analysis did not show that those who are revealed to be more parochially altruistic are *generally* more anti-immigration than those who are revealed to be more egoistic, it is still striking to find that people who incur personal costs to help others are on average as anti-immigration as are those who merely wish to advance their own self-interest. This is an especially notable finding considering that, similar to those who donate to global charities, those who donate domestically are genuine altruists who are more likely to participate in politics and support domestic redistribution than those who do not donate.

On a more theoretical level, the fact that egoists agree with parochial altruists on immigration in some cases but not others casts further doubt on the view that voters use information about potential group impacts as a mere heuristic for self-interest. This finding also suggests that the widespread sociotropic concerns about the potential impacts of immigration that have been documented extensively in previous research are driven at least in part by parochial altruism.

The incentivized game described here provides a new way of measuring revealed nationalist (vs. cosmopolitan) preferences as the in-group bias (or its absence) in altruistic behavior. Given the low variation in self-reported attitudes (e.g., voters almost unanimously report strong national and weak supranational attachments), revealed measures can fruitfully complement the existing empirical literature on the subject of (supra)national identity.[8] Accordingly, my 2018 UK study indicates that individual donations to domestic versus global charities are predictive of anti-immigration attitudes and political behaviors even after statistically controlling for conventional national and global identity.

Of course, people's underlying beliefs about policy impacts may be endogenous to parochial altruism owing to motivating reasoning.[9] That is, some may say they believe that immigration has good or bad consequences *because* they care more about the world or their country. Consistent with this idea, the results of my 2018 study indicate that humanitarian altruists are much more likely to view freer immigration as globally *and* nationally beneficial than do parochial altruists or egoists. As a result, it is essential to consider experimental evidence for my argument so that I can manipulate beliefs about policy impacts to make them independent of people's parochial altruism and other predispositions.

To that end, the next chapter builds on the findings of an original conjoint experiment examining the causal effect of popular beliefs about the impacts of immigration policy and the relative importance of genuine concern for national interest versus racial biases. Overall, my findings demonstrate the striking conditionality of current opposition to immigration for most citizens who, despite their various prejudices, are generally willing to accept freer immigration if it benefits their country.

4

NATIONAL INTEREST RANDOMIZED

When Would Most Voters Support Immigration?

H OW CAN THE CAUSAL CONNECTIONS AMONG NATIONALISM, altruism, and immigration policy attitudes be uncovered? More practically, under what conditions (if any) might most voters—those who genuinely care about their compatriots—support freer immigration?

Ideally, answering these questions would involve experimentally manipulating people's intrinsic prosocial motivations independently of the immigration-related attitudinal outcomes of interest, which is difficult to do outside of the lab setting. And though the literature provides a variety of more or less unobtrusive ways to prime altruism, in-group bias, and national identity, criticism of the robustness of the results of such priming studies has been growing.[1]

Instead, I examined the influence of altruistic and nationalistic motivations by manipulating people's perceptions of the impact of hypothetical immigration policies and looking at their policy choices using a conjoint survey experiment. Overall, this new experimental evidence further confirms the notion that voters intrinsically value the well-being of others in political decisions in addition to their self-interest and other concerns. However, it also convincingly shows that voters value their national interest more than that of any other collective interest, whether global or even local. When it comes to immigration attitudes, my findings imply that voters are willing to support pro-immigration policies when they are explicitly designed to benefit their country.

My goal in this chapter is to estimate the relative effect of people's personal and social incentives on their immigration policy preferences. Previously, I hypothesized that voters' beliefs about the national impacts of immigration policies should matter beyond considerations of self-interest and that these impacts should be more influential on people's immigration attitudes than other potential group impacts. Next, I wanted to determine how much people's opinions on immigration are driven by their selfish and prosocial motivations alongside other factors like racial prejudice.

EXPERIMENTAL DESIGN: CONJOINT ANALYSIS

To do so, in my 2018 online survey of English citizens, I randomized policy impacts using a conjoint analysis in which respondents chose between alternative immigration admission policies. I employed an established method for eliciting preferences underlying trade policy attitudes, complemented that with a multidimensional choice experiment technique, and then applied it to the issue of immigration *policy* preferences as opposed to preferences for *individual immigrants*, as has been explored in earlier research.[2]

As illustrated in figures 0.1 and 0.2 in the introduction, most voters currently oppose freer immigration. According to the logic of parochial altruism (see Hypotheses 2a–c), however, voters would be more supportive of freer immigration if (all else being equal) they perceived it to be nationally beneficial. In other words, people should be more supportive of pro-immigration policies explicitly designed to be beneficial to their country. But what about a similar policy that might substantially undermine personal or global prosperity? Are voters willing to prioritize the interest of their country over their self-interest and the interest of the entire world? Further, what roles do racism and other important noneconomic considerations play?

To answer these questions and determine whether nationalism can play a positive role in immigration policy preferences, I employed a popular conjoint analysis technique. This experimental survey tool was originally used in marketing research to determine how much people value various attributes of consumer products like soda. It is now increasingly being applied to social and political research to figure out how much people value various attributes of political alternatives.[3]

Conjoint analysis works by breaking down complex decision scenarios (whether related to products or policies) into their basic components (i.e., attributes and levels) and then varying combinations of those components to identify respondent preferences among the different options presented. When all components and their combinations are independently randomized, we can be sure that when respondents say they prefer policy A over policy B, it is *because* of the distinct attributes of policy A.

In my conjoint experiment of hypothetical immigration policy choice, I asked respondents to choose their preferred immigration policy in each of five pairs of policies with randomized attributes (so that each respondent sequentially selected five out of ten distinct policies). For each conjoint task question, respondents were forced to choose one option of the pair, even if they disliked both. All policy attributes were randomly selected from discrete, predefined levels indicating distinct implications for the number of immigrants from various regions, as well as (economic) self, local, national, and global consequences of various magnitudes. As long as the relevant decision-making alternatives are adequately specified in the conjoint experiment, the results should predict real-world behavior.[4]

Respondents were provided with the following instructions for the conjoint task:

> Immigration control policies have a significant but different impact on the well-being of each particular individual, their community and sometimes even the world as a whole (including the effects on prices, jobs, wages, and taxes). Now, suppose Britain is holding a popular vote about two competing policy proposals concerning the regulation of immigration from different regions. In each case, suppose that the experts estimate with a good degree of precision that the policy choice will affect some overall measure of economic well-being over the next decade (but has no other effects that matter).

Please examine each table carefully before answering the questions that follow.

The task included the following six attributes and levels of randomization:

Number of immigrants: allow almost none, allow some, allow many, allow almost all

Sending region: Western Europe, Eastern Europe, Asia, Middle East, Africa

Your household wealth: decreased by 5–6 percent, decreased by 1–2 percent, no change, increased by 1–2 percent, increased by 5–6 percent

Your city or town's wealth: decreased by 5–6 percent, decreased by 1–2 percent, no change, increased by 1–2 percent, increased by 5–6 percent

British wealth: decreased by 5–6 percent, decreased by 1–2 percent, no change, increased by 1–2 percent, increased by 5–6 percent

Global wealth: decreased by 5–6 percent, decreased by 1–2 percent, no change, increased by 1–2 percent, increased by 5–6 percent

Figure 4.1 provides an example of a policy choice a respondent would have seen.

Scenario 1 out of 5		
	Policy proposal 1	**Policy proposal 2**
Number of immigrants	Allow some	Allow almost none
Sending region	Asia	Western Europe
	Consequences:	
Global wealth	Increased by 1–2%	No change
Your household wealth	Decreased by 5–6%	Decreased by 5–6%
British wealth	Increased by 1–2%	No change
Your city or town's wealth	Decreased by 5–6%	Increased by 1–2%

If you had to choose, which of these two policy proposals should be enacted?

FIGURE 4.1 An example of the randomized conjoint policy-choice task.

Source: Original England Qualtrics survey, 2018.

The sequence of attributes 3 to 6 ("your city or town's wealth," "British wealth," and "global wealth") was randomized. The relatively small number of attributes and levels ($4 \times 5 \times 5 \times 5 \times 5 \times 5$) ensured that most respondents were able to assess these hypothetical policies adequately. While some effect magnitudes used in the study were arguably more realistic than others, respondents' answers to an open-ended follow-up question gave no indication that their perceptions of policy feasibility affected their choices. Further, removing atypical policy profiles or conditioning on prior beliefs about the impacts of immigration does not change the main results.

Importantly, as opposed to numerous existing conjoint experiments on attitudes toward various *individual immigrants*, my design allows for the examination of the relative importance of various (potentially correlated) motivations that underlie attitudes toward various *immigration policies*. In other words, in addition to eliciting public preferences for *whom to admit*, this design accounts for public preferences for *admission numbers*. This point is crucial because it has long been known that voters sympathetic toward particular immigrant groups may still oppose their immigration when they feel the numbers are too high.[5] Considering a choice between immigration policies, as opposed to between individual immigrants, is also arguably more realistic and informative since, perhaps besides the curious case of historical naturalization referenda in Switzerland, immigration policymaking is almost never done at the individual level.[6]

One key advantage of such an experimental design is its ability to disentangle the causal connection between attitudes about immigration and beliefs about policy consequences, which is generally hard to do in real-world politics owing to motivated reasoning.[7] Given that all policy attributes were simultaneously randomized and their effects are measured on the same scale, the design allowed me to estimate and compare the responsiveness of (counterfactual) immigration preferences to various personal and collective interests. In turn, I was able to examine the relative importance of (potentially correlated) egoistic and more or less parochial altruistic motivations that underlie immigration attitudes. To avoid confounding altruism with a variety of group-based psychological mechanisms related to reciprocity and other social norms, the design deliberately does not pose explicit trade-offs between one's in- and out-groups.[8]

The addition of the "number of immigrants" and "sending region" attributes further helped account for other potential concerns that affect voters' decision-making. Most prominently, it is possible that— because of their categorical racial prejudice—respondents may have decided to reject policies that would increase immigration even if, as explicitly stated, they were economically beneficial for everyone. Further, people may want to limit immigration from certain regions because of perceived security concerns or their preference for more culturally homogeneous or integrated communities.[9] Since the data are on the individual level, it was also possible to assess whether various subgroups of voters would respond differently to specific policy consequences or their combinations.

To test my hypotheses regarding the relative importance of various motivations and the predominance of altruistic nationalism in policy choice, I followed the standard empirical approach to analyzing conjoint experiments.[10] In particular, I estimated the average marginal component effects (AMCEs) of various attributes on policy choice and rating using simple linear regression. The AMCEs represent the average difference in the probability of choosing a policy when comparing two attribute values (e.g., a policy proposal for immigration from Western Europe versus Africa); the average is taken over all other possible attribute combinations.

Finally, to examine the difference in possible effects by various individual characteristics of interest such as altruist type, I compared the respondents who chose to donate the potential prize money to charity with those who chose to keep it, as identified in the economic game from the previous study. To that end, I also replicated my results by calculating marginal means, which indicate the predicted probability of choosing a policy profile with a particular attribute value (e.g., a policy proposal for immigration from Western Europe) averaged across all other attributes and respondents.[11] Therefore, the AMCEs I discuss in this chapter show the average difference in the predicted probability of choosing a policy between two marginal means (e.g., for immigration from Western Europe versus Africa). All the main and alternative conjoint hypotheses, as well as the analysis plan, were preregistered in the Evidence in Governance and Politics (EGAP) registry.[12]

THE EFFECT OF SELFISH VERSUS ALTRUISTIC INCENTIVES

Figure 4.2 illustrates the experimental results based on the estimates from the benchmark ordinary least squares (OLS) regression (appendix B, table B.4) of policy choice on various economic consequences for all participants. Given that there are almost no substantively significant interactions between treatments, most of the effects I discuss

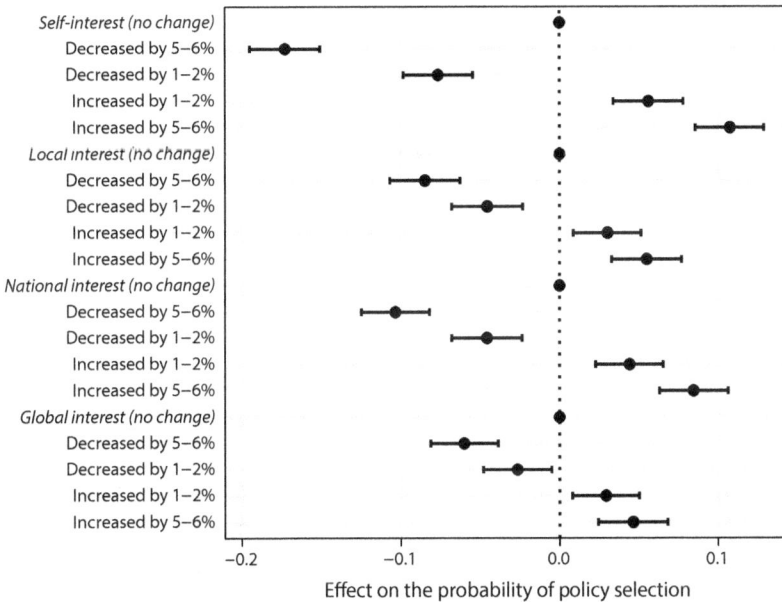

FIGURE 4.2 Effects of immigration policy consequences on policy selection. The plot shows the effects of the randomly assigned policy consequences on their probability of being selected. Estimates are based on the empirical model from appendix B, table B4 (column 2). The bars represent 95 percent confidence intervals.

Source: Original England Qualtrics survey, 2018.

in this chapter are independent of one another as stipulated in the theoretical model.[13]

As may be expected by political economy theories, respondents' preferences were highly responsive to personal policy consequences (i.e., whether a policy would harm or benefit them and their household). Specifically, the difference in the probability of policy selection between the worst and best possible self-interest outcome is about 28 ± 2 percentage points (figure 4.3). This means that out of every 100 policy choices between the explicitly most and least personally lucrative options, 64 (or 28 more) would favor the most lucrative option, while only 36 would favor the least lucrative option, regardless of other policy characteristics.

While a policy's impact on household wealth is by far the strongest single predictor of respondent support, the results also indicate that people care about collective consequences *in addition* to personal consequences. In fact, contrary to theories of pure egoism, the combined *independent* effect of local, national, and global interests is even greater than the effect of self-interest alone (44 ± 3 percentage points). Put differently, an average voter may decide to incur a cost (or forgo a benefit) to herself if a political option is clearly beneficial (or detrimental) to everyone, *despite the predominance of her selfish motivations*.

If greater sensitivity to collective interests elicited in the conjoint task is indeed indicative of genuine altruism, rather than acting as a group heuristic for self-interest, we should also expect it to be more pronounced among the altruists who were revealed independently in the economic game. As indicated by figure 4.3, those who chose to donate to charity were less responsive to changes in household wealth and more responsive to a combination of collective (i.e., local, national, and global) interests. The comparison of coefficient differences between the two indicates that revealed altruists are more likely to prioritize collective over personal interests in their policy choices. While these differences are not large, they are consistent with the interpretation of respondents' donation decisions as indicative of only marginally greater altruism.

This is the exact comparison that I specified in my preanalysis plan. A more direct comparison of all altruist types with policy

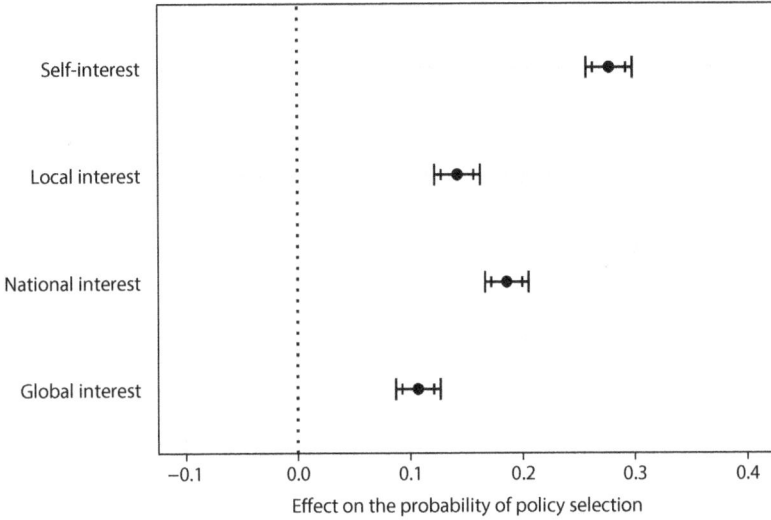

FIGURE 4.3 Effects of best and worst immigration policy consequences on policy selection. The plot shows the effects of the randomly assigned best and worst policy consequences on their probability of being selected. Longer and shorter bars represent 95 percent and 84 percent confidence intervals, respectively.

Source: Original England Qualtrics survey, 2018.

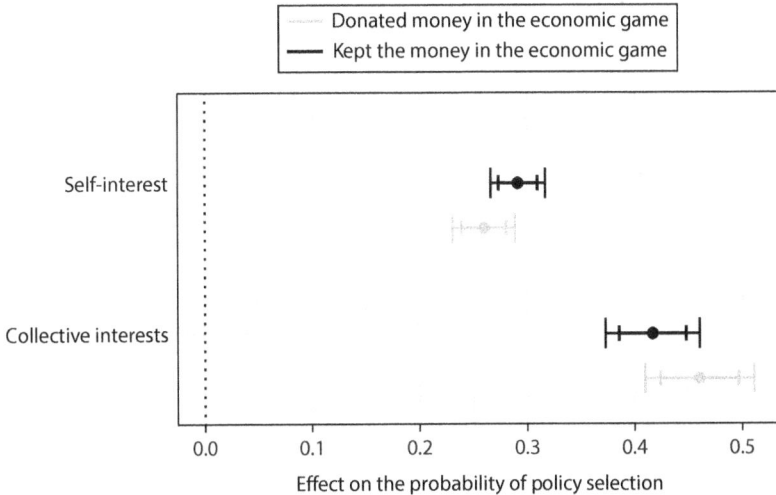

FIGURE 4.4 Effects of policy consequences on policy selection by revealed altruism. The plot shows the effects of the randomly assigned best and worst personal and collective consequences on their probability of being selected by respondents' choices to donate or keep the potential prize money from the economic task. Collective interests were calculated as a combination of local, national, and global interest treatments. Longer and shorter bars represent 95 percent and 84 percent confidence intervals, respectively.

Source: Original England Qualtrics survey, 2018.

consequences on different levels would have been impractical given the small sample size of the humanitarian altruist group and the noisiness of the preference elicitation procedure. It is important to note, however, that even those who chose to donate primarily to global charities appear to have been more responsive to national than global wealth in the conjoint task. As emphasized in earlier research, truly humanitarian, rather than parochial, altruism is empirically rare. But, similar to the results described in chapter 3, those who do have some genuine humanitarian motivations still prefer nationally over globally beneficial immigration policies.

THE DOMINANCE OF NATIONAL INTEREST

Though people respond to prosocial incentives, it is clear that they care about some groups more than others. To better compare the effects of national interest against other collective consequences, figure 4.3 gives the experimental estimates of the difference between the best and worst possible policy outcomes (i.e., a 5–6 percent increase vs. a 5–6 percent decrease).[14]

In line with my theoretical expectations, respondents clearly prioritized parochial over global relative gain, despite the fact that the latter is much greater in absolute terms. Further, when it comes to various parochial impacts, the probability difference in selection for national interest was the most influential (19 ± 2 percentage points), as expected. While respondents also cared greatly about their local community, the average effects were less prominent (14 ± 2 percentage points). The results for global interest were also quite striking. While it is not particularly surprising that the independent effects of global interest are rather weak (11 ± 2 percentage points), their very existence is noteworthy.

Of course, it is possible that these results were found because of scope insensitivity[15] and that people would be more sensitive to global gains if they were presented in absolute terms. However, this possibility does not explain why respondents were more sensitive to national than local impacts. That is, contrary to the common understanding that people necessarily prioritize groups that are spatially closer, national membership seems to dominate over local allegiances.

Conventional ideas of omnipresent tribalism notwithstanding, the evidence thus suggests that voters are willing to take at least some *global* concerns into account, even when choosing *national* policy.

Another pattern that emerges from figure 4.2 is the consistent dynamic of both self-regarding *and other-regarding* "loss aversion."[16] While outside the scope of my theory, this tendency may further exacerbate the political implications of parochial altruism and the tragedy of the global commons: a 1–2 percent decrease in national wealth trumps the positive effect of a 5–6 percent increase in global wealth, but a 1–2 percent decrease in global wealth does not trump a 1–2 percent increase in national wealth when it comes to people's preferred policies.

THE EFFECT OF THE NUMBER AND ORIGIN OF IMMIGRANTS

As emphasized earlier, it is possible that immigration preferences are also determined by people's categorical rejection of certain racial outgroups and other related concerns. As shown in figure 4.5, respondents' immigration policy preferences were indeed responsive to the number of immigrants and their sending region *even when specified policy consequences were taken into account.* In particular, the independent negative effect of increasing immigration ("allow almost all" or "allow many") compared to limiting immigration ("allow some" or "allow almost none") is considerable (13 ± 3 percentage points). In addition, non-European immigration had a negative effect (7 ± 3 percentage points).

How should we interpret the magnitude of the observed effects? On one hand, the estimates are both statistically and substantively significant. For instance, all else equal, a policy that allows almost all immigration was supported as much as a policy that causes a 5–6 percent decrease in national wealth. Meanwhile, a policy that allows non-European immigration was supported as much as a policy that causes a 1–2 percent decrease in national wealth. The more detailed subgroup analysis further suggests that policies of freer immigration are especially discounted among people with higher racial prejudice (see figure 4.6). In line with this finding, respondents with strong

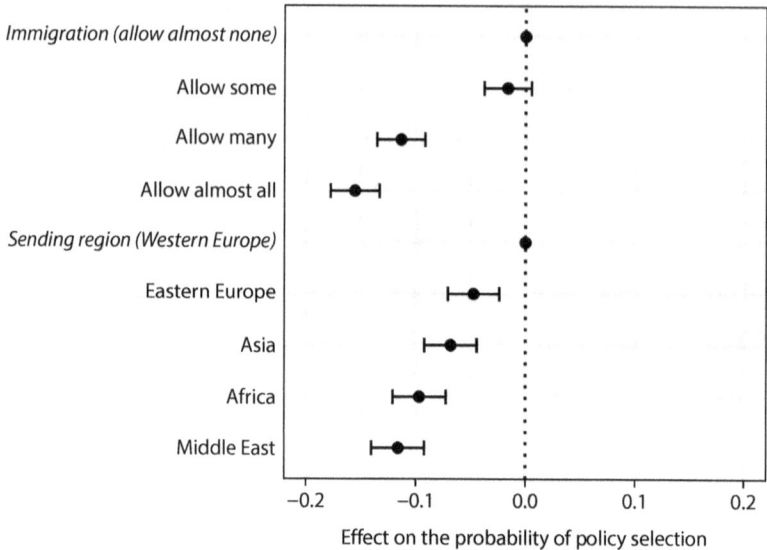

FIGURE 4.5 Effects of immigration policy attributes on policy selection.
The plot shows the effects of the randomly assigned policy characteristics
on the probability of the policies being selected. The attributes represent the
categorical measures for immigrant number and sending region. Estimates
are based on the empirical model from appendix B, table B4 (column 2).
The bars represent 95 percent confidence intervals.

Source: Original England Qualtrics survey, 2018.

racial preferences were also slightly less responsive to both personal and social incentives. In other words, some people are willing to trade off their personal and even national material well-being to live in a more racially homogeneous community.

On the other hand, the effects of the number of immigrants and their sending region are much less influential than various policy consequences as a whole for most voters. In particular, the former explains less than one-third as much variance in policy selection as does the latter (2 percent vs. 7 percent). Albeit less so, the same holds true *even for racially prejudiced voters.*

Of course, one may argue that the explanatory power of racial and demographic factors was artificially minimized here owing to the presence of fewer available attributes (compared to material

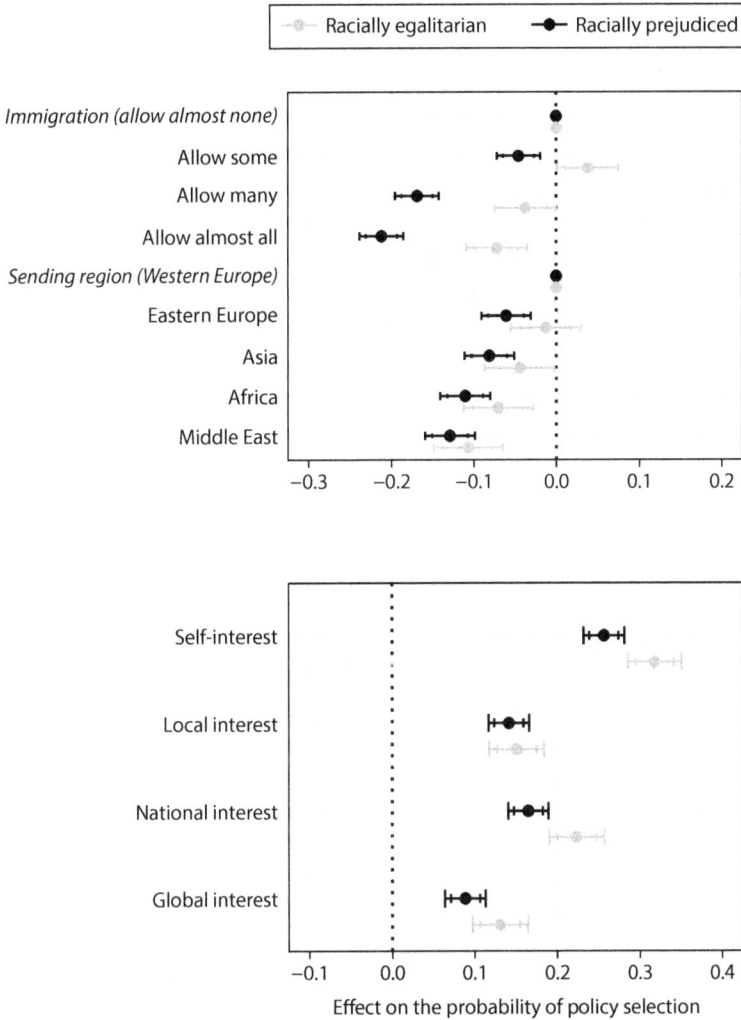

FIGURE 4.6 Effects of policy attributes on policy selection by racial prejudice. The plots show the effects of the randomly assigned policy characteristics on the probability of the policies being selected by respondents' racial prejudice. Estimates are based on the sample restricted to native-born white respondents. Longer and shorter bars represent 95 percent and 84 percent confidence intervals, respectively.

Source: Original England Qualtrics survey, 2018.

consequences). However, it is important to note that the effects of the number of immigrants and their sending region were completely negligible in my identical U.S. study.[17] That is, the categorical rejection of immigration because of taste-based, racial prejudice or related preferences is likely present among some voters, but it is far from pervasive.

To better understand what drives people's immigration preferences in my conjoint experiment, I asked respondents to explain their choice in their own words afterward. A few people did state that they wanted to see immigration reduced regardless of the consequences (e.g., "I favor a reduction in immigration, even if it means an impact to household wealth"; "Immigration should be decreased by all means necessary"). But in line with my quantitative analysis, most people emphasized a combination of personal and national concerns.

* * *

In the real world, the role of selfish versus prosocial motivations is often confounded by the fact that people are more uncertain about the personal than collective consequences of various policies. As a result, when voters respond positively to the prospect of economic growth, for example, the extent to which they use that response as a group heuristic for their self-interest is unclear. As a methodological innovation introduced here, I adopted a new conjoint analysis tool to differentiate between these distinct motivations when it comes to immigration policy choice.

All in all, any independent effect of national interest detected in such design can be considered an indication of pure (parochial) altruistic motivations at work. Further, even if some (egoistic) voters, in fact, support nationally beneficial immigration policies merely as a group heuristic for improving their own pocketbook, that could only reinforce the popularity of and thus the practical need for such policies. As indicated by the similarity between the UK and U.S. results, the dominant role of national interest in people's political decision-making extends across advanced democracies.

Of course, my study has a few limitations, including those related to all survey research and hypothetical choice experiments more generally. For the interested reader, at the end of the chapter, I describe a number of more technical empirical tests, the results of which show no change in my substantive findings. I also describe additional exploratory analyses that also support my argument and its generalizability.[18]

I should also mention that, in focusing on changing immigrant admission numbers and material consequences, the conjoint experiment did not address important policy preferences with regard to immigrant integration and rights. For instance, it is likely that voters may support freer immigration if the selected immigrants are willing to assimilate or if they would have fewer rights.[19] If these or other noneconomic concerns were indeed the most dominant, however, one would expect my survey respondents to have been significantly more responsive to sending region and number of immigrants in the conjoint task.

In this respect, my evidence also contributes to a better understanding of the role of racial prejudice in immigration politics. The very existence of racial bias in the results is not surprising given the abundant evidence on the cultural and demographic drivers of anti-immigration attitudes. Nonetheless, one may argue that when people are asked about immigration in a survey, they may have unobserved expectations about policy consequences. Contrary to that notion, the conjoint task setup employed here explicitly specified both policy consequences and sending region using random assignment. The results of the conjoint experiment can thus reveal biases regarding various sending regions while controlling for policy consequences. As a result, these estimates are arguably more precise at capturing the scope of racial prejudice and related policy-specific demographic concerns in determining public attitudes toward immigration than traditional survey methods that simply ask about immigration support from different regions.

Overall, the results of my theoretically driven choice experiment suggest that, conditional on the perceived economic consequences, immigration preferences are only mildly responsive to the number of immigrants or their sending region. Instead, in line with my preregistered expectations, voters' immigration preferences are highly responsive to their perceived national interest *in addition* to their self-interest.

While some may reasonably think of prioritizing national over global interest as a type of prejudice, it is clearly not the same as simply disliking or discriminating against foreigners because of their racial origin. Although the particular numbers may be specific to the experimental design used in the study, it is likely that the influence of racial prejudice is far less pronounced in immigration preferences than that of both selfish and prosocial motivations.

According to the estimated probability of policy selection based on the benchmark model, all survey respondents' concerns notwithstanding, when they had a choice, respondents chose policies increasing immigration from non-European countries when they believed that those policies would benefit themselves and their compatriots 70 percent of the time. At the same time, only 30 percent of the time did respondents choose policies decreasing immigration when those policies could significantly hurt their country. Of course, inferring majority preferences from conjoint choices is notoriously tricky since such choices do not differentiate between preference intensity and prevalence.[20] Still, in line with the survey evidence from the chapter 3, the conjoint experiment results here strongly suggest that most people are willing to support freer immigration when it is nationally beneficial.

Consequently, despite current political realities, the prevailing sentiment of "my country first" could in principle be employed to *increase* immigration levels. Put differently, the common altruist's dilemma of immigration introduced earlier could be resolved so that the *currently closed* borders of compassion become much more *open*. That said, this evidence reinforces the idea that people's humanitarian motivations are real, but such motivations are never sufficient to sustain majority support for freer immigration admission policies.

NATIONAL INTEREST MATTERS: ADDITIONAL ANALYSES

To confirm the robustness of the results of my conjoint experiment, I conducted several additional empirical tests and found no change in the substantive findings. First, considering that respondents may have found some policy profiles, such as harsh restrictions on European immigration, atypical or unrealistic, I checked the effects of policy consequences within each category of number of immigrants and sending region. Second, given that people may interpret the conjoint task differently based on their preexisting attitudes, I conditioned the results on respondents' prior beliefs about immigration impacts. Third, I used policy rating on a scale ranging from 1 to 7 as an alternative dependent variable to that of policy selection. Fourth, I added fixed effects for respondent IDs and policy pair numbers in addition to clustering standard errors by respondent. Fifth, I controlled for the time respondents spent on each policy pair. Sixth, I replicated all subgroup estimations using marginal means instead of AMCEs as the main quantity of interest.

I then conducted a number of exploratory analyses that also support my argument and its generalizability. First, while no substantive interaction effects of self-interest implications and other policy attirubutes were identified, one can still argue that respondents responded to social good in the conjoint task mostly as a heuristic for personal consequences. As shown in figure 4.7, however, the unconditional importance of collective interests held across the subsamples of both gains and losses for self-interest (as viewed by the respondents). In other words, people are likely to prefer policies that are collectively beneficial regardless of whether they believe the policies will harm or benefit them personally. At the very least, this finding suggests that individuals do not use collective interest only as a proxy for personal gain. It is worth noting that people do seem to care slightly less (more) about national interest when they know that a policy is personally detrimental (beneficial). While this pattern was not explicitly predicted by my theory, it is consistent with the idea that national interest is generally more important to people than are other collective interests.

Second, I compared people's responses to various consequences by age. Given that older people have more predictable income than younger people thanks to state pensions (at least in the United Kingdom), one could argue that they should be less reliant on collective interests as a heuristic for their own income than are younger people.[21] In contrast, if sensitivity to the wealth of others is indicative of altruism, we should expect older people to be similarly sensitive to collective interests but less responsive to personal interest since they

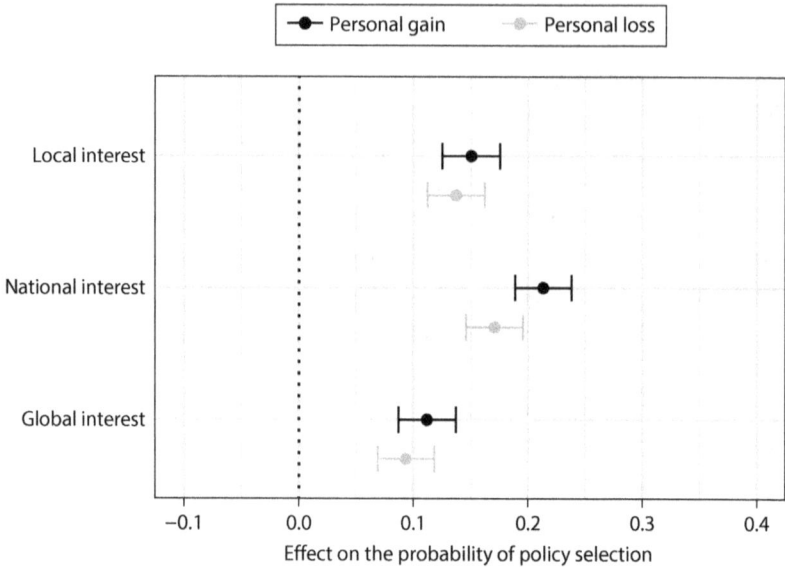

FIGURE 4.7 Effects of policy consequences on policy selection by personal gain versus loss. The plot shows the effect estimates of the randomly assigned best and worst personal and collective consequences on the probability of a policy being selected based on personal gain (black estimates) versus loss (gray estimates). The personal gain (loss) condition included only policies that are beneficial (detrimental) or inconsequential to one's wealth. The bars represent 95 percent confidence intervals.

Source: Original England Qualtrics survey, 2018.

are less likely to benefit from such gains compared to younger people. It is worth noting that the conjoint task explicitly specified that "the policy choice will affect some overall measure of economic well-being over the next decade." The results here are more consistent with sensitivity to collective interests as indicative of altruism than as a group heuristic for self-interest.

Third, I replicated the results of the UK survey with a smaller U.S. study using a similar conjoint design. The dynamic of parochial altruism is not specific to immigration politics in the United Kingdom, and the general findings appear to replicate across cases. The U.S. results are distinct only in terms of the noneffect of number of

immigrants and sending region, which may arguably be a consequence of relying on a less representative sample. Given the variety
of differences between the United Kingdom and the United States, as
well as in the UK and U.S. samples, it is remarkable how similar the
effect coefficients are in both cases. Nonetheless, as emphasized earlier, it is likely that *national* parochial altruism (as opposed to *racial*
or *sectarian* parochialism) is contingent on strong all-encompassing
national identities that are arguably unique to modern and relatively
affluent states.

Fourth, some may argue that the importance of self-interest may
have been exaggerated in the conjoint task since information on
the personal effects of policies is rarely available in the real world.
Conversely, others may argue that the importance of collective interest was exaggerated because of its social desirability. Though the
conjoint technique is generally considered to be robust to this concern, I compared U.S. respondents in terms of low versus high self-
monitoring (a common measure of people's tendency to provide
socially desirable responses).[22] The differences were minor, and in
fact it seems that people consider selfish responses to be *more* and
nation-regarding responses to be *less* socially desirable. While somewhat surprising, this finding aligns with the idea of self-interest as a
prevalent social norm.[23]

These results are not specific to immigration policy. Using a similar experimental setup in a different UK sample (of 534 native-born
English respondents recruited via Prolific Academic in March 2018),
I conducted a conjoint analysis of environmental policy choice in
which voters traded off their personal and collective wealth against
the volume of carbon emissions (as opposed to number of immigrants). As with the studies discussed in this chapter, I found that
people are most responsive to the personal consequences of a policy,
then to its national and local consequences, and finally to the global
consequences. Overall, these results indicate that most voters are
similarly motivated by nationalism as parochial altruism across policy domains.

PART II

PERSUASION BY DESIGN

HOW DEMONSTRABLY BENEFICIAL POLICIES MAKE IMMIGRATION POPULAR

5

MAKING IMMIGRATION POPULAR

From Framing to Policymaking

ACCORDING TO THE EVER-INCREASING NUMBER of empirical studies, including my own research, public attitudes toward immigration are primarily shaped by so-called sociotropic perceptions: what people believe about the impact of immigration on society rather than on their personal fortunes. But where do these sociotropic perceptions come from? Why do they matter for some voters more than others? And what does it all mean for making freer immigration popular? What if people politely say they want policies benefiting their country, but what they really mean, as some critics suspect, is that they oppose foreigners who speak different languages or compete for jobs?

Part I of this book showed decidedly that people's sociotropic concerns about immigration are genuine and that those concerns cannot be reduced to self-interest or prejudice in disguise. Rather, my new experimental and revealed preference evidence indicates that many voters in today's advanced democracies can be described as *altruistic nationalists*. They are generally willing to give up something personally if it helps others, but they are especially inclined to help those from their own country. Nonetheless, because of their upbringings and predispositions, individuals vary significantly in terms of how much they care about others in general and their compatriots in particular. As a result, most people—and especially those who are inclined to prioritize national interest in their policy preferences—support tough rules on immigration if they think such restrictions are necessary to protect the well-being of their fellow citizens. Contrary to conventional wisdom, genuine prosocial motivations are common, but they do not translate straightforwardly into pro-immigration attitudes.

However, my evidence also suggests that concern for fellow citizens, which currently makes many people apprehensive about immigration, could actually *encourage* people to support it if current policy circumstances change. While only a small percentage of people are in principle willing to relax existing immigration restrictions, most say they are eager to do so, at least for those immigrants who would contribute to the nation economically or otherwise. I have also found that, despite their current skepticism and various biases, most voters across all possible groups would support a new policy significantly increasing immigration if it were clearly designed to benefit average citizens. Put simply, most people should be able to support more open immigration admission policies if they believe those policies are good for their country.

I hope you still remember my theoretical model of parochial altruism in politics from chapter 1. Apart from voters' diverse altruistic and parochial predispositions, I assumed that people decide among various policies based on the perceived consequences of those policies. At this point, you may rightly wonder, Why do people believe that certain policies, including current immigration policies, are bad for their country, and can these (mis)perceptions be changed?

Unlike predispositions, people's beliefs about how certain policies will impact their country are clearly not something they are born with. So, it is only natural to assume that these beliefs come about from some combination of information sources, which may be viewed as either benevolent education or malevolent propaganda depending on one's pre-existing stance on immigration. However, what I fear is often overlooked by observers is that these beliefs must also reflect, at least to some extent, the policies that are actually in place and their real consequences, even if not entirely accurately perceived.

When I first published some of this evidence on altruistic nationalism as a driver of immigration attitudes in the form of an academic paper a few years ago[1] and received my first reactions from a wider audience, I noticed that many people were interpreting my argument primarily in terms of its implications for policy communication and elite messaging. If it is true that voters care deeply about their compatriots, as some have referenced and interpreted my work, then policymakers should be able to make immigration more popular by creating more effective narratives emphasizing the benefits of immigration to receiving countries. While I do not think that this interpretation is wrong, I have long felt that it is incomplete since it overlooks the actual policies in place.

Meanwhile, others continue to question how realistic hypothetical preferences for more nationally beneficial immigration policies are in real-world politics. After all, despite international migration's enormous benefits to both receiving and sending countries, few voters are unabashedly pro-immigration, and few political parties run on an explicitly pro-immigration platform. Instead, anti-immigration forces always seem to have a competitive edge. Elected officials often dismiss the possibility of liberalizing even the most beneficial immigration pathways as not electorally viable, fearing backlash from immigration-skeptical constituents.[2]

Some have also justifiably asked how this work can align with my previous research showing that changing people's minds on immigration is incredibly hard.[3] This collaborative research suggests that most observed changes in immigration attitudes likely stem from random fluctuations in survey responses rather than from substantive opinion shifts. Drawing on the best available longitudinal survey data across countries, my colleagues and I found that most people maintain their general stance toward immigration, even in times of economic or refugee crises. These findings imply that any change in communication strategy for immigration is unlikely to significantly alter public pro-immigration sentiment on its own.

Over the past several years, I have thought a lot about the practical implications of widespread altruistic nationalism and sociotropic concerns for successful persuasion and productive policy changes on immigration issues. Part II approaches these implications by setting out a framework of what I call "durable persuasion by demonstrably beneficial policymaking." Drawing on the voter preference evidence presented in part I and the literature on good governance and policy feedback, I consider the few systematic ways in which freer immigration, or consistently high immigration flows, can become legitimate in the electorate.

Overall, I conclude that having long-running, selective immigration policies that attract needed workers or otherwise *demonstrably benefit* citizens are a necessary and major contributory condition for this to happen. No matter how smart policy communication is, what ultimately matters are the policies on the ground. At least descriptively, the only major countries where freer immigration is practiced and popular are those with a highly selective immigration system. There are also no major countries with a highly selective system where immigration is relatively unpopular.

In the rest of this chapter, I assess what it takes for persuasion efforts on freer immigration to be successful and long-lasting. I start with a discussion of framing strategies as the most immediate practical implications of the argument presented in this book. According to this interpretation, for freer immigration to be popular, policy communication should be framed predominantly in terms of national interest. I show that, while such strategic communication is a good start, it is ultimately not enough to ensure sufficient support for immigration owing to the constant availability of alternative competing frames. I then show that even more complex interventions, such as correcting misperceptions about immigration or reducing prejudice against immigrants—assuming they can be at least somewhat successful—are also insufficient to secure the public endorsement of more open immigration admission policies. The primary reason for this is that people's perceptions, no matter how mistaken they may be, are and must be grounded in their interests and the political reality.

Chapter 6 provides a proof of concept for the general idea of persuading voters by implementing new policies. In particular, I use new data on historical changes in immigration policy and politics from across European countries and the United States to examine what actually happens when governments adopt pro-immigration reforms broadly aimed at benefiting the nation. Despite the common fear of populist backlash, I show that pro-immigration policy changes are generally not associated with either greater popular concerns about immigration or populist voting, at least in the short run. If anything, broad pro-immigration reforms can only further legitimize immigration in the electorate in the medium to long term.[4]

Of course, not all pro-immigration reforms will be equally persuasive to voters, especially in the long run. So what is needed in addition to messaging efforts and broad pro-immigration reforms, as I argue in chapter 7, is a much more durable form of persuasion through both responsive and responsible policymaking. Governments are more likely to convince their citizen constituencies that immigration is good for them when they consistently enact policies that have tangible and clear benefits for their citizens and communities. First, building on the idea of conditional immigration preferences introduced in part I, I show that any counterfactual persuasion effects from reducing prejudice on people's support for freer immigration are likely trumped by the impact of enacting demonstrably beneficial policies. In line with this result, I then show descriptively that only the countries that have historically prioritized labor and needed skills in their immigration policies have managed to achieve general public acceptance of freer immigration.

Chapter 8, a qualitative chapter, illustrates how this dynamic plays out in the real world. In particular, I contrast the national interest-based and humanitarian-based approaches to immigration policy reform and compare the historical evolution of immigration politics and public opinion in Canada and Sweden. Both countries have been deemed immigration success stories in the past, but only Canada has been able to maintain its expansive policies and public support for them. As the increasingly evident collapse of Sweden's generous humanitarian policies shows, voters will accept freer immigration only when they see that it has worked for them and their country over time. In sum, the evidence presented in part II suggests that, while providing accurate information and reducing prejudice in the electorate are worthwhile, only demonstrably beneficial pro-immigration reforms can secure public support for consistently high immigration rates.

WHY COMMON PERSUASION EFFORTS FAIL

A great number of individuals and organizations are rightly interested in persuading people that *immigration of all kinds*, not just highly skilled immigration, is generally beneficial to all parties and thus should be freer. But despite all existing well-meaning efforts to provide accurate information and reduce prejudice to achieve this goal, most voters around the world are still skeptical about allowing higher immigration flows. It is important to review why these efforts, however important they may be, cannot be fully sufficient on their own, as well as why any effort to change people's minds on immigration is an uphill battle.

This is one of the questions that my coauthors, Dillon Laaker and Cassidy Reller, and I tried to answer in previous research.[5] Our study was motivated by the observation that, whereas many immigration advocates find it difficult to sway people's views on the issue, immigration scholars usually assume such views are flexible. To resolve this puzzle, we conducted the first comprehensive assessment of the stability and change of immigration attitudes across a number of receiving countries over the past several decades. Importantly, unlike most previous studies that looked at public opinion changes in the aggregate, we considered nine panel, or *longitudinal*, datasets that tracked the same individuals over time and measured their opinions on various aspects of immigration policy.

Our study used several methods to assess stability and change in immigration attitudes. We started with a straightforward test comparing the shares of respondents who kept articulating the same immigration views over time in various surveys. Depending on the survey context, immigration questions, and the amount of time that had passed, we found that *71 to 94 percent of respondents did not change their opinion much* throughout the survey. In some particularly long-running surveys like the Swiss Household Panel, most respondents even reported the same pro- or anti-immigration stance after a decade. We then combined multiple survey questions to estimate people's underlying immigration attitudes and used various statistical models to reduce the impact of potential measurement errors related to people's misunderstanding of survey questions. We found that the average stability of attitudes was even stronger after accounting for this possibility.

The apparent stability of immigration attitudes is particularly remarkable given that the time covered by our surveys includes the global recession, Brexit, the 2016 election of Donald Trump, and the 2015–2016 European refugee crisis. In other words, we demonstrated that immigration attitudes are not very sensitive to changes in economic conditions, migration flows, or political environments. This finding is further corroborated by another recent paper I coauthored that reveals that even the COVID-19 pandemic, despite halting most global immigration, has had a minimal impact on people's long-term views on the issue.[6]

Why are people's views on immigration so stable? Most of all, our research supports the central role of socialization and deep-seated predispositions. Most people's stance on immigration policy simply reflects their early life experiences and personality traits, such as those related to racial prejudice or parochial altruism. Acknowledging this, our study questioned the role that (mis)information and contextual factors play in people's immigration attitudes, and we found that these factors explain only a small amount of difference in these attitudes. While major political events or large campaigns may shift people's views on particular immigration issues in the short term, those changes are small, and people eventually revert back to their initial beliefs.

However, all this evidence does not necessarily imply that people cannot change their minds following some underlying change in the objective conditions in the longer term. As described earlier, people who unconditionally oppose or support freer immigration no matter what are rare. Policymakers and advocates can and should try to change people's minds by meeting voters where they are: acknowledging their current concerns about immigration, recognizing the persistence of their biases, and making compromises on immigration reforms that will be appealing despite these preconceptions. In particular, the evidence on altruistic nationalism presented in part I implies that many voters who currently oppose freer immigration can be persuaded to change their minds if they believe that immigration is to their country's benefit.

In this respect, most voters across the Atlantic have already been persuaded, perhaps even *pre-suaded*, that certain types of immigration—such as that of skilled workers—are beneficial and desirable.[7] Importantly, people do not need to be convinced of this fact through any benevolent information campaign or malevolent elite manipulation; they already recognize such immigration as legitimate and its advantages as undeniable. Further, as I illustrate over the next few chapters, this acceptance goes way beyond attracting top talent. Rather, it extends to most other forms of immigration that are explicitly and directly beneficial to their country, including the immigration of immediate relatives, students, and temporary workers and bilateral agreements designed to fill specific job vacancies.

Consequently, the most sustainable way to persuade voters to support freer immigration in a representative democracy is for responsible governments to open selective legal immigration pathways that actually and demonstrably benefit citizens. When the benefits of certain forms of immigration are clear and people have confidence in those benefits, they are more likely to accept other forms of immigration, even when its benefits are less obvious or in situations that demand it, such as a refugee crisis.

WHY IMPROVING POLICY MESSAGING IS NOT ENOUGH

Many studies show that framing pro-immigration reforms so that they appeal to values that voters hold dear may be an effective messaging strategy to increase public support for freer immigration.[8] Voters care deeply about national interest, so it is reasonable to believe that emphasizing the benefits of immigration to the country should be conducive to its popular support, especially if it comes from a source people trust.[9] In a competitive political environment where voters are constantly exposed to anti-immigration counterframes from various sides, however, such an approach would require constant repetition and media dominance to be effective.[10]

Still, one may rightly point out that communication centered on national interest has already been quite common among governments and immigration agencies.[11] Indeed, politicians and policymakers across the political spectrum often assert that their proposed policies benefit the country and its citizens. However, there are many important exceptions. For example, the Swedish Migration Agency, examined later on, commonly and deliberately frames its immigration goals in humanitarian terms. In addition, some scholars and advocates argue that even within governmental agencies, national interest rhetoric may be counterproductive or ethically questionable.[12]

National interest rhetoric may also be less common among in the context of pro-immigration nonprofits and advocates where the humanitarian and rights-based arguments in favor of immigration are increasingly gaining traction.[13] Some advocates, for example, are understandably concerned that using the rhetoric of national interest may undermine humanitarian support for freedom of movement by perpetuating the idea that only those immigrants who benefit their adopted countries deserve rights and respect.[14] From this perspective, relevant stakeholders should instead always strive to communicate that all immigrants are human beings who deserve help regardless of their potential contribution.

While certainly admirable and well intentioned, these idealistic notions are arguably misguided, especially when taken to an extreme. It has been increasingly recognized that humanitarian or rights-based frames alone are not very effective, even on their own terms.[15] At the same time, people's sense of obligation to their compatriots is not going anywhere anytime soon. As extensively shown in part I, very few people are willing to benefit foreigners *before* their compatriots, and almost none are willing to do it *at the expense* of their compatriots. Yet nationalists are more willing to increase immigration when it benefits their country than are cosmopolitans when it does not.

Many observers have written convincingly and at length about how immigration serves as an ultimate wedge issue, enabling right-wing politicians to capitalize on people's prejudices and amplify immigration problems for electoral gain.[16] So, at the very least, the evidence presented so far implies that, when it comes to making immigration popular, it is a bad idea for advocates to *de-emphasize* the benefits of immigration to receiving countries. Similarly, it is a bad idea to *de-emphasize* the importance of an orderly, legal admission process and the need for immigrants to integrate successfully into society. If there is no compelling national interest narrative in favor of freer immigration, voters confronted with choosing between narratives focused on preventing border chaos and those focused on aiding less fortunate foreigners will invariably find the former more persuasive.

Regardless of what one believes about the merits of framing immigration in terms of national interest or any other important value, however, such communication considerations can only matter so much. After all, counterframing is always a possibility, and most arguments either for or against immigration clearly invoke multiple complementary frames. I am also not familiar with any evidence suggesting that appeals to national interest can reduce the effectiveness of humanitarian arguments, or the other way around.

On the brighter side, the underlying stability of immigration attitudes also implies that it is hard for any particular communication strategy to make voters more anti-immigration. When far-right politicians use anti-immigration rhetoric in their campaigns, they can usually raise the issue's salience only among those who are already anti-immigration.[17] And there is little evidence that using populist or other divisive rhetoric to frame immigration issues matters much for persuasion. People vote for right-wing populists because they *already* agree with the populists' substantive policy position that immigration is harmful, not because they find their rhetoric particularly appealing.[18]

While people do respond to elite cues and at times are willing to change their minds based on elite messaging, this generally works only for issues that do not affect people personally and only when the messaging comes from trusted copartisan leaders.[19] Unfortunately, as I show in my most recent research, those who oppose immigration also tend to care more about it than those who support it.[20] While there is some evidence that center-right politicians taking pro-immigration positions may be persuasive,[21] it is difficult to imagine widespread pro-immigration messaging being adopted by parties that are currently anti-immigration or by politicians incentivized to stoke anti-immigration views among their base.

According to the vast literature in social sciences (as discussed in chapter 2), a key reason that many voters currently believe that immigration is harmful is not because of insufficient emphasis being placed on its benefits or too much populism being present in policy communication. The reason is *prejudice*, broadly conceived, including both ignorance of basic immigration facts and animus against foreign out-groups.

WHY PROVIDING CORRECT
INFORMATION IS NOT ENOUGH

As the discussion so far implies, even consistently positive framing and reframing of immigration would likely not be sufficient to change people's preferences in a durable way. However, according to extensive recent reviews of information experiments, lasting change is more likely to be achieved by introducing new knowledge that can expand people's understanding of the issue rather than merely repackaging existing information.[22]

Across countries, voters are quite ignorant about immigration in that they have false empirical beliefs about the issue. In particular, most people exaggerate the number of immigrants in their country, their various unfavorable characteristics, and their potential differences from the native-born population. They overestimate their negative effects and underestimate their positive effects on the economy and society, from welfare use and tax contributions to crime and assimilation.[23] Voters across the political spectrum also often lack any knowledge of immigration admission and related policies currently in place.[24]

Among possible information interventions, nonjudgmental and verifiable narratives from a source people find credible that can generate new knowledge in favor of increasing immigration[25] should be preferable to fact-checking approaches that attempt to correct people's misperceptions about immigrants and their costs.[26]

In line with the argument of this book, new relevant knowledge and narratives that align with respondents' national interest concerns by providing information about economic or other benefits to citizens should be more effective than those that appeal to humanitarian concerns—*even among cosmopolitans*. For instance, some recent research has found that information about how immigration can help address population decline may be persuasive for those who are currently ambivalent about the issue.[27] And others have found that sharing information about economic benefits can persuade people across the political spectrum.[28]

In my most recent research, I also found that informing individuals about the broad benefits of increasing legal immigration or the threats of not doing so significantly affects people's attitudes. Not only does it convince more people to support immigration, but it also deepens the commitment of those already in favor of it.[29] Even from a purely normative democratic perspective, it may be useful for voters to be informed about what immigration is or is not, what policies are currently in place, and how these policies can or cannot help their country.

Unfortunately, a lack of relevant knowledge is only one barrier to greater acceptance of immigration. According to even the most optimistic estimates from the literature, effective information interventions can durably shift only a small percentage of marginal voters on the issue and mostly only in the short term.[30]

Some may argue that information campaigns can never be fully successful in democracies in which voters are not incentivized to be more knowledgeable about politics in general.[31] That said, when voters are somewhat informed about immigration issues, as in the case of Canada examined later on, that policy knowledge may be a consequence rather than a cause of good policymaking.[32]

Ultimately, however, even if all people were perfectly informed about immigration, support for more open policies would not necessarily be overwhelming. After all, an underappreciated fact is that even those who already support immigration are not necessarily aware of its effects or the workings of particular policies in detail.[33]

WHY REDUCING PREJUDICE AGAINST IMMIGRANTS IS NOT ENOUGH

Although information provision can sometimes be effective for policy persuasion, there is one important and extremely evident reason that the case of immigration is different. That is that immigration involves the movement of *foreigners*, an out-group: people who most likely look different, speak a different language, and have a different culture.[34] As a result, a vast literature documents the importance of ethnic, racial, nationalist, and other forms of group prejudice and animus in the formation of immigration policy preferences.[35]

A logical implication of this literature is that reducing prejudice should make people more open to increasing immigration. But reducing prejudice against out-groups in general—or immigrants in particular[36]—is perhaps even more difficult than sharing knowledge or correcting misperceptions.[37] Nonetheless, there are several promising avenues to do this.

First, prejudice can be reduced somewhat by correcting certain misperceptions themselves, especially when it comes to voters' erroneous beliefs about immigrants' adherence to social norms.[38] Second, prejudice can be reduced by engaging in empathy-based or perspective-taking approaches that encourage citizens to better understand and relate to immigrants.[39] Finally, there is evidence that meaningful intergroup contact can reduce prejudice at least against existing immigrants who are already living in a new home country.[40]

Still, as with factual ignorance, there are important reasons to believe that it is not possible to remove prejudice against foreigners completely. Nativism and xenophobia—and outright hostility to foreigners—have been around for all modern if not all known human history.[41] At the same time, ethnocentrism, which arguably fuels these feelings, is a stable personality characteristic that simply cannot be changed much.[42]

Ultimately, however, a world without prejudice against immigrants would not necessarily bring about more open policies or even support for such policies. First, while anti-immigrant and anti-immigration attitudes (as well as xenophobic, nativist, racist, and ethnocentric attitudes) are correlated, their correlation is far from perfect. Many people who do not support freer immigration do not hold much prejudice toward immigrants. And many people support more open policies despite being prejudiced.[43]

An important reason for such a discrepancy is the recently documented immigration "stock premium."[44] According to this finding, public support for more open immigration admission policies (to bring future immigrants) is systematically lower than public support for more positive policies toward existing immigrants (who are already at least in part an in-group). Another important reason is that, as demonstrated in part I, people can support policies based on their perceived personal and national interests (alongside other values and principles), not just group prejudice.

All in all, while there is some evidence that prejudice toward immigrants can be slightly reduced and that policy preferences toward freer immigration can be improved through information campaigns, neither approach is sufficient to markedly transform public opinion regarding immigration. Going back to the evidence presented in part I, we can see that even among educated, left-leaning UK voters who hold no explicit racial prejudice, support for more open immigration admission policies is often low. This finding suggests that, even in a world of highly knowledgeable and unprejudiced individuals, freer immigration is unlikely to be universally accepted or even to have majority support.

WHY MAKING BETTER IMMIGRATION POLICIES IS NECESSARY FOR PERSUASION

Of course, none of this means that providing people with credible information about immigration and its national benefits or reducing prejudice against immigrants is not important in itself. After all, as shown in part I, the vast majority of anti-immigration voters oppose immigration *conditionally* and thus are persuadable in principle. But, to the extent that much work has already been done in these areas, it is also crucial to understand what is currently missing from attempts to make freer immigration more popular in affluent democracies.

As I argue, the commonly missing component is *meeting voters where they are* in terms of demonstrating how different immigration policies can better align with voters' personal and social incentives. Only when voters are *confident* that immigration policymaking is in their country's interest can they accept more open immigration admission policies, including those helping vulnerable migrants fleeing adversity. This acceptance can only occur when people not just hear from experts that immigration is beneficial, but also see and experience firsthand that it is good for them. In other words, what is currently often missing from persuasion efforts is better, responsible, and *responsive* policymaking that demonstrably addresses voters' concerns.

The long-standing ideal of responsible democratic governance requires the adoption of policies that promote the national interest in the long run regardless of whether those policies are supported by most voters.[45] The process of figuring out such nationally benefi-cial policies—especially in the divisive field of immigration—is not easy and it necessarily involves political compromises. As a result, policymaking usually involves years-long deliberations among demo-cratically elected legislators from different parties, expert decision-making among appointed agencies, and occasional judicial review by local and national courts. Despite all these efforts, the political elites still often end up being wrong about which policies are better for their country (which we come to know with the benefit of hindsight).

In contrast, the ideal of responsive democratic governance empha-sizes the alignment of public policy with voters' stated preferences. The idea is that the best way to govern is to do what people say they want. The hope is that, even when voters cannot be fully informed about most issues, implementing policies in line with their stated preferences will generally also align with their interests. However, people often fail to advance, articulate, or even understand their own interests.[46] It is no wonder that the merits of more direct forms of democracy, as opposed to more representative systems, are still debated today.

The tension between these two approaches to democratic gover-nance—the technocratic and the populist—is especially common in immigration politics. According to the sincere beliefs of most political elites, it is true that increasing immigration would gener-ally advance the national interest of receiving countries. To the extent that voters are currently (rightly or wrongly) skeptical about immigra-tion in general, it is also true that increasing immigration would not be a responsive policy.

One way to solve this tension might be for elites in power to del-egate more immigration policymaking to independent agencies, similar to how monetary policy is regulated by central banks in many countries.[47] However, this is unlikely to be politically feasible, even on the margin, in most contexts today in which immigration is already heavily politicized and unpopular. So, what can policymakers and advocates do *now* to ensure more open immigration policies?

Outside of immigration, some scholars have recognized that pub-lic policies can be successful in a democracy only when they can gen-erate their own support.[48] Moreover, others have argued that policies implemented by representative governments not only reflect but also significantly shape voters' views on various issues. This usually happens either by changing people's incentives and their personal experiences with policies or by sending authoritative institutional signals about what is accepted as normal in society.[49]

In this respect, when government policies are already evidently responsive to people's views, the government also gains benefit of the doubt from voters in terms of their confidence in the ability of the government to enact responsible policies.[50] Citizens are more likely to trust in their government's decision to implement unpopular policies when those governments are actually trustworthy. When voters trust the government, they may become more receptive to their arguments, such as those about the less obvious benefits of certain policies as argued by experts.[51] The idea of good governance often similarly means finding the right balance between implementing technically sound policies and being responsive to the citizenry.

The evidence presented here implies that the tension between responsible and responsive immigration policymaking can be reduced significantly if the government enacts policies that are *demonstrably* beneficial to receiving countries, like opening up new selective pathways for foreign workers to fill *specific* labor shortages. As I argue and explore in more detail in chapter 7, such selective liberalization of immigration—a commonly preferred technocratic solution—is still in line with the public opinion or conditional majority preferences in many countries. Moreover, it may also be the only viable path to broadly and durably legitimize freer immigration.

THE POWER OF DEMONSTRABLY BENEFICIAL POLICYMAKING

So, what exactly does it mean for a policy to be demonstrably beneficial? I define *demonstrably beneficial (DB) policies* as a subset of actually beneficial policies—as may be imperfectly estimated by researchers—that are *explicitly* and *straightforwardly* beneficial to countries and their citizens. First, DB policies must be *explicitly* beneficial in terms of their official or stated goals. Second, DB policies must be *straightforwardly* beneficial in terms of being apparent to most of the electorate or anyone without special knowledge of particular policy domains. Put simply, demonstrable benefits are the positive effects of policies on countries that most citizens can easily recognize.

In the context of immigration, I use *DB* to redefine and rebrand the often ambiguous and contested category of "selective policies." While selective policies often focus on skill selection in the name of national interest, they can also involve race-based or other illiberal ways to select migrants. As a result, selective policies can be conflated with restrictive policies, even when they open new legal pathways for immigration. In contrast, DB policies can comprise a much broader spectrum of pro-immigration policies, from increasing labor migration of individuals with various skill levels to facilitating various types of family, student, and humanitarian migration.

In his influential critique, Gary Freeman argues that many liberal immigration policies in Western democracies are *clientelistic*, catering to specific interest groups as opposed to advancing broader national interest. According to this critique, immigration mostly has concentrated benefits accruing to immigrants themselves and their employers who need labor while its diffuse costs are borne by the general public. However, it is unclear how accurate this critique is.[52] Regardless, DB policies are by definition *programmatic* in terms of being implemented according to transparent rules that benefit the public at large.[53] As a result, DB policies do not require extensive explanations, unique framing strategies, or any clientelistic conspiracy on behalf of policymakers for voters to understand their value or accept them.

Importantly, the demonstrable benefits of immigration can extend beyond purely economic considerations, encompassing longer-term cultural effects and the potential for migrants to integrate successfully into their new societies. In other words, DB policies are not solely about attracting economically valuable migrants but also about fostering conditions under which most immigration can be seen as orderly, integrated, and beneficial in line with voters' preferences (for more details, see chapter 7). The emphasis on demonstrable benefits highlights the importance of policies that make the positive impacts of immigration on receiving countries clear to most voters, regardless of their knowledge or political persuasion.

Defined this way, the idea of DB policies provides a useful lens to reinterpret the results presented in part I. As a reminder, I showed that people, especially those who care about their compatriots, are more likely to support immigration when it is (experimentally manipulated to be) explicitly and straightforwardly beneficial to receiving countries. They are more likely to support hypothetical policies increasing immigration when those policies are more beneficial compared to both less beneficial policies and other possible factors driving immigration policy preferences.

While there is a significant overlap between *actually* and *demonstrably* beneficial policies, they are not always the same. Experts may disagree on the actual national benefit of various immigration policies, and even when they agree, these policies may not be demonstrably beneficial from the voters' perspective. Many pro-immigration policies endorsed by experts are not explicitly designed to benefit receiving countries, and even when they are, the benefits may be indirect or based on assumptions that voters may not share or understand.

Although I am putting forward the idea of DB policies as a distinct analytic category of policies for the sake of conceptual clarity, the extent to which certain policies are actually beneficial and the extent to which the benefits are demonstrable are empirical questions. It is also undoubtedly a matter of degree. However, demonstrable benefits are decidedly not subjective or just in the eyes of the beholder. Experts can estimate the actual benefits or costs of a policy, and representative polling can estimate their "demonstrableness." In practice, a policy proposal can be deemed demonstrably beneficial if, in a hypothetical or real survey, most respondents agree that enacting it will be good for the country. Unfortunately, many existing immigration policies across OECD countries today may not meet this criterion.

One example of this dynamic is the ongoing academic debate about the fiscal consequences of immigration. Few experts or citizens doubt the fiscal benefits of skilled immigrants who are highly paid and taxed, but the effects of permanent low-skilled immigration are much more controversial. According to most existing estimates from the United States and other OECD countries, low-skilled immigrants tend to have negative direct effects on public finances since they pay less in taxes than they consume in terms of government services. And this notion is likely reflected in common public perceptions of immigrants' fiscal burden. However, recent evidence from the United States also suggests the possible indirect net fiscal benefits of low-skilled immigration. The argument is that low-skilled immigrants tend to work in sectors that induce additional demand for and allow native-born citizens to move to higher-skilled occupations, making the nation more productive overall.[54]

This idea of indirect benefits makes perfect sense to academics like myself who already support freer immigration. There should also certainly be more research on these and other general effects, as well as greater effort among advocates to communicate those effects to the public. However, these findings are based on many technical assumptions that some experts may disagree with and that most people may not understand (e.g., regarding the marginal costs of various public goods or foreign–native labor complementarity). Further, even experts do not yet know how well these findings may apply to economies outside of that of the United States. Ultimately, regardless of its actual merits, the general policy of permanently admitting more low-skilled immigrants without connecting it to any particular national need is decidedly not demonstrably beneficial and is thus unlikely to be popular among voters.

Importantly, I am not just changing the goalposts from making freer immigration popular in general to making a certain type of immigration popular in particular. The idea of persuasion through enacting better policies that are demonstrably beneficial is not just about appeasing negative attitudes toward low-skilled immigration by allowing only high-skilled immigration. The good news is that there are ways to attract more immigrant workers of all skill levels— which experts say host countries desperately need—in more demonstrably beneficial ways. As I discuss in more detail in the following chapters, this must be done through deliberate, targeted policy efforts, such as those related to filling specific labor shortages, regional programs, and labor mobility partnerships, for which the goal of advancing the national interest is clearly evident to anyone.

Of course, what exactly constitutes the national interest often remains elusive. Voters and their representatives, as well as experts themselves, often vehemently disagree about whether various policy alternatives serve the national interest.[55] These disagreements are especially strong when considering noneconomic factors that are difficult or impossible to quantify. When advocates claim that "we are a nation of immigrants" (or that "we need to prioritize real Americans first," for that matter), they are essentially saying that adopting more open (or more restrictive) immigration policies should factor into national interest considerations, independent of the economic impacts of immigration.

What almost no one argues, except perhaps a few stanch antinationalists, is that representative democratic governments should forsake or even downplay the pursuit of national interest. The evidence presented here so far suggests that, though there may be debate over which policies best advance the national interest, most voters view national interest as paramount beyond their personal interests. In addition, most voters consider national interest to outweigh both more universalistic and more particularistic considerations, at least in the context of formulating national immigration policy within a representative democracy.

This point is important because pro-immigration policies are in fact often promoted and implemented independently of or even in opposition to national interest. For example, refugee resettlement in high-income countries can be championed explicitly by its advocates and by governments for its humanitarian benefits. Of course, some might still argue, at least rhetorically, that such policies are also beneficial to receiving countries. But, while potentially bolstering the receiving economy through population growth over the long term, such policies do not generally yield immediate, visible benefits that voters can easily recognize. The potential indirect benefits, such as increased innovation, cultural enrichment, and the eventual economic contributions of successfully integrated refugees or their descendants, require time to manifest and are often contingent on the implementation of other economic policies. These potential and indirect benefits can also be offset by direct resettlement costs to host communities.[56]

Another relevant example here is employment bans for refugees and asylum seekers. These bans often have an ambiguous mix of national interest and humanitarian justifications, from deterring future migration to protecting vulnerable migrants from abuse. While they are still prevalent in many countries, there is growing recognition among experts and stakeholders that banning people from work, regardless of their legal status, is counterproductive for both migrant integration and host societies.[57]

Ironically, though employment bans are often motivated by a desire to reassure the public that refugees will not compete for their jobs, they may have the opposite effect. When refugees are unable to support themselves, they may be understandably perceived as a drain on the social welfare system. While I am not aware of any public opinion studies on the issue, the general idea of spending taxpayer resources on migrants and then not allowing them to contribute to the host society by willingly sharing their labor strikes me as being very similar to a rare instance of a *demonstrably harmful* policy.

However, it is also true that some policies perceived as obviously beneficial to their country by some voters, such as increasing punitive border control measures, may not be perceived as such by experts, who may also consider various unintended consequences and the cost ineffectiveness of such measures.[58] Such discrepancies between actually and demonstrably beneficial policies are common in most public policy domains. What makes immigration unique is that public attitudes toward it are more likely to be determined by people's sociotropic perceptions than by rare personal experiences devoid of tangible implications for their material self-interest.

Consequently, the notion of DB policies is useful because it underscores the centrality of national interest in the formation of voters' perceptions about immigration and other public policies in democracies. It also fruitfully highlights the fact that not all actually beneficial impacts of immigration policies are directly observable or understood by voters, who may lack the interest or capacity to understand these impacts. In other words, DB policies are particularly instrumental for making immigration popular because of their inherent clarity of being "in our interest."

Of course, one may reasonably wonder how realistic the voter preferences for hypothetical freer immigration policies revealed in part I are. Indeed, not all major reforms are greeted with acceptance: citizens can and often do protest and vote incumbent governments out of office if policy changes clash too much with their preferences. Concerns about a voter backlash to even programmatic reforms are especially prevalent in the context of immigration policymaking in which people's stated preferences are often very restrictive. Chapter 6 addresses this concern by examining what happens when governments enact pro-immigration reforms and showing that persuasion by policymaking is both possible and common.

In chapter 7, I also show that various proxies of DB immigration policies at the national level, such as the share of work-related versus non-work-related immigration flows, correlate strongly with voters' perceptions of the benefits of immigration to receiving countries. In turn, this finding indicates that the actual presence of DB policies, as opposed to just smart policy rhetoric, is what may generate support for immigration in the electorate. In chapter 8, I trace this process historically using the qualitative case studies of Canada and Sweden. While some politicians have incentives to demonize immigration for electoral gains, it is much easier to do so successfully in contexts in which immigration policies are not demonstrably beneficial, as in Sweden today.

Unfortunately, while they are necessary, better policies alone are not sufficient to make immigration popular. According to the extensive policy feedback literature, not all policies can generate support, and those that do typically see only modest improvements in public attitudes toward them over time.[59] Further, public feedback on the implementation of even well-intended policies—especially when it comes to salient, divisive issues like immigration—can often be negative and self-correcting or, as some political scientists call it, "thermostatic."[60] Ultimately, given common attitudinal stability and political polarization, even policies that are clearly and personally beneficial may not succeed much in generating positive public opinion feedback.[61] Making immigration popular is a challenging task no matter what, but implementing DB policies is the only way to achieve that goal.

6

BACKLASH VERSUS LEGITIMATION

Do Programmatic Pro-immigration Reforms Backfire?

A S WE HAVE SEEN, many people in the United States, Europe, and other rich democracies do not like immigration. Yet it is still happening and even growing, so some people choose to vote for anti-immigration parties and candidates. So, what should democratic governments do when faced with a potential populist backlash against immigration?

The former U.S. presidential candidate Hillary Clinton—a pro-immigration politician who had previously remarked on her "open borders dream"[1]—once recommended to Europe's governments to curb their "generous and compassionate" immigration policies. According to Clinton, European openness to immigration was clearly "inflaming voters and [had] contributed to the election of Donald Trump and Britain's vote to leave the EU."[2] Similarly, a great number of otherwise immigration-friendly politicians and scholars across the political spectrum have repeatedly attributed the rise of populism to *public backlash against immigration* and the corresponding political failure to sufficiently restrict immigration. Despite a lack of solid empirical evidence, popular arguments against pro-immigration reforms based on particular instances of alleged immigration backlash have been extremely influential among policymakers.

Further, some anti-immigration parties and candidates also oppose liberal democratic norms and institutions. According to an increasingly popular argument, mainstream politicians and other stakeholders could and should address this potential threat to liberal democracy by implementing more restrictive immigration policies.[3] For many, this is not a merely hypothetical issue: the consequences of the 2016 election of Donald Trump, such as the attack on the United States Capitol on January 6, 2021, provide a vivid example of how public backlash to freer immigration can undermine not just immigration but also democracy.

So, do significant pro-immigration reforms that increase legal immigration pathways for foreign-born workers cause voter backlash by increasing anti-immigration concerns and right-wing populist voting? Of course, it is possible to find examples to support this idea, but the relevant question is whether such consequences are systematic. In this chapter, I use new historical data on changes in immigration policy and politics to examine whether past pro-immigration reforms—or at least those broadly aimed at benefiting average citizens—have in fact been counterproductive in practice.

To test for possible backlash effects, I estimated the impact of *programmatic* pro-immigration policy changes on voting behavior and public attitudes by leveraging the variation in the timing of immigration reforms in European countries over the last four decades. Programmatic policies are the policies implemented according to transparent rules to benefit the public at large, so I particularly focused on legal *labor* immigration admission reforms. Work-related immigration is the broadest cross-nationally comparable category that is most often explicitly devised to advance the national interest.[4] It is also a major immigration category that is conventionally viewed as nationally beneficial by most economic research, even though it includes the immigration of workers across all skill levels.[5] Given that most work-related immigration is facilitated by family ties and that many legislative reforms affect both work and family migration, my main analysis combined both categories, which together include most of the immigration occurring in high-income countries.[6] While there are valid reasons to expect that voters would retaliate against the liberalization of immigration by voting for anti-immigration parties, it is also possible that voters can accept such liberalization as legitimate—if it benefits their countries.

I complement the evidence I present with a discussion of my latest related research demonstrating the possibility of a "reverse" pro-immigration backlash to the rise of the populist right wherever it occurred in the same set of European countries. I also talk about recent research I have done on generalizing the "no backlash" finding by replicating it in a vastly different U.S. context and looking at how voters respond to high-profile pro-immigration reforms, including the U.S. Deferred Action for Childhood Arrivals (DACA) policy regarding unauthorized migration, using a natural experiment.

Overall, I found that changes in pro-immigration policies do not affect changes in populist right-wing voting or immigration concerns within countries. If anything, pro-immigration policies may be related to more positive voter attitudes both within and between countries. While counterproductive political backlash to immigration is certainly plausible, and a real concern for policymakers, it is likely confined to narrow types of unauthorized and otherwise mismanaged immigration. Taken together, the evidence presented in this chapter suggests that, at least when it comes to generally beneficial programmatic reforms, pro-immigration policy changes are more likely to generate their own support because of legitimation than backfire because of backlash.

WHAT IS AND IS NOT PUBLIC BACKLASH?

Broadly, *public* or *voter backlash* refers to a strong, adverse reaction to a particular policy advancement perceived as excessive by a significant segment of the population that may ultimately be *counterproductive* to the advancement of the policy. This adverse reaction may relate to changes in public attitudes toward certain (usually disadvantaged) groups, as well as related policies or their behavioral manifestations. While these changes do not have to be political, the public backlash to various policy advancements in today's democracies is often challenged electorally when people can and do vote for policies and politicians with an aim to reverse such advancements.

While a variety of scholars across disciplines employ the concept of backlash, there is little agreement about its precise definition.[7] Nonetheless, most analysts agree that not every negative response to political change constitutes backlash, especially if it remains within the bounds of ordinary democratic politics. Reasonable criticism and debate or mere disagreement by some segment of the public does not amount to backlash. For backlash to be meaningful, it must be substantial and broad-based, not limited to a small fringe in a large, diverse democracy.

Finally, any analytically fruitful backlash argument necessarily states that a significant adverse reaction against a particular advancement may be, at least in principle, *counterproductive* to the goals of the advancement in either the short or long run. Importantly, when the backlash argument is invoked, the advancement should be counterproductive *because* of the popular adverse reaction to it, independent of any actual economic or social effects of such advancement. In sum, a political backlash argument can be viewed as an empirically testable claim about voter response to a change of the following kind: "Regardless of its merits, if your cause advances too much now, you may eventually get less than otherwise would be the case due to the more active resistance of those who disagree with your cause."

Throughout history, backlash arguments have been applied—both popularly and academically—to a variety of disadvantaged groups and causes, including the abolition of slavery, women's suffrage, racial equality, and same-sex marriage. Of course, backlash arguments can be and are often factually mistaken, and they can be strategically employed by the opponents of a cause to undermine it. One reasons for that is that, though falsifiable in principle, the "excessiveness" of any advancement is context dependent and largely subjective. In the case of social status or other zero-sum rivalries, for instance, any advancement of lower-status groups beyond the status quo may be perceived as excessive by higher-status groups.

Further, the idea of backlash necessarily implies some uncertainty and a *counterfactual* argument about what would have happened to the cause and related behaviors without a particular advancement. As a result, the inherent ambiguity about what constitutes the appropriate time frame and the counterproductive reaction makes it difficult for reasonable observers to agree about whether a backlash has indeed occurred.

When it comes to the harsh government restrictions on international labor mobility in today's high-income democracies, backlash arguments usually try to convey the idea that any significant pro-immigration advancement beyond the status quo has the potential to encourage more people to adopt restrictive views on the issue or vote for anti-immigration politicians in the present electoral cycle, which can undermine or even reverse progress toward the pro-immigration advancement.

BACKLASH TO IMMIGRANT PRESENCE VERSUS IMMIGRATION POLICIES

What constitutes a pro-immigration advancement that might result in voter backlash? Most prominently, scholars have conceptualized anti-immigration backlash as an adverse voter response to the rising physical presence of immigrants in terms of racial *demographic change*. While this rather intuitive idea—often dubbed "group threat," as outlined in chapter 1—has been studied extensively in the social science literature, the existing observational evidence is far from conclusive.[8] At the same time, experimental studies that randomly assign demographic composition are difficult to conduct and thus rare in the literature. Further, studies that have found some backlash effects usually focused on rapid flows of forced or otherwise unauthorized immigration, not the presence of immigrants in general. The effects found in such studies are also likely to be short term, not long term.[9]

More problematically, a focus on immigration-induced demographic change arguably misses a significant aspect of the issue since the presence of immigrants (whether actual or anticipated) is evidently neither necessary nor sufficient to cause voter backlash.[10] Even if one grants the possibility that rapid immigration flows increase the probability of populist voting, this factor alone can only explain a small fraction of the differences we see in voting results across contexts. In addition, from the perspective of policymakers, the evidence regarding the effect of immigrant presence on voter behavior is not very helpful because immigrant presence has many complex causes beyond migration policy.[11] However, the extent to which immigration policy itself influences political behavior beyond its effects on immigration levels is still unclear.[12]

To illustrate this point, consider the implications of the argument that immigration backlash contributed to Brexit. Even if one explicitly focuses on the effects of immigration-related demographic change, such a causal argument also necessarily contains an implicit counterfactual claim that if the United Kingdom's immigration *policy* had been sufficiently more restrictive, then the country would have had fewer immigrants and thus Brexit would not have happened.

In other words, to the extent that anti-immigration voters react negatively to increases in immigrant presence, they should also react negatively to any pro-immigration policy change that would facilitate those increases. Of course, voters may fail to react if they or even lawmakers themselves underestimate the significance of a certain policy (as was prominently the case with the 1965 Immigration Act in the United States). Such critique, however, is arguably applicable to any political stimuli in the world of uncertainty and bounded rationality.

To give an even more extreme example, a hypothetical UK government decision to suddenly end all border enforcement could plausibly cause significant opposition among some voters regardless of how many people actually immigrated (or wanted to immigrate) there simply because of the existence of at least some sociotropic opposition to losing control over immigration among the British public.

As I argue, however, it is unclear how unconditional most current anti-immigration public preferences really are. For instance, a UK government decision to adopt an open border policy with Canada or Australia with an explicit aim of increasing the exchange of talent and mobility between these countries might have been quite popular with the public regardless of how many people would actually take advantage of the opportunity.

A real-world example of such a targeted immigration proposal is CANZUK, an advocacy organization that advocates for free movement and increased cooperation among Canada, Australia, New Zealand, and the United Kingdom.[13] Although the idea has generated interest among various political figures and think tanks, it has not yet gained significant political traction among policymakers. Nevertheless, the very existence of CANZUK highlights the potential for more mutually beneficial immigration arrangements to garner public support, even in the face of generally restrictive attitudes toward immigration.

EXPECTATIONS: TESTING FOR IMMIGRATION POLICY BACKLASH AND LEGITIMATION

So, how do voters respond to pro-immigration reforms? To answer this question, I built on the policy feedback literature and related research exploring the possibility of voter backlash to other contentious laws and policies such as same-sex marriage legislation. The literature recognizes that, in addition to simply reflecting public opinion, government policies can generate their own support by changing people's incentives or by sending authoritative institutional signals about what is accepted as normal in society.[14]

In the case of gay rights, while many observers have speculated about the possible backlash to the proliferation of same-sex marriage legislation, most studies have been unable to detect such an effect. Further, across various contexts and empirical strategies (from survey experiments and event studies to difference-in-differences approaches), scholars have found that, if anything, legal advances in gay rights have increased their public acceptance by signaling that they are a new norm.[15]

As emphasized earlier, it may be analytically fruitful to consider the hypothesized popular backlash to pro-immigration policies as being independent of their actual societal effects as long as immigration is generally disliked by a significant number of voters (because of its perceived negative effects or simply racial prejudice). In other words, any consistent backlash argument is not about the consequences of pro-immigration policy changes per se but rather about the *net* attitudinal or behavioral responses of voters to the proposed changes. To that end, I focused primarily on the more proximate manifestations of immigration backlash in terms of *aggregate* attitudinal and voting responses, rather than the reactions of particular voter subgroups or other possible broad effects (e.g., those related to an increase in ethnic violence, a decrease in social cohesion, lower economic growth, or more restricted immigration).

Departing from the existing studies of the effect of policy feedback on political behavior, I specified the following empirical expectations with regard to the possible backlash effects of pro-immigration reforms. First, the backlash argument stipulates that pro-immigration reforms can increase anti-immigration attitudes in the electorate within the course of an electoral cycle. This idea has been present in both the popular media and the academic literature, and it also aligns with evidence documenting attitudinal change with regard to same-sex marriage among some voters.

Unlike the case of same-sex marriage, however, both absolute and relative public preferences toward immigration have been relatively stable or growing only slightly more positive in Europe since the start of opinion polling.[16] That said, most recent immigration reforms have been relatively minor, and it is hard to find an immigration advancement equivalent to the legalization of same-sex marriage. Consequently, an alternative plausible expectation is that, unless the change is radical (which was not the case within the limits of my European dataset), immigration policy cannot significantly affect immigration attitudes, which are normally stable. To the extent that significant policy change does occur sometimes, it is also possible that pro-immigration reforms can alter the underlying social norms and legitimize advancements in immigration across the electorate—countervailing backlash-induced increases in anti-immigration attitudes or even decreasing them.

Second, the backlash argument stipulates that pro-immigration reforms increase the share of the populist vote in the electorate probabilistically. Although it is usually assumed that this relationship is necessarily mediated by immigration attitudes, other causal pathways are possible, such as those related to racial prejudice and anti-elitist views.[17] Consequently, at least for the purposes of this chapter, I assume that both expectations are independent of each other; that is, immigration reforms can affect immigration attitudes even if they are not related to the populist vote.

DATA AND METHODS: DETERMINING THE EFFECTS OF
IMMIGRATION POLICIES ON POLITICS

Here, I provide a more detailed technical explanation of my panel county-year research design and the data I used to test for potential backlash and legitimation effects. Put simply, the question I aimed to answer was as follows: *As immigration policy liberalizes within a country, how does that liberalization relate to changes in aggregate voter attitudes or behavior over time?*

Unlike with other government policies, the causal identification of immigration reform effects is complicated by the fact that they are predominantly "assigned" at the national level and thus cannot easily be randomized. At the same time, since immigration policy changes also likely reflect the preferences of voters and parties in power alongside other unobserved factors, any cross-sectional associations (or the lack thereof) are likely subject to reverse causality and omitted variable bias. The standard econometric solution to these problems is to produce plausible causal estimates of policy effects by using longitudinal or panel data.

To test for voter backlash to pro-immigration reforms, I gathered a cross-sectional time-series dataset linking the best available voter behavior, public opinion, and policy data at the country–year level for 1980 to 2010 across twenty-four European countries. Recent advances in data collection and various scaling methods allowed for a detailed examination of the backlash dynamic across both countries and time. Unlike related research on policy backlash, I did not use *individual-level* public opinion data since such data have much more limited coverage.[18] While useful for examining potential heterogeneous effects by voter characteristics (which I discuss later), individual-level data do not provide any advantage over aggregate-level data in the immigration setting in which all policy reforms happen at the *country–year* level.

The most prominent set of statistical techniques for this purpose is related to either unit, time, or unit-and-time (i.e., two-way) fixed-effects regression models, which can account for unobserved confounding factors under a number of more or less realistic assumptions. These models have been especially popular in the policy literature as a possible generalization of the difference-in-difference technique, which identifies policy treatment effects by simply comparing the average change in the outcome variable over time for the treatment group with that of the control group (assuming parallel trends in the outcome). Given that the conventional two-way fixed-effects models have recently been contested, I used the simpler country unit fixed-effects models as my baseline specification.[19]

As for the main dependent variable, I relied on the well-established immigration conservatism index (for 1989 through 2010), standardized to vary from 0 to 1.[20] Based on the aggregation of dozens of major public opinion survey questions regarding immigration (e.g., "Do you think immigration should be decreased?"), this index indicates the general restrictiveness of the electorate toward immigration in a given country and year.

To complement this attitudinal variable with the more long-running measure of voter preferences, I also relied on the Timbro Authoritarian Populism Index (for 1980 through 2010). This index provides a comprehensive measure of the share of votes cast for *right-wing* populist parties in European national legislatures (in each country-year since the last elections) as coded by the Chapel Hill Expert Survey.[21] The index includes data for parties such as Alternative für Deutschland (AfD) in Germany, the Front National in France, Lega in Italy, and the UK Independence Party (UKIP) in the United Kingdom. These are the parties that have been explicitly anti-immigration or otherwise attractive to the anti-immigration electorate in line with the backlash argument explicated earlier. I also corroborated my analysis using the alternative coding of far-right populist parties from the PopuList project and the alternative immigration index and found no change in the substantive results.[22]

For the main independent variables, I relied on the comprehensive Immigration Policies in Comparison dataset (for 1980 through 2010).[23] Unlike other migration policy data sources, IMPIC allows for a fruitful comparison of absolute levels of immigration policy openness across countries and years. To capture the idea of policy reforms or shocks, I also calculated annual changes in IMPIC score for all countries in the dataset. As stated earlier, since my primary focus is possible voter responses to liberalizing major legal immigration pathways that broadly serve the national interest, my main empirical specifications included only the "labor migration" and "family reunification" components of IMPIC (while excluding humanitarian and irregular migration policies). Unfortunately, a more recent analysis or fine-grained differentiation of skilled economic policies is not possible with this otherwise excellent resource. In some specifications, I also included control variables common to this literature: share of immigrants, unemployment rate (log), and per capita GDP (log).

CROSS-SECTIONAL ANALYSIS: THE TRAJECTORIES OF IMMIGRATION POLICY AND PUBLIC OPINION IN EUROPE

Do pro-immigration reforms fuel anti-immigration attitudes and populism? To answer this question, I started with a naive descriptive analysis documenting the basic trajectories of populist voting and immigration policy across time and countries. As can be seen from figure 6.1, both the share of populist voting and immigration policy openness have gradually increased in Europe over the last forty years. Although some version of this stylized fact has often been used by political commentators to draw a connection between these two variables, that does not mean that there is in fact any *causal* relationship between them or even that the same correlated trend has held within each country. After all, we know that, if anything, immigration attitudes have only warmed during these years across the continent.[24]

Many between-country differences exist in the trajectories of immigration policy openness, immigration attitudes, and populism (figure 6.2). Though countries like Germany and Switzerland show a notable trend similar to that of Europe as a whole (i.e., increasingly freer immigration policy and attitudes but rising populism), several countries have had different experiences. Slovakia, for instance, has seen a slow liberalization to its immigration system and attitudes and a fall in the populist vote. Meanwhile, Greece has experienced a growth in restrictive policies and attitudes alongside rising populism. And Portugal and Spain have managed to

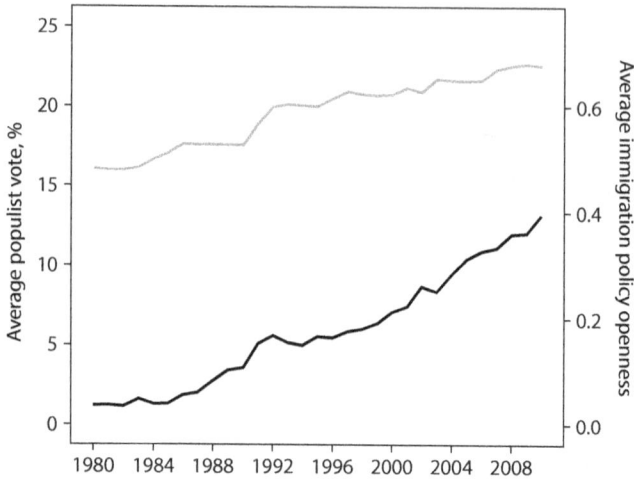

FIGURE 6.1 Immigration policy openness and populist voting across Europe, 1980–2010. The black line indicates average populist voting; the gray line indicates openness to immigration.

Sources: Timbro (share of populist voting); Caughey et al. 2019 (anti-immigration attitudes).

liberalize their immigration system without experiencing any significant populist wave.

Setting aside variation across time, it appears that the positive relationship between immigration policy openness and populism holds cross-nationally. In particular, as shown in figure 6.3, few countries with restricted immigration experienced any significant populist vote, whereas countries with more open immigration experienced a lot of variation in populism. Interestingly, however, immigration policy openness is negatively correlated with restrictive immigration attitudes.

To understand the link between *changes* in immigration policy openness and populist voting, I also examined the annualized "first differences" of these variables. As can be seen from figure 6.4, the basic bivariate link between annual change in immigration policy openness and populist voting (during election years only) is still positive. When it comes to the link between immigration policy openness and anti-immigration attitudes, however, it is still negative.

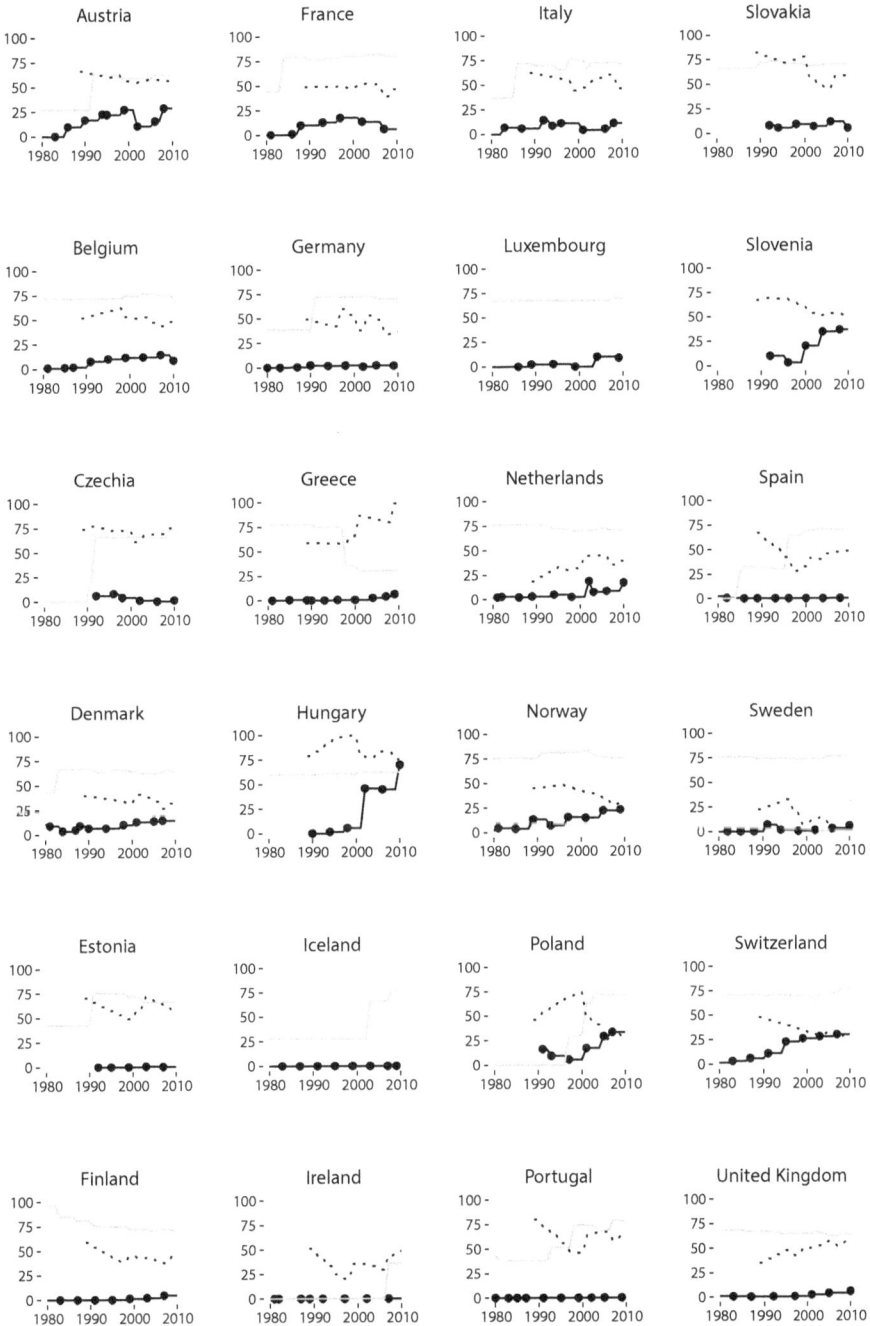

FIGURE 6.2 The trajectories of immigration policy openness, immigration attitudes, and populist voting across European countries, 1980–2010. The black lines indicate share of right-wing populist voting with major election years marked by points. The dotted lines indicate anti-immigration attitudes. The gray lines indicate immigration policy openness.

Sources: Timbro (share of populist voting); Caughey et al. 2019 (anti-immigration attitudes); IMPIC (immigration policy openness).

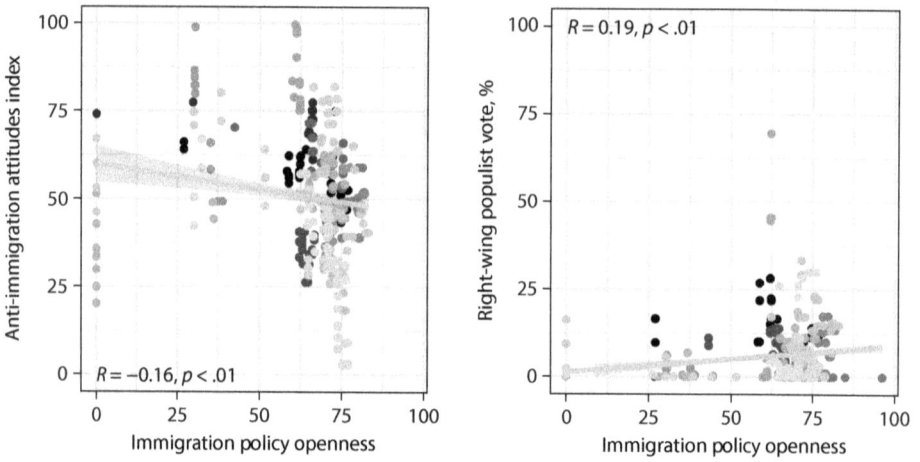

FIGURE 6.3 Immigration policy openness, immigration attitudes, and populist voting across European countries and years (1980-2010). The graphs depict the bivariate relationship between immigration policy openness and anti-immigration attitudes (left) or populist voting (right) at the country-year level. All points are shaded by country.

Sources: Timbro (share of populist voting); Caughey et al. 2019 (anti-immigration attitudes); IMPIC (immigration policy openness).

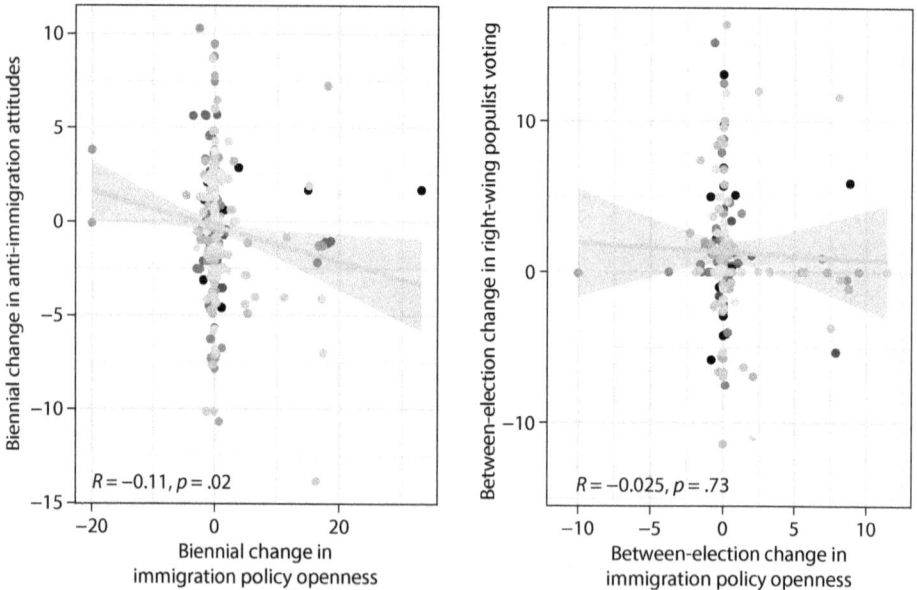

FIGURE 6.4 Short-term changes in immigration policy openness, immigration attitudes, and populist voting across European countries (1980-2010). The graphs depict the relationship between first differences in immigration policy openness and anti-immigration attitudes (left) or populist voting (right) at the country-year level.

Sources: Timbro (share of populist voting); Caughey et al. 2019 (anti-immigration attitudes); IMPIC (immigration policy openness).

However, when one compares the amount of accumulated pro-immigration policy change with populist voting (or anti-immigration attitudes) over the last forty years (figure 6.5), the relationship is clearly negative across countries for both variables. Although such analysis is evidently underpowered and subject to reverse causality concerns, it is descriptively true that in the long run, the countries that liberalized their immigration systems the most experienced the least growth in populist voting and anti-immigration attitudes. Importantly, none of the bivariate relationships explored so far nec-essarily implies that changes in immigration policy *cause* (or do not

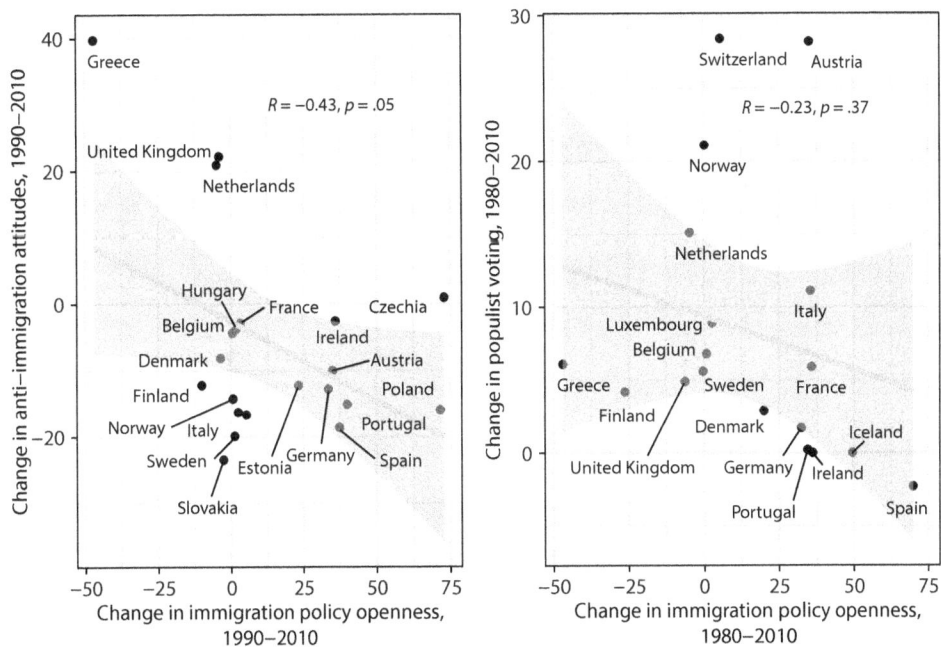

FIGURE 6.5 Long-term change in immigration policy openness, immigra-tion attitudes, and populist voting across European countries. The graphs depict the relationship between long-term change in immigration policy openness and anti-immigration attitudes (left) or populist voting (right) at the country level.

Sources: Timbro (share of populist voting); Caughey et al. 2019 (anti-immigration attitudes); IMPIC (immigration policy openness).

cause) changes in immigration attitudes or populist voting within particular countries.

PANEL DATA ANALYSIS: THE LEGITIMIZING EFFECTS OF PRO-IMMIGRATION REFORMS?

After establishing the theoretical and empirical possibility of back-lash (as well as possible counterexamples) in the descriptive analysis, I took advantage of the cross-sectional time-series nature of my data-set and fitted a set of fixed-effects linear regressions to estimate the possible effects of pro-immigration reforms on attitudes and voting *within* countries. Such analysis allowed for the accounting for various country-specific confounding factors such as those related to culture and institutions.

Table 6.1 summarizes the results of these empirical models.[25] Overall, voters' attitudes did not become more restrictive in response to

TABLE 6.1 The relationship between pro-immigration policy changes and anti-immigration attitudes

	ANTI-IMMIGRATION ATTITUDES					
	(1)	(2)	(3)	(4)	(5)	(6)
Immigration policy openness	−0.271***	−0.239*	−0.303**			
	(0.073)	(0.106)	(0.107)			
Change in immigration policy openness				0.089	0.072	0.077
				(0.049)	(0.066)	(0.074)
Country fixed effects	Yes	Yes	Yes	Yes	Yes	Yes
Year fixed effects	No	Yes	Yes	No	Yes	Yes
Control variables	No	No	Yes	No	No	Yes
Observations	462	462	441	462	462	441
Adjusted R^2	0.793	0.791	0.803	0.759	0.766	0.771

Source: Caughey et al. 2019 (anti-immigration attitudes); IMPIC (immigration policy openness).
Note: All models are OLS panel regressions with country fixed effects (European countries, 1989–2010). Robust standard errors clustered by country are given in parentheses.
*p < .05, **p < .01, ***p < .0010

pro-immigration policy changes. If anything, it appears to be the opposite: immigration policy openness and pro-immigration reforms were associated with *more positive* immigration attitudes. In other words, when countries open up legal pathways for more immigrant workers and family members, such liberalization on average leads to more positive immigration attitudes among voters. The positive relationship between immigration policy openness and voter preferences is particularly remarkable since it holds after accounting for fixed effects and other control variables.

Nonetheless, it would be premature to claim any causal effects since the potential for reverse causality here is high. For instance, one could argue and show that improvements in immigration preferences in public opinion polls encourage or make it easier for policymakers to pass pro-immigration reforms. At the same time, none of the more volatile policy change variables are significantly correlated with immigration attitudes. Overall, though the robustness of the positive "legitimizing" relationship between policy openness and attitudes may reasonably be disputed, it is notable that none of the results are consistent with the idea of a counterproductive backlash to immigration policy.

Although immigration reforms do not seem to cause an attitudinal backlash, it is still possible that they can affect populist voting. As can be seen from table 6.2, the general openness of immigration systems is indeed positively correlated with the populist vote, which could be predicted by the backlash argument. However, these effects are substantively small, and none is statistically significant after accounting for all differences between countries. Put differently, the passage of broadly selective pro-immigration reforms is not followed by a rise in populism, at least within the European context examined here.

One can also reasonably worry about reverse causality here. To the extent that populist parties may restrict immigration as soon as they come to power, for instance, this potential for immediate policy changes could arguably bias estimates against finding any contemporaneous backlash effect of pro-immigration reforms. More broadly, if some limited populist electoral success could influence the subsequent position of mainstream parties by lowering their resolve to pass pro-immigration reforms, this potential shift in mainstream party

TABLE 6.2 The relationship between pro-immigration policy changes and populist voting

	POPULIST VOTE, %					
	(1)	(2)	(3)	(4)	(5)	(6)
Immigration policy openness	8.910	1.543	3.140			
	(5.002)	(5.116)	(4.569)			
Change in immigration policy openness				−2.068	−0.769	−0.916
				(2.423)	(2.744)	(2.464)
Country fixed effects	Yes	Yes	Yes	Yes	Yes	Yes
Year fixed effects	No	Yes	Yes	No	Yes	Yes
Control variables	No	No	Yes	No	No	Yes
Observations	656	656	626	638	638	610
Adjusted R^2	0.490	0.568	0.610	0.482	0.573	0.613

Source: Timbro (share of populist voting); IMPIC (immigration policy openness).
Note: All models are OLS panel regressions with country fixed effects (European countries, 1980–2010). Robust standard errors clustered by country are given in parentheses.
$*p < .05, **p < .01, ***p < .001$

behavior could also bias the results downward. According to my analysis, however, most immigration reforms are not more likely to happen during election years, and those that do overwhelmingly occur before national elections. After all, many significant changes to an immigration system are usually planned in advance and sometimes take years to negotiate. That said, the most recent evidence indicates that populist parties fail to shift the positions of mainstream parties on the issue or to change immigration policies themselves when in power.[26]

IS THERE A PRO-IMMIGRATION COUNTER-BACKLASH TO ANTI-IMMIGRATION BACKLASH?

So far, I have discussed the concept of immigration-related backlash solely as a potential hindrance to the pro-immigration cause. However, given the dynamic nature of politics, for every reaction from immigration opponents, there may also be a counterreaction from immigration supporters. The idea of backlash is not limited to adverse reactions to progressive causes and groups. In fact, many instances of potentially counterproductive backlash to various policy changes are in response to conservative advancements. A recent example is the U.S. Supreme Court's anti-abortion decision overturning *Roe v. Wade*, which disproportionately motivated and helped (the pro-choice) Democrats in the 2022 midterms and beyond.[27]

In this sense, the concept of voter backlash can also be understood as an extreme form of "thermostatic" public opinion in which the public reacts to policy changes in the direction opposite to that of the policy in question.[28] Specifically, when people witness a high-profile policy change, they adjust the "thermostat" of their opinion in the direction of their actual policy preferences. For example, if the government increases spending, voters in general, and particularly those who want less spending, are more likely to express their desire for reduced spending.

In the case of immigration, a high-profile pro-immigration reform could lead to more people voicing anti-immigration opinions and voting for anti-immigration parties to reverse the changes they disagree with. While thermostatic backlash may not necessarily indicate a fundamental long-term shift in individuals' underlying preferences, it can still be counterproductive if it brings success to anti-immigration politicians and parties. There is some evidence that this can happen in the case of some pro-immigration policies that aim to increase the number of asylum seekers or unauthorized immigrants.[29]

However, observers often forget that the thermostatic backlash dynamic should work both ways. Pro-immigration policies may be unpopular and polarizing, but so are unnecessarily restrictive anti-immigration policies and right-wing populism more generally. Recent prominent examples of such a dynamic include the seemingly pro-immigration reactions of the U.S. public to the 2016 election of Donald Trump and of the UK public in the aftermath of Brexit.[30]

In my recent research with James Dennison, we tested whether these notable cases of pro-immigration reaction to anti-immigration politics could be generalized to a larger set of populist radical right successes across countries. We argued that greater populist success (for reasons not necessarily related to immigration) could actually have a positive relationship with immigration attitudes, reflecting people's desire to reemphasize anti-prejudice norms and their rejection of populist anti-immigration politics. Using the same European country–year data and similar methods to those described earlier, we found a robust relationship between the electoral success of populist radical right parties and a subsequent positive change in immigration attitudes among the public.[31] That is, when anti-immigration parties and politicians become successful, a significant proportion of the electorate "thermostatically" reacts by adjusting their stated preferences toward immigration in a positive direction (table 6.3). In other words, we found that a growing proportion of Europeans and Americans are becoming more pro-immigration in their attitudes precisely in reaction to the rise of the far right they dislike.

Given the general stability of immigration attitudes and the limitations of such an observational design, it is important not to overstate the magnitude or the independent causal nature of these possible

TABLE 6.3 The relationship between the electoral success of populist parties and anti-immigration attitudes

	ANTI-IMMIGRATION ATTITUDES					
	(1)	(2)	(3)	(4)	(5)	(6)
Right-wing populist vote, %	−0.271***	−0.179**	−0.186**			
	(0.054)	(0.055)	(0.057)			
Far-right populist seats, %				−0.283***	−0.231***	−0.235***
(Alternative measure)[a]				(0.054)	(0.057)	(0.062)
Country fixed effects	Yes	Yes	Yes	Yes	Yes	Yes
Year fixed effects	No	No	Yes	No	No	Yes
Control variables	No	Yes	Yes	No	Yes	Yes
Observations	616	595	595	601	595	595
Adjusted R^2	0.762	0.779	0.773	0.766	0.783	0.776

Sources: Timbro (share of populist voting); Popu-List (populist seats), Caughey et al. 2019 (anti-immigration attitudes).
Note: All models are OLS panel regressions with country fixed effects (European countries, 1989–2017). Robust standard errors are given in parentheses.
*p < .05, **p < .01, ***p < .001

effects. Still, the available evidence strongly suggests that, at the very least, populist success does not make the electorate more anti-immigration in the aggregate. Even as a simple descriptive fact, this is an important point because much previous research has suggested that populist success can lead to more negative attitudes owing to the breaking down of anti-prejudice norms and more prominent anti-immigration party cues.[32]

IS THE "NO BACKLASH" FINDING GENERALIZABLE? LESSONS FROM A NATURAL EXPERIMENT IN THE UNITED STATES

Does the finding about the absence of a backlash effect generalize to other contexts, types of immigration, and methods? According to my argument in this book, pro-immigration policies should not generate backlash as long as they are demonstrably beneficial. However, some might reasonably argue that I found no backlash effect simply because voters are unaware of most pro-immigration policy changes passed in their national legislatures and because such changes are often obscure. The aggregate country–year data also misses potential short-term and polarizing subgroup changes that can still be politically consequential. Another important concern is that causal evidence can be tricky in this context since immigration policies are not randomly assigned.

At the same time, others may wonder whether the findings about the liberalization of legal pathways for work-related immigration in Europe apply to other contexts and immigration policies. For instance, given the evidence and discourse about the backlash to refugees and the border crisis, it is reasonable to think that policymakers may not be able to address unauthorized immigration constructively.

In my latest collaborative research, Marcel Roman and I addressed these concerns by examining how voters respond to pro-immigration reforms from a very different angle and in a very different context.[33] Specifically, we used all publicly available granular survey data to examine what happened to people's opinions after President Obama announced and implemented DACA, one of the most high-profile recent immigration policies in the United States, in 2012. DACA provided temporary work authorization and protection from deportation to hundreds of thousands eligible young people who had come to the United States as children but did not have legal immigration status.

To investigate the possible backlash to DACA, we compared the responses of voters from a dozen high-quality surveys conducted just before and after one of the salient events (i.e., the announcement of DACA or its implementaiton) in terms of their anti-immigration attitudes and incumbent approval (i.e., approval of Obama). This is a so-called unexpected-event-during-survey research design. As long as the event was salient and unexpected (which we confirm), and as long as the respondents were not systematically different from one another, we could treat this event as a natural experiment. Respondents who answered a survey before the announcement of DACA on June 15, 2012, or its implementation on August 15, 2012, were considered the control group, and those who answered a survey after the announcement or implementation of DACA were considered the treatment group. If a backlash effect were present, we would have expected the treatment group to have more negative immigration attitudes and incumbent evaluations than the control group.

One can imagine an argument for why this policy could have backfired. Although DACA enjoys relatively wide support among voters now,[34] that was not the case at the time of its announcement in 2012. In fact, it faced harsh criticism from Republican politicians and many voters who viewed it as an illegal usurpation of the authority of Congress. Further, immigration issues were already politically polarized at the time, and DACA dealt particularly with a subset of unauthorized immigrants: the least popular and most politically salient immigrant group in the United States.

Many observers thus believed that DACA could have provoked or did provoke a significant backlash among voters, contributing to a rise of anti-immigrant sentiment and support for restrictionist policies. For example, Donald Trump capitalized on this criticism. On the 2016 campaign trail, he regularly promised to end the program and subsequently did after assuming office, further contributing to the perception of a strong counterproductive backlash against pro-immigration policies.[35]

However, one can imagine that granting legal status to children who are undocumented through no fault of their own, and who are already integrated into communities and fully assimilated into the American fabric, would be a no-brainer for many people. Despite the fact that some may find DACA controversial, it is demonstrably beneficial relative to the status quo: the people in question are already here and are productive members of the nation. Doing nothing or even deporting them would clearly harm their U.S. citizen families, friends, and communities. So, no backlash or even legitimation is also possible following the implementation of even initially controversial pro-immigration legislation. And that is indeed what we found.

In our analysis, we assessed the impacts of the announcement and implementation of DACA on voters' anti-immigration attitudes and evaluations of Obama, using all high-quality publicly available survey data we could find. The effects estimated from seven surveys that happen during these high-profile events revealed that neither the announcement of DACA nor its implementation triggered significant voter backlash against Obama or immigration. Specifically, across all surveys and outcomes examined, the average effect of the announcement of DACA and its implementation for both anti-immigration attitudinal outcomes and and incumbent approval outcomes was almost precisely estimated at zero.

To assess whether this finding generalizes, we conducted a similar analysis for three more surveys that happened during the announcement of the Deferred Action for Parents of Americans and Lawful Permanent Residents (DAPA) in November 2014, yielding the same null results. We also conducted subgroup analyses by partisanship and ideology to examine whether our null result was masking countervailing effects conditional on political dispositions favoring or disfavoring pro-immigrant policies. The average effects of all these high-profile pro-immigration events on pro-incumbent evaluations and anti-immigration attitudes were statistically null for both Democrats (liberals) and Republicans (conservatives).

These results provide strong evidence against the backlash hypothesis. One could argue that there was no backlash effect in this case because DACA is relatively limited in scope or because voters tend to be more sympathetic toward migrants who are already here, like the "Dreamers" (i.e., the young people affected by DACA).[36] Still, this study addresses several limitations identified earlier. By using granular survey data and a natural experiment, we captured the immediate effects of highly salient policies on public opinion, minimizing the influence of confounding factors. The subgroup analyses by partisanship and ideology further strengthened our findings, demonstrating that the absence of a backlash effect is not driven by countervailing reactions among various political groups.

* * *

According to most evidence, the enormous benefits of more open global labor mobility outweigh its many possible costs.[37] Still, most voters in rich countries—even those who are highly educated and unprejudiced—oppose increasing immigration, often (com)passionately so. Many scholars and policymakers reasonably worry that any significant relaxation of existing restrictions would face harsh voter resistance and thus potentially be counterproductive.[38] Further, given the complexity of the issue, even the best-intentioned and sound reforms can backfire on their own merits. It is also unlikely that there will ever be an ultimate policy solution that satisfies all relevant parties, even among those who are already pro-immigration.

However, it is important not to overthink the issue. Backlash effects can certainly be real. But they are most plausible when it comes to immediate, short-term attitudinal outcomes, not distant outcomes of institutional change. They are also most plausible when policy triggers are salient and out of touch with most voters.[39]

Building on the best available public opinion and policy data from Europe over the last forty years combined with a recent natural experiment conducted in the United States, this chapter provides a data-driven assessment of such concerns. Overall, the results presented here indicate that existing pro-immigration reforms have not been counterproductive in terms of increasing anti-immigration attitudes or voting.

Specifically, despite the gradual increase of both populism and pathways for legal immigration over the last four decades, the timing of existing pro-immigration reforms is not related to the increases in the populist vote in subsequent elections. Similarly, pro-immigration reforms are not related to any negative changes in immigration attitudes. If anything, it appears that most pro-immigration reforms may further legitimize freer immigration in the electorate. To the extent that most current legal immigration is already restricted, the evidence thus suggests that most relaxations of such restrictions would be unlikely to cause a backlash.

Of course, immigration reforms are rarely independent of prior voter behavior. Consequently, one could argue that the backlash effect has not occurred in recent years because even the most significant pro-immigration reforms in Europe and the United States over the past several decades have been relatively conservative, perhaps owing to governments being mindful of possible negative effects within the existing political equilibrium.[40] Even with this limitation in mind, the evidence presented here challenges the common claim that pro-immigration policy advancements may be counterproductive or conducive to the rise of populism, at least when it comes to opening pathways for legal immigration or selective regularization of immigrants without legal status.

The fact that moderate pro-immigration reforms do not generally cause a counterproductive backlash is a rather weak standard for evaluating the possible political effects of immigration. It does not mean, for instance, that even these moderate reforms command full support among citizens. As we have seen, it also does not mean that such reforms necessarily lead to greater public acceptance of immigration in general or a relatively more open immigration admission system in particular.

Still, if backlash does not emerge in the short term, it is unlikely to emerge in the long term.[41] This notion is further supported by recent evidence of a "reverse backlash" effect in which people react in a pro-immigration way when policies are anti-immigration.[42] In the case of DACA, we know that the policy has been able to gain substantial popularity in the long run despite the initial criticism and all the subsequent political challenges.[43]

However, it is clear that not all legal pro-immigration reforms are equally able to generate their own support in the electorate. For example, in line with the main argument of this book, selective pro-immigration reforms that explicitly focus on increasing high-skilled or otherwise demonstrably beneficial immigration may have the most legitimizing impacts among those who currently oppose immigration (especially those who are more altruistic and nationalistic). Conversely, some of the more controversial pro-immigration enforcement and humanitarian policies that contribute to the public perception of a lack of control over immigration or potential economic burdens may generate voter backlash even among those not particularly hostile to international labor mobility.

Unfortunately, to the best of my knowledge, none of the available immigration policy indices is detailed enough to convincingly test for such plausible differentiated effects in the panel data. It is also worth noting that the temporal coverage of these indices ends before the peak of Europe's refugee crisis and the politicization of the issue, which arguably limits the external validity of the analyses presented here.

The next two chapters address these limitations by reevaluating and providing new evidence about what is needed from immigration policymaking for successful, durable persuasion. Still, the evidence presented here suggests that the immigration debate could have been more productive if we had talked about the relevance of a more specific backlash to *mismanaged* migration or to *large-scale unauthorized* migration, rather than anti-immigration backlash in general.

7

THERE IS NO SHORTCUT

Why Does Immigration Have to Be Demonstrably Beneficial to Be Popular?

I N CHAPTER 6, I showed that broad programmatic pro-immigration reforms generally do not lead to a quantifiable backlash among voters, even those predisposed to be more skeptical. Some policy changes, however, can generate significant opposition among people affected by the changes.

Germany's Skilled Immigration Act (*Fachkräfteeinwanderungsgesetz*, or FEG) came into force on March 1, 2020. Alongside a number of pro-immigration provisions, the act was designed primarily to make it easier for foreign skilled professionals and those with vocational training from outside the European Union to work in Germany.[1] The law was later updated to include a Canadian-style point-based system, and the new regulations came into force on November 18, 2023. These regulations effectively allowed people from all over the world to get an "opportunity card" to enter Germany before getting a job offer as long as they qualified in terms of having a sufficient number of points. Heralded a milestone in Germany's immigration policy by Horst Seehofer, the federal minister of the interior from 2018 to 2021, the law was supposed to be a win for everyone. What could possibly go wrong?

A lot apparently. By the end of March 2020, shortly after the law was enacted, thousands of mostly unemployed, university-educated

Germans took to the streets to protest across the country—despite the harsh COVID-19 restrictions at the time. Led by an unlikely coalition of both populist left and right parties, these people were rallying against the anticipated influx of foreign professionals whom they saw as a dire threat to their jobs and identity. Signs and banners carried messages like "Stop the skilled invasion!" and "We don't need foreign engineers; we have real German ones right here!"

The protesters claimed that they were not against immigrants or immigration per se but against only highly skilled immigrants and expats whom they called *Fremdbesserwissers* (literally "foreign know-it-alls"). Fearing that these foreigners would take their jobs, they accused the potential immigrants of being overqualified, overpaid, and overzealous in their work performance. They argued that high-skilled immigrants from Asian countries in particular were taking away high-quality jobs that rightfully belonged to native-born citizens, and they demanded that the government stop the unnecessary immigration of any foreigner with a competitive skill set.

If you are unaware of these protests and you think they sound farfetched if not absurd, it is because none of them happened. While the Skilled Immigration Act is real, the German people's reaction to it that I have just described is not. I made this story up simply to illustrate how weird it sounds to have a public backlash against skilled foreign professionals who are clearly beneficial to the national economy. In fact, despite the contentious politics of immigration and widespread prejudice against foreigners, I am not aware of a single large-scale protest against skilled immigration reforms ever happening anywhere in the world.[2]

To be clear, like all immigration, skilled immigration has winners and losers. It is likely that some individuals and groups will always oppose even high-skilled immigration policies, such as those increasing the number of H1-B visas for skilled foreign workers in the United States.[3] If such opposition is concentrated and influential, it may stall or reverse reform efforts. But opposition to skilled immigration, unlike people's general dislike of immigration, is never broad.

Germany's Skilled Immigration Act went through a lengthy, tumultuous legislative process, ultimately achieving only 52 percent final support in the Bundestag, the German federal parliament, most of

which came from the center parties. It received numerous endorse-
ments from the usual suspects of business and medical associations,
as well as harsh criticism from trade unions and even some humanitarian immigration groups.[4] Despite all the politics, however, the act
has never become a prominent national issue in the electorate. I am
not aware of any public polls that asked German voters about their
opinion of this legislation, but it is safe to say that most people have
likely not heard or thought much about it.

Why have German voters—including those who compete directly
with skilled immigrants or dislike immigration for any other reason—
completely ignored this consequential pro-immigration legislation?
Why did even committed anti-immigration voters not even think of
protesting along the lines I hypothetically considered earlier despite
their vocal opposition to accepting more immigrants during the refugee crisis a few years earlier? At this point, it may seem intuitive that
skilled immigration is simply not controversial enough among voters
to become a significant political issue. What is less intuitive, however,
is how broad the range of potentially popular policies is and what the
lack of significant public opposition to selective pro-immigration
reforms implies for successful persuasion efforts in support of freer
immigration and for policymaking efforts in general.

VOTERS PREFER BENEFICIAL IMMIGRATION

To understand what exactly demonstrably beneficial immigration policymaking should entail, it is important to reconsider people's conditional support for alternative immigration policies. While various
survey questions about people's support for different types of immigration or immigrant groups are usually used to adjudicate the causes
of opposition to immigration in general, it may be useful to take these
stated preferences at face value.

Most prominently, it has been extensively documented that *most
groups* of voters have a preference for policies that increase the number of skilled and educated economic immigrants. Such preference
for "skill-selective" policies holds true in terms of increasing both
absolute immigrant numbers and their relative number compared

to other types of immigrants.[5] This preference is also close to being universal: it holds true in affluent democracies across the Atlantic and beyond Europe and the United States.[6] Such policies also appear to have majority support even among Leave voters in the context of a post-Brexit United Kingdom and among Republican voters in the post-Trump context of the United States.[7] In fact, according to a recent comprehensive U.S. study from June 2024, 71 percent of those who support Trump favor increasing high-skilled immigration. As a result, in many countries, public support for attracting a greater number of skilled immigrants is shared by a supermajority of all voters.[8] Underlying such preference is usually people's stated and revealed belief that such immigration is beneficial to receiving countries.[9]

The overwhelming popular support for increasing immigration—when it is skill selective—is both extremely general and robust. Although this general finding is often used as evidence that people form their immigration preferences based on sociotropic concerns, it can also be considered evidence that immigration *can* be popular.

Of course, some rightly suspect and have shown that preference for essentially better-off immigrants may also, to some extent, imply prejudice or otherwise discriminate against racially different and lower-status immigrant groups who would not be eligible to immigrate under more selective policies.[10] However, people's preferences toward some regions of origin and biases against others may arguably be driven at least in part by (mis)perceptions about "typical" immigrants from those regions and their characteristics. Some research, for instance, shows that the "skills premium" in public support is generally greater for non-European immigrants, which implies that some opposition against them is driven by voters' stereotypes about their potentially lower skills or contribution.[11]

While voters may hold certain stereotypes about various immigrant groups and their potential contributions, it is important to recognize that these stereotypes are often inaccurate owing to the widespread positive self-selection of migrants under current restrictive policies.[12] However, the accuracy of these stereotypes—in terms of the correlation between group averages in desirable characteristics like contributions in taxes and people's respective perceptions of them—can vary depending on the context and the selectivity of the immigration policies in question. For example, recent research based on fine-grained administrative data from the Netherlands, a generous welfare state with a moderately unselective immigration system, documents that immigrants' fiscal contributions vary systematically in terms of their fiscal costs and benefits based on their admission category, education, and other background characteristics.[13] Although individuals should never be reduced to their demographic characteristics, the fact that the generally more popular educated immigrant groups show greater fiscal benefits aligns with the idea that people's immigration preferences are driven by sociotropic concerns about immigrants' potential contributions to society.[14]

PREFERENCE FOR DEMONSTRABLY BENEFICIAL IMMIGRATION IS MUCH BROADER THAN IT SEEMS

The often overlooked fact about people's conditional preference for demonstrably beneficial immigration is that it goes far beyond attracting the best and the brightest. This preference thus does not have to be racially discriminatory or otherwise illiberal in either its intent or result (apart from the general discrimination by citizenship status inherent in any immigration policy). In terms of immigration purposes, for instance, *any* type of work-related immigration is generally viewed more favorably than family and humanitarian immigration, especially when those types of immigration are unauthorized. This preference holds regardless of immigrants' racial background or voters' personal characteristics.[15]

Although it can be controversial in certain contexts, student migration is overwhelmingly popular.[16] Whether it is temporary for study purposes or permanent, this popularity stems from the fact that students bring money into publicly financed universities, reinvigorate the towns where they stay, and are expected to be skilled after they graduate. According to the most recent data from the United States, most respondents have very positive perceptions about the impact of international students on their communities and the country as a whole, despite their general skepticism about the merits of freer immigration. Consequently, they also overwhelmingly support attracting international students and making it easier for them to

stay in the country after graduation. Interestingly, the most prominent concern people have about international students is not about
their impact on the host country but about the fact that students may
return home to benefit their home countries instead of the country
where they studied.[17]

Recent research indicates that voters tend to favor immigrants who
make economic contributions, regardless of their skills, education,
or legal status. For instance, one study found that the skills premium
is completely eliminated when voters are informed that prospective
high-skilled immigrants plan to engage in low-skilled jobs.[18] This
finding also aligns with studies showing that immigrants' economic
contributions enhance the perception of them as deserving within
the welfare state context.[19] At least descriptively, we also know that
voters who are aware of how their countries' immigration systems
select immigrants to benefit citizens tend to be more supportive of
freer immigration.[20]

In other words, and in line with the results of the conjoint experiment presented in chapter 4, voter preference for skill-selective and
educated immigration appears to be more about advancing perceived
national benefit than about attracting high-status individuals of a
certain racial origin. This is an important point because, in principle,
there are many ways in which any immigrant—including refugees
and those without a degree—can learn a skill and make a valuable
contribution. Indeed, there is more to labor needs than attracting
top talent, and many employers in high-income countries evidently
struggle to fill vacancies considered low- or middle-skilled.[21]

But demonstrably beneficial policies that most voters accept as
desirable are not just about work-related migration and immigrants'
economic contributions. An overwhelming majority of voters also
implicitly support the immigration of immediate relatives. Indeed,
if push comes to shove, even the staunchest anti-immigration supporters of Donald Trump would probably acknowledge that American citizens have a right to sponsor and bring their foreign spouses to
the country—after all, Donald Trump did it himself! This view makes
perfect sense from the perspective of altruistic nationalism because
it recognizes that allowing citizens to unite with their loved ones
from abroad clearly improves the well-being of existing citizens.

Of course, voters may quibble about the merits of distant family migration, sometimes termed "chain immigration," but the migration of close family members is already popular. I am not aware of any polling on the issue of close family migration, and the likely reason for that is that nobody thought of asking people about it because it is not at all controversial. It is instructive, however, that some of my recent research shows that telling U.S. respondents about how difficult even family migration is makes them a bit more pro-immigration more generally.[22] Further, other recent evidence indicates that voters generally support the immigration of immediate relatives or dependents of potential immigrants who are skilled.[23] This finding suggests that people understand the impracticality and undesirability of expecting professionals from abroad to uproot their lives and leave their families.

Finally, from some of the latest research by my colleagues, we now also know that many of those who currently oppose increasing immigration are willing to compromise and conditionally support it if new policies credibly promise not just more selective admissions but also better integration of immigrants or border control.[24] Despite the possible differences in the mechanisms underlying those preferences, people's views on these distinct issues are largely based on their genuine sociotropic perceptions of what is good for their country. Importantly, demonstrably beneficial integration and law enforcement policies that would allow freer immigration do not necessarily have to be punitive, illiberal, or otherwise unacceptable to responsible democratic governments. The good news here is that such policies can be and often are programmatic,[25] potentially allowing for an even broader scope of admission pathways to become popular among the electorate.

PREFERENCE FOR DEMONSTRABLY BENEFICIAL IMMIGRATION TRUMPS OTHER PERSUASION FACTORS

So, how important are national interest concerns for immigration preferences compared with prejudice and other factors? Building on my original survey of English voters introduced in part I, I approached this question by comparing expected support for increasing immigration in general with increasing nationally beneficial immigration in particular among various groups of voters. To do so, in addition to the standard item asking whether immigration should be increased or decreased, I asked respondents whether they would support "a policy significantly increasing immigration that is specifically designed to benefit average British citizens through greater selection and taxation of immigrants" (figure 7.1a). To see if these results were generalizable, I then asked whether Britain should make immigration much easier for those "who would contribute to economy" *or* "regardless of their contribution to the economy" (figure 7.1b).

As I showed previously, racially egalitarian, university-educated, and left-leaning voters are more supportive of freer immigration than their counterparts. However, this support never reaches the majority, at least in the post-Brexit context of the United Kingdom. At the same time, majority support for increasing nationally beneficial immigration is always present regardless of voter characteristics or the wording of survey questions. Perhaps most remarkably, most (53 percent) are willing to support increasing immigration (provided it is nationally beneficial), even among the generally anti-immigration group of uneducated, racially prejudiced, *and* right-leaning voters.

In addition to the common demographic characteristics related to immigration support, I considered people's genuine desire to help others regardless of concern for national interest, as revealed by their decision to donate potential prize money to global charities. Figure 7.1 shows that committed humanitarian altruists are indeed more supportive of freer immigration than are other groups. Still, even among this select group, support does not reach the majority, and support is much higher for nationally beneficial immigration. In other words, humanitarian intentions are never sufficient to sustain the popular legitimacy of freer immigration.

Overall, when voters are asked to consider more open immigration admission policies that are explicitly and straightforwardly beneficial to their countries, they are favorable toward the idea no matter the sending region. Independent of political context and individual characteristics, most voters support increasing immigration that advances their national interest.

(a) Support increasing immigration, %

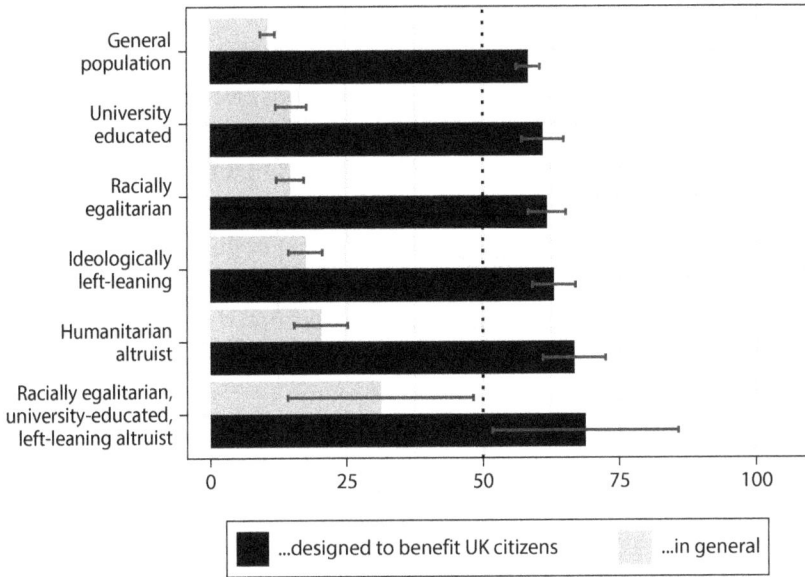

Legend:
- ...designed to benefit UK citizens
- ...in general

(b) Support making immigration easier, %

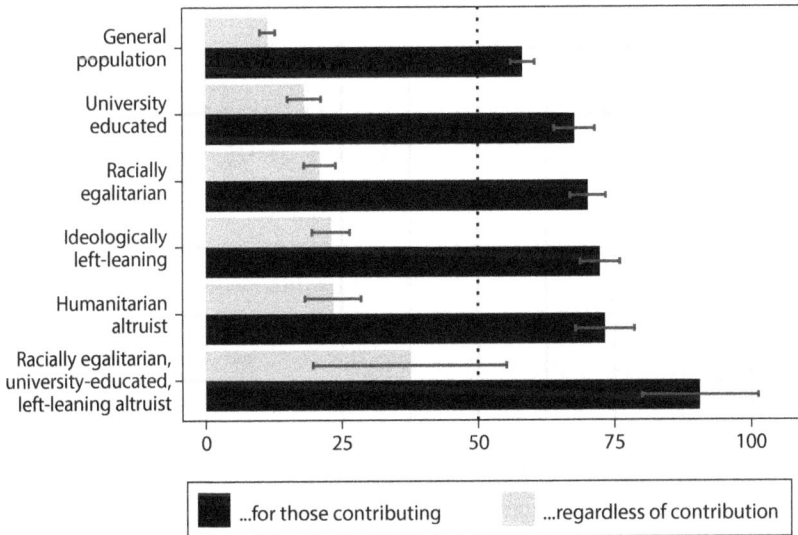

Legend:
- ...for those contributing
- ...regardless of contribution

FIGURE 7.1 Conditional preferences for freer immigration. (a) Respondent support for increasing immigration levels. (b) Respondent support for making the immigration process easier.

Source: Original England Qualtrics survey, 2018.

Of course, survey responses can be influenced by the wording of questions, and it is possible to elicit more positive attitudes toward immigration by using language that is suggestive or socially desirable. As a somewhat far-fetched example, if respondents are asked, "Are you more supportive of good immigration than bad immigration?," few people would probably say "No," even if they don't really support any immigration. Further, people may sometimes report more positive attitudes toward specific immigrant groups than toward immigration in general.[26] However, the significance of my rather intuitive finding that voters strongly support immigration policies that benefit their countries lies in the fact that attitudes toward freer immigration of any kind is typically the immigration-related questions least likely to elicit positive responses from respondents in any context.[27] This finding also suggests that implementing meaningful, demonstrably beneficial pro-immigration policy changes has the potential to legitimize freer immigration, despite the general evidence of immigration attitude stability.

DEMONSTRABLY BENEFICIAL IMMIGRATION SYSTEMS ARE MORE POPULAR

What does people's conditional preference for demonstrably beneficial immigration imply for policy persuasion? One way to think about this issue is that any durable persuasion effort must ultimately be grounded in the political or institutional reality and its change. While people tend to underestimate the benefits of immigration to their countries, their (mis)perceptions may also have a grain of truth, as discussed earlier.

I should emphasize that most immigration can ultimately be beneficial to receiving countries with the right policies in place.[28] Still, the impact of immigration as it is managed now is not always positive, and this impact varies significantly across countries and immigrant groups.[29] At the same time, while all human life should rightly considered to be sacred and priceless, governments around the world routinely assign value to statistical lives to determine which policies will be better for their citizens. Although most economies require all kinds of workers, and immigrants can often be "overeducated,"[30] there is a significant consensus that skilled, educated economic immigration is particularly beneficial.[31] As a result, skill-selective policies can be credibly viewed as preferable by both governments and voters alike.

To see whether that is indeed the case, I considered a variety of possible indicators to capture the demonstrable immigration benefits and burdens accrued to receiving countries. In particular, I considered the shares of highly educated (i.e., college or more) and low-educated (i.e., less than high school) immigrants, the share of work-related immigration flows, foreign-born unemployment, and policy selectivity. Next, I explored the relationship of these indicators with the share of people who believe that immigration is beneficial to their countries based on the comprehensive 2017 Ipsos Global Trends survey of fourteen OECD countries.[32] I looked at the most directly related public net perceptions that "immigration is good for [the country's] economy" and a broader assessment of whether immigration has a positive societal impact (ranging from public services to culture) based on several related questions (with very high correlation between items, $r = 0.93$). The reason that these survey items are preferable to alternatives is that they directly assess people's empirical beliefs as opposed to their policy preferences or other complex attitudes, which may be confounded by a host of other factors.

As can be seen in figure 7.2, the correlation between immigrant skill and voters' immigration attitudes is substantial: people who live in countries that have attracted educated immigrants are more likely to believe that immigration *in general* is good for their countries. Meanwhile, the share of low-educated immigrants is reversely correlated with this perception. Canada, the United Kingdom, Australia, and the United States are the only four countries where a majority agrees that immigration is good for the country economically. Importantly, with the possible exception of the United States, in no OECD country with a predominantly low-educated immigrant population are economic perceptions net positive.

I then considered the relationship between public perceptions of immigration and share of work-related immigration flows (as opposed to family, humanitarian, and other types of immigration). To do that,

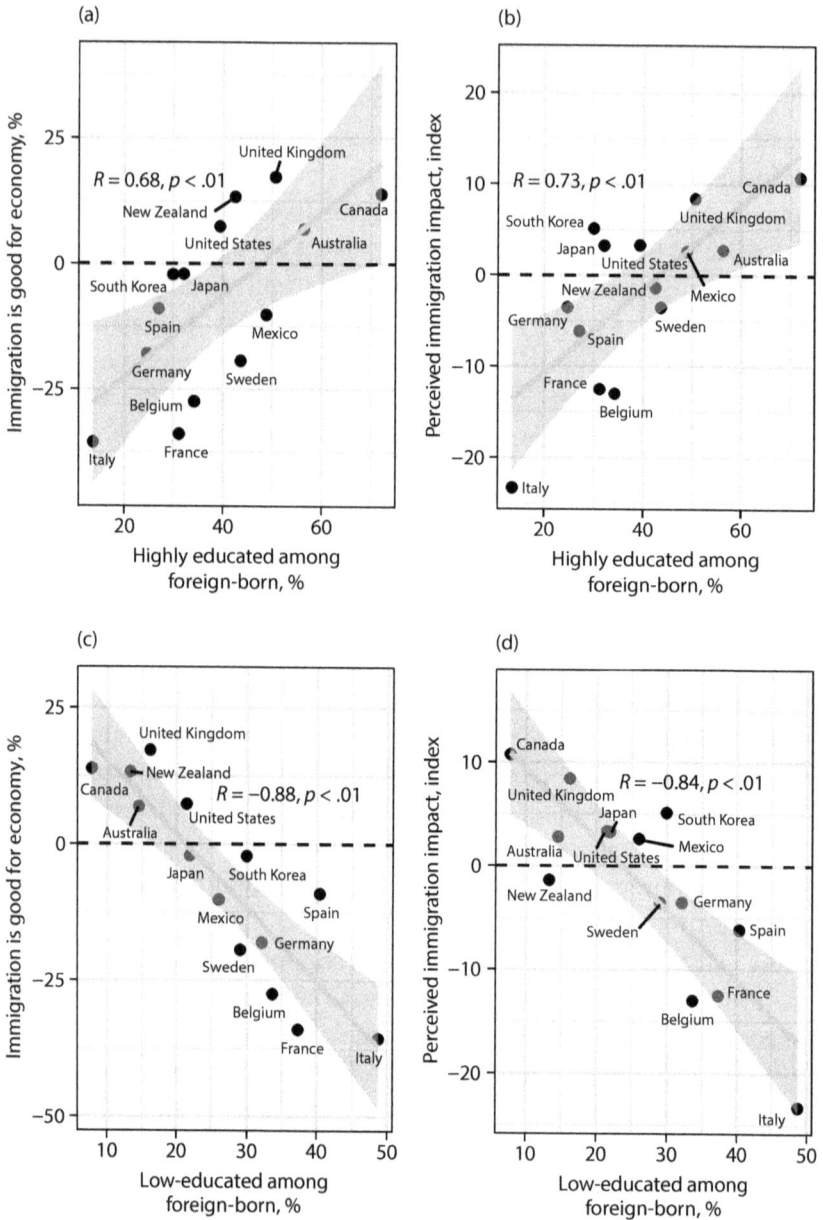

FIGURE 7.2 Immigrants' level of education and voters' perceptions of the impact of immigration. (a) Perceptions of the economic impact by percent high-educated among foreign-born. (b) Perceptions of the general impact by percent high-educated among foreign-born. (c) Perceptions of the economic impact by percent low-educated among foreign-born. (d) Perceptions of the general impact by percent low-educated among foreign-born.

Sources: OECD 2017 (immigration stocks); Ipsos 2017 (immigration attitudes).

I combined the numbers of new temporary and permanent work-related immigrants and divided that by the total number of immigration flows in 2011 using a recently compiled dataset.[33] Although these data are available only for a single year, they should still give a good picture of immigration systems, which normally do not change very fast. To get at the possible flip side of attracting work-related immigrants, I also looked at the share of unemployed immigrants.

As shown in figure 7.3, these relationships are substantively similar. People are more likely to view immigration as beneficial in countries with more work-related immigration policies and fewer unemployed immigrants. It is likely that the relationship would have been even stronger if I had had data on the share of skilled immigration flows. The United States is again a notable outlier in that perceptions of immigration are more positive than may otherwise be expected for the first indicator. While some may point out the long-standing U.S. tradition of being a nation of immigration, an arguably more plausible explanation is that the United States also attracts the vast majority of top talent from around the world, a fact not captured by simple metrics of education and visa mix.[34]

Finally, I directly examined the link between public perceptions of immigration and the degree to which countries explicitly prioritize high-skilled over low-skilled workers in their labor immigration admission policies. To do that, I relied on another new dataset that compares regulations for admitting foreign workers of various skill levels based on labor market tests, job offer requirements, and points tests across twenty countries from 2000 to 2010.[35] Since it takes time for policies to have an effect and for voters to notice that effect, I averaged the available selectivity scores across years. Figure 7.4 shows a remarkably strong association: in no skill-selective country are perceptions of immigration negative (or vice versa).

To summarize this cross-national evidence more effectively, I combined standardized versions of all various approximations of demonstrably beneficial immigration policies into a simple average index and plotted it against the net index of citizens' perceptions of the impact of immigration. The relationship between these two broad measures across the included OECD countries is, as before, exceptionally strong (with a correlation coefficient of 0.85, $p < .01$).

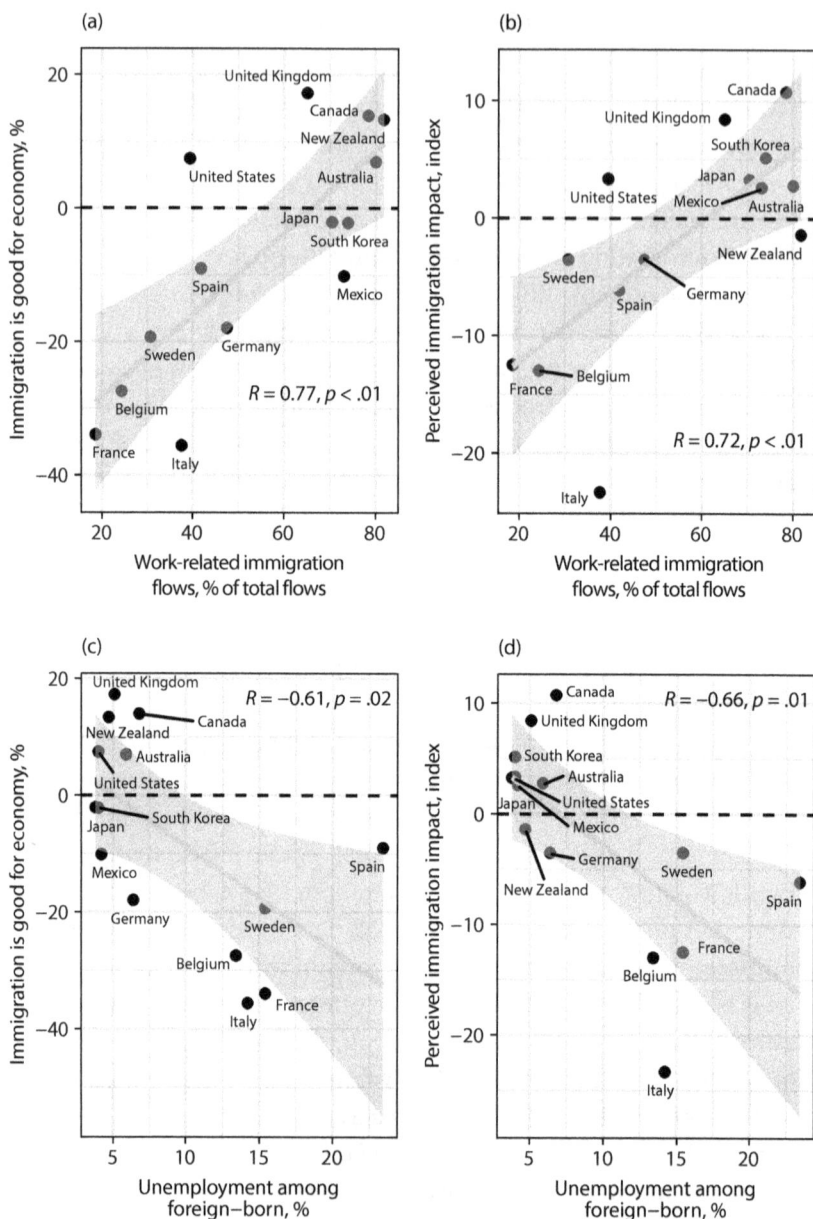

(a)

Immigration is good for economy, %

20 — United Kingdom
Canada
New Zealand
United States   Australia
0 - - - - - - - - - - - - - - - - -
Japan
South Korea
Spain
Mexico
−20 —   Germany
Sweden
Belgium $R = 0.77, p < .01$
France Italy
−40 —

20   40   60   80
Work-related immigration
flows, % of total flows

(b)

Perceived immigration impact, index

Canada
10 —
United Kingdom
South Korea
Japan
United States Mexico Australia
0 - - - - - - - - - - - - - - - - -
New Zealand
Sweden
Germany
Spain
−10 —
Belgium
France
$R = 0.72, p < .01$
−20 —
Italy

20   40   60   80
Work-related immigration
flows, % of total flows

(c)

Immigration is good for economy, %

20 — United Kingdom $R = -0.61, p = .02$
Canada
New Zealand
Australia
United States
0 - - - - - - - - - - - - - - - - -
Japan   South Korea
Mexico
Spain
−20 — Germany
Sweden
Belgium
France
Italy
−40 —

5   10   15   20
Unemployment among
foreign−born, %

(d)

Perceived immigration impact, index

Canada
10 —
United Kingdom
South Korea
Australia
Japan   United States
0 - - - - - - - - - - - - - - - - -
Mexico
Germany
Sweden
New Zealand
Spain
−10 —   France
Belgium
$R = -0.66, p = .01$
Italy
−20 —

5   10   15   20
Unemployment among
foreign−born, %

FIGURE 7.3 Immigrants' work and voters' perceptions of the impact of immigration. (a) Perceptions of the economic impact by percent work-related immigration flows. (b) Perceptions of the general impact by percent work-related immigration flows. (c) Perceptions of the economic impact by percent unemployed among foreign-born. (d) Perceptions of the general impact by percent unemployed among foreign-born.

Sources: OECD 2011 (immigration flows); OECD 2017 (unemployment); Ipsos 2017 (immigration attitudes).

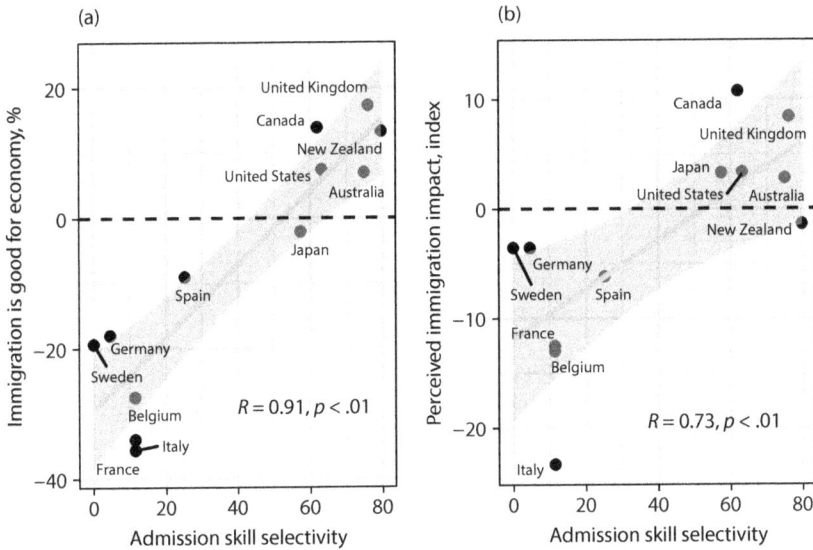

FIGURE 7.4 Immigration skill selectivity and voters' perceptions of the impact of immigration. (a) Perceptions of the economic impact by policy selectiveness. (b) Perceptions of the general impact by policy selectiveness.

Source: Admission Skill Selectivity Index, 2000–2010; Ipsos 2017 (immigration attitudes).

As can be seen clearly in figure 7.5, there are effectively only two types of affluent democracies: those where immigration is both demonstrably beneficial and relatively popular and those where immigration is neither demonstrably beneficial nor popular. There is simply no exception or possible third option.

Taken together, these correlations provide evidence that for freer immigration to gain and sustain legitimacy, it must be selective in terms of demonstrable benefit to citizens. Of course, these findings are based on data from a small number of participants and cross-national correlations from only a handful of OECD countries with numerous confounding factors. Unfortunately, it is simply not possible to conduct an experiment in which the selectiveness of immigration admission policies across national governments can be randomized and people's perceptions of those policies can be monitored over many years.

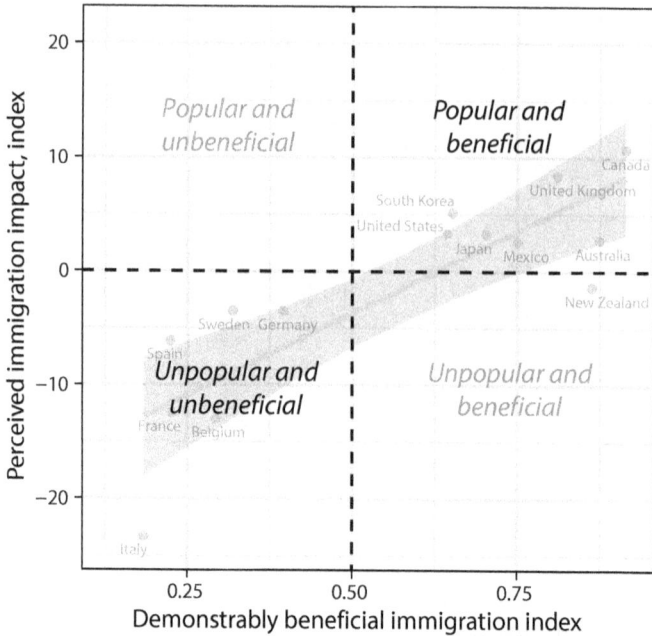

FIGURE 7.5 Demonstrably beneficial immigration index and voters'
perceptions of the impact of immigration.

Sources: Combined administrative data (DB Immigration Index);
Ipsos 2017 (immigration attitudes).

In chapter 8, I address some of the concerns regarding possible
reverse causality and omitted causes by qualitatively tracing the
sequencing of immigration reforms and changes to public opinion
in Canada and Sweden. Still, the evidence presented here aligns well
with more rigorous quasi-experimental research at the subnational
level showing that the exogenous growth in skilled immigration[36]
and the better integration of refugees into the labor market[37] can
cause voters' attitudes toward immigration to grow more positive. It
is also important to note that the cross-national correlations between
the perceived impact of immigration and the usual suspects, such as
gross domestic product (GDP) per capita, the size of the foreign-born
population, or Inglehart's self-expression values, are almost precisely
estimated to be zero. Finally, it is instructive that, at least descriptively,

not a single country has managed to achieve a net positive view of the impact of immigration without having a predominantly or disproportionately skilled population of existing immigrants or a skill-selective immigration policy for admitting future immigrants.

HOW DEMONSTRABLY BENEFICIAL REFORMS CAN LEGITIMIZE ALL TYPES OF IMMIGRATION

It is understandable that demonstrably beneficial or more open yet still selective immigration may sound to some like a hard-hearted oxymoron. Indeed, one may reasonably wonder whether more open immigration admission policies toward only some groups of immigrants are truly open. Yet it is important to remember that the status quo is restrictive even for the highest-skilled immigrants in most OECD countries.[38] While potential migrant beneficiaries of selective liberalization may not be the worst-off people in the world, selective immigration policies are likely to improve millions of human lives in both receiving and sending countries through increased productivity, higher wages, and remittances.[39]

Even more important, there is a case to be made that the countries that are more open toward skilled economic immigration are also at least descriptively more open toward other types of immigration. To examine this possibility, I plotted the demonstrably beneficial immigration index against the total share of immigrants accepted. As shown in figure 7.6a, the relationship is positive. This means that countries that accept relatively more skilled immigrants as a share of their *immigrant* population also accept more immigrants of all kinds as a share of their *total* population, compared to countries that place less emphasis on skilled immigration. Further, accepting relatively more skilled immigrants does not seem to come at the expense of humanitarian immigration. There is no significant association between how demonstrably beneficial an immigration system is and the *population* share of humanitarian migrants (figure 7.6b).

The United States, for example, has a much more humanitarian immigration focus than does Canada.[40] Pro-immigration advocates may rightly celebrate the humanitarian commitments of the United States. Yet since Canada generally accepts much higher immigration

(a)

(b)

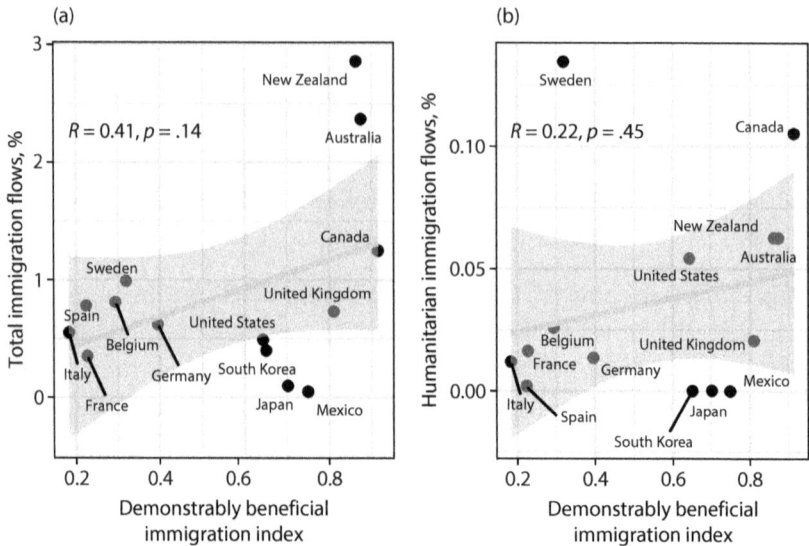

FIGURE 7.6 Demonstrably beneficial immigration index and immigration flows. Total immigration and humanitarian immigration flows are given in terms of the percentage of the national population. (a) Total immigration flows by demonstrably beneficial immigration. (b) Humanitarian immigration flows by demonstrably beneficial immigration.

Source: Combined administrative data (DB Immigration Index); OECD 2011 (immigration flows).

flows than does the United States, it is also able to accept a greater number of humanitarian immigrants as a percentage of its population. As a result, from the perspective of vulnerable populations fleeing persecution and violence, Canada may be even more helpful than the United States. In other words, even for those who care about the humanitarian aspects of immigration policy, it is important not to lose sight of how important overall immigration flows and popular support for them are.

✳ ✳ ✳

Many scholars and politicians argue that governments have been out of touch with their voters when it comes to immigration issues.

Influenced by businesses, nongovernmental organizations, academics, and other pro-immigration interest groups, governments continue to accept hundreds of thousands of immigrants and ignore dissenting public opinion on the issue.[41] More recently, it is increasingly recognized that businesses are no longer much interested in immigration, that most immigration policies are in fact quite restrictive, and that this state of affairs is largely in line with ambivalent public opinion.[42] Ultimately, despite all the news headlines about mass immigration and border chaos, very few OECD countries allow more immigrants than a small fraction of 1 percent of their population each year. Moreover, immigration has been so politically controversial that even the most pro-immigration politicians prefer not to alter the status quo given the potential voter backlash.

This chapter argues that there is one tried-and-tested, yet still largely neglected, way out of this inefficient political equilibrium. This solution involves governments significantly expanding skilled and other demonstrably beneficial economic immigration by increasing existing quotas, making the process easier, and actively encouraging such immigration. Given the vast untapped potential benefits of freer immigration and voters' conditional preference for demonstrably beneficial immigration, this strategy constitutes both a responsible *and* responsive policy agenda for representative democratic governments to pursue.

Of course, even expanding skilled immigration may prove politically difficult as well illustrated by the continuous failure to expand the H-1B visa program in the United States. While this program has attracted considerable negative attention among certain labor and anti-immigration interest groups, very little of this negativity has been picked up by the general public.[43] In this respect, as highlighted by the fictitious backlash account presented at the beginning of this chapter, it is notable that there has not been a single significant bottom-up political movement against overly generous immigration policies for skilled professionals anywhere in the world.

Overall, the descriptive evidence presented here suggests that affluent democracies with relatively high, economic-oriented immigration flows on average have more positive public perceptions of the impact of immigration than do affluent democracies with relatively low, humanitarian-oriented flows. Despite these policy and opinion differences, both types of countries ultimately accept similar proportions of humanitarian immigrants relative to their population. This is simply because the countries with economic-oriented immigration flows accept many more immigrants of all kinds than those with primarily humanitarian-oriented flows. From a certain perspective, countries with selective immigration policies can simply "afford" to accept more immigrants, including those fleeing war and persecution.

Although providing accurate information to voters is essential, only demonstrably beneficial pro-immigration policies can secure durable public support for consistently high immigration rates. There is no easy shortcut to ensuring that voters see immigrants as contributors to their communities or making immigration popular; doing so requires years of hard policy work and compromises for governments and advocates alike. In the next chapter, I illustrate this principle by providing a detailed qualitative comparison of the historical evolution of immigration policies, politics, and public opinion in Canada and Sweden.

8

HOW (NOT) TO DESIGN POPULAR IMMIGRATION POLICIES

Comparing Reforms in Canada and Sweden

THE EVIDENCE PRESENTED in the previous chapters suggests that, while counterproductive backlashes to legal pro-immigration reforms are rare, not all pro-immigration policies are alike in terms of generating public support. In particular, countries with more skill-selective, utilitarian immigration systems paradoxically tend to accept more immigrants of all kinds and have more positive immigration attitudes than do countries with less selective, humanitarian systems. That is, at least descriptively, only demonstrably beneficial pro-immigration policies can secure durable public support for consistently high immigration rates.

This chapter illustrates this dynamic by comparing the increasingly divergent historical experiences of Canada and Sweden in terms of designing their immigration policies and legitimizing them to the public. While some have compared the two countries with respect to immigration, most research has focused on integration and welfare state outcomes, not public support for freer immigration.[1] Although I discuss the evolution of Canada's and Sweden's immigration policies and the expert assessments of their success, my focus is on whether these countries' governments have been able to generate public support for their relatively open policies with consistently high immigration flows.

As I will describe later, despite many commonalities, these two cases arguably exhibit the maximum possible difference in my key outcomes of interest: their approaches to immigration admission policy and the resultant legitimacy of their policies in the electorate. All in all, Canada's immigration policy has the most explicit emphasis on national interest among high-income democracies as evidenced by its famous point-based system and the correspondingly high proportion of skilled economic immigrants. In stark opposition to Canada and most other countries, Sweden espouses an unusual universalist approach that focuses on admitting a large number of humanitarian immigrants and ensuring their equal treatment. While Canada has gradually managed to channel its large supply of immigrants from around the world into an impressive machine of economic selection and nation-building, Sweden has built a global image of extraordinary generosity by providing a home to a disproportionate number of refugees, asylum seekers, and their families. Though it may be hard to compare the ethical and welfare implications of these distinct systems, it is increasingly clear that Canada has been much more successful than Sweden in securing popular support for its expansive immigration policy despite the favorable, elite-backed conditions for such support in both countries.

In addition to being established parliamentary democracies with advanced capitalist economies, Canada and Sweden share many features commonly emphasized as important for immigration support such as a commitment to multiculturalism. Both countries have also been considered moral superpowers, routinely topping various global rankings, including the Social Progress, Commitment to Development, Good Country, and Globalization Indexes. Meanwhile, because of their relative geographic isolation and peripheral positions on major migration routes, especially when compared to the United States and Mediterranean countries, neither Canada nor Sweden has experienced significant unauthorized immigration that voters may find controversial. Most relevant to immigration politics, however, are the high levels of racial tolerance and social liberalism among Canadian and Swedish voters.[2] It is thus not surprising that potential immigrants from all over the world name Canada and Sweden among their most desired destinations.[3]

Of course, these countries are not the same. As a larger settler-colonial state, Canada has naturally had much more experience with immigration than the old Kingdom of Sweden. Canada's deep linguistic and religious divisions at the time of its founding also mean that it has had a longer tradition of accepting cultural differences. Even today, the French-speaking province of Quebec maintains a culture, institutions, and immigration policies distinct from those of English-speaking Canada but within the country's federal system.[4]

Sweden has historically had stronger labor unions and welfare state institutions than has Canada, which may have constrained more expansive immigration. Sweden's electoral system of proportional representation is arguably also more conducive to the rise of anti-immigration political parties than is Canada's pluralist system in which parties are more incentivized to attract immigrant voters.[5]

Despite these important differences, amid the social transformations of the mid-twentieth century, both countries experienced a critical juncture for the development of their immigration systems. In particular, the Canadian and Swedish governments faced significant domestic and international political pressure to open up their countries to the world and reform their explicitly racist immigration policies. However, policymakers in each country consciously chose very different paths: taking a utilitarian perspective, Canada prioritized skilled immigrants, whereas Sweden prioritized humanitarian immigrants and their equal treatment. An informed comparison of the increasingly divergent political outcomes of these reforms is thus ideal for better understanding the role of policymaking in generating popular support. Table 8.1 provides a comparison of Sweden, Canada,

TABLE 8.1 Necessary conditions for making immigration popular

STRUCTURAL CONDITION	SWEDEN (IMMIGRATION IS CONTESTED)	CANADA (IMMIGRATION IS POPULAR)	UNITED STATES (IMMIGRATION IS CONTESTED)
Educated, tolerant voters	Yes	Yes	Yes
Multicultural institutions	Yes	Yes	No
Low rate of unauthorized immigration	Yes	Yes	No
Demonstrably beneficial policies	*No*	*Yes*	*No*

Note: U.S. values are grayed out as they are included here for comparison purposes only.

and the United States with regard to the structural conditions necessary to make immigration popular (U.S. values are given for informational purposes only).

When observers try to explain why immigration is much more popular in Canada than in the United States, they often point to the presence of multiculturalism or the absence of unauthorized immigration in Canada. However, this explanation is overdetermined, as it is unclear whether the popularity of immigration in Canada results from one of those factors, from the presence of a demonstrably beneficial policies (as I argue in this book), or a combination of all these factors. Notably, none of these factors—apart from a demonstrably beneficial policy—can explain why immigration is much more popular in Canada than in Sweden, despite both countries having educated and tolerant voters, multicultural institutions, and low levels of unauthorized migration. Therefore, a comparison of the two countries can be used to highlight the crucial role of policy design in shaping public attitudes toward immigration.

HOW CANADIAN IMMIGRATION POLICIES GENERATED THEIR OWN SUPPORT

THE OPEN SECRET OF CANADIAN SUCCESS

In general, it is difficult to define policy success in an objective way. It may be especially difficult to do so when it comes to the success of immigration policies since so many people disagree even on their very purpose. However, if there is one country where immigration policies can be decisively considered successful, it is Canada.

One fruitful way to define policy success is to consider whether a certain policy consistently achieves its goals while conferring legitimacy among relevant stakeholders.[6] The modern post-1960 Canadian immigration policy regime does exactly this. It consistently fulfills its main objectives of promoting economic and population growth in Canada by attracting high levels of skilled immigrants. It also legitimately serves important family reunification and humanitarian goals while constantly adapting to changing economic and social realities.

According to a recent comprehensive assessment by the OECD, Canada has "the most carefully designed and long-standing" set of immigration policies that "serve as a benchmark" for other countries.[7]

Perhaps most impressively, however, Canada has been able to generate and maintain a broad public consensus in support of high levels of immigration even in times of crisis when its peer countries succumb to anti-immigration politics. In fact, Canada is the only high-immigration democracy in which all current national political parties across the ideological spectrum support high immigration levels without facing any credible challenge on the issue from the populist right.[8] Importantly, few, if any, experts believe that this success has been the result of uniquely successful persuasion or prejudice eradication campaigns by pro-immigration advocates or the government. Instead, analysts have suggested the following three distinct reasons for Canada's exceptional public acceptance of immigration.[9]

The first commonly cited reason is Canada's embrace of multiculturalism at both the institutional and grassroots levels. Canada was the first country to adopt official multiculturalism policies in 1971—later codified in the Canadian Multiculturalism Act of 1988—which many citizens now endorse or even view as a part of their national identity. At the legislative level, these policies affirm Canada's bilingualism, promote cultural diversity, and combat group discrimination. As a result, common cultural concerns about racially different immigrants who undermine native culture may have less power in today's Canada.[10] But similar multicultural policies have also been present in many other immigrant-receiving countries, including those with much less popular immigration. In particular, according to the Multiculturalism Policy Index, Canada and Sweden equally rank second in the world in terms of their multicultural policies for immigrant minorities; they are surpassed only by Australia.[11] Further, despite the high levels of stated support for multiculturalism in the abstract, Canadian attitudes toward specific cultural policies, ethnic and racial diversity, and discrimination do not appear to be much different from those of its peer countries.[12]

The second reason relates to Canada's advantageous geographic positioning with its sole land border facing the more affluent United States. This positioning ensures that the border and the foreign population can be effectively controlled by precluding unauthorized or otherwise unwanted immigration. However, while undoubtedly important, such favorable geography and the related absence of border security as a salient issue are not unique to Canada. Many much less pro-immigration European countries outside the Mediterranean region, for instance, similarly receive very few irregular migrants or deal much with border issues.[13] It is also worth noting that the Canadian government has responded harshly to even relatively minor unauthorized immigration throughout the years, including recent encounters at Roxham Road, an unofficial Canada–U.S. border crossing in Quebec that has become an entry point for thousands of asylum seekers.[14]

This point brings me to the third—and arguably the most consequential—reason: Canada's immigration policies themselves. It is worth clarifying what these entail, however. In explaining why immigration is so popular in Canada, various observers have emphasized everything from Canada's point-based system in general to its particular features, such as skill selection, transparency, flexibility, and efficiency. In line with my argument in this book, I contend that the main reason that Canadians accept freer immigration is that their immigration admission policies have been explicitly and straightforwardly designed to advance the national interest.

Indeed, the benefits of Canada's policy of selecting a large number of immigrants who will benefit the Canadian economy and society based on their individual characteristics are easy for the government to communicate and for voters to understand. It also helps that the individual characteristics favored by the point system are transparent and make intuitive sense: the system prioritizes younger, educated, skilled, or otherwise wanted individuals as demonstrated by their occupation, job offer, or provincial nomination.

As discussed in chapter 7, such deliberate prioritization of the national interest in immigration policy is incredibly persuasive both in the short and long term. In the short term, voters can understand and agree with the criteria and purposes of immigration. In the long term, voters can see the favorable outcomes and understand that they are clearly attributable to immigration. For some, this can be the realization of continued economic growth and national development.

For others, it can be as simple as the availability of diverse food options or the ability to receive high-quality services made possible by foreign-born doctors and other professionals.

With time, these and other signals of immigrant selection and benefits trickle down to uninformed voters. Although Canadians are no more politically knowledgeable or engaged than are citizens of other countries, they do have a much better understanding of their immigration policy and its selectiveness.[15] Concerns about the welfare burden of immigrants that are common elsewhere are almost absent in Canada because its immigration system has been designed explicitly to prevent significant immigrant reliance on social benefits and people are aware of that.[16] As a result, unlike the governments of many of Canada's peer countries, the Canadian government can credibly claim that immigration is beneficial, and Canadian citizens can largely trust these claims.[17]

Contrary to many commentators, however, I do not want to suggest that the positive support for immigration in Canada is about the point-based system or its implementation per se. In fact, one can imagine an employer-led or minimum qualification requirement system that would likely have the same effect on the legitimacy of a country's immigration system. At the same time, one can also imagine a much less popular point-based system that would reward immigrants' humanitarian needs instead (e.g., for the purposes of refugee resettlement). However, what ultimately matters is the *demonstrable* prioritization of national interest in the design and implementation of immigration policies.

THE THORNY HISTORY OF MAKING IMMIGRATION POPULAR

The success of Canada's immigration policy is no accident. It can be traced back directly to the initial design of the modern immigration system as formulated in the famous 1966 White Paper. This paper was commissioned by the government to reorient the immigration system from its problematic racist past. From the outset, the paper stipulated that immigration should "involve no discrimination by reason of race, colour or religion." It then made very clear that "without a substantial continuing flow of immigrants, it is doubtful that

[Canada] could sustain the high rate of economic growth and the associated cultural development which are essential to the maintenance and development of [Canadian] national identity."[18] The paper further argued for boosting population growth and ensuring a greater alignment of immigration policy and long-term economic Canadian interests by liberalizing the recruitment of skilled immigrants of *all origins* and restricting less skilled immigration based on family ties.

Despite its progressive aspirations, upon its release, the proposal sparked strong opposition from various organized groups. Interestingly, it was particularly opposed by existing immigrant, ethnic, and religious groups who were relatively disadvantaged by the proposed rules that de-emphasized family sponsorship. Despite this initial setback, Jean Marchand, the minister of the newly established department of Manpower and Immigration, and other civil servants behind the reform set up a task force to make revisions that would satisfy both the government and civil society. The eventual proposal, which was well received by the media and the general public, divided immigration flows into the (family) sponsored and (economic) unsponsored categories and introduced the famous point-based system to assess immigrants for the latter group.[19]

These new regulations, approved and implemented by the government the following year and codified in the Immigration Act of 1976, were much less selective and much more family-forward than was the initial proposal. As a result, selective economic migration became the dominant category, overtaking family migration, only much later in the 1980s (figure 8.1). Still, the post-1960 reform efforts managed to completely transform the way immigration works in Canada and in many other countries that were later influenced by the Canadian model.[20]

It is important to acknowledge the key role of bureaucrats in shaping Canadian immigration policy through much trial and error.[21] Canadian immigration policy has traditionally been in the hands of appointed officials whose discretion was limited by only a few government stakeholders. Indeed, one reason that the post-1960 reforms were possible is the relative insulation from electoral politics of the civil servants responsible for them.[22] As a result, the

Number of residence permits approved yearly

Types of residence permits approved yearly

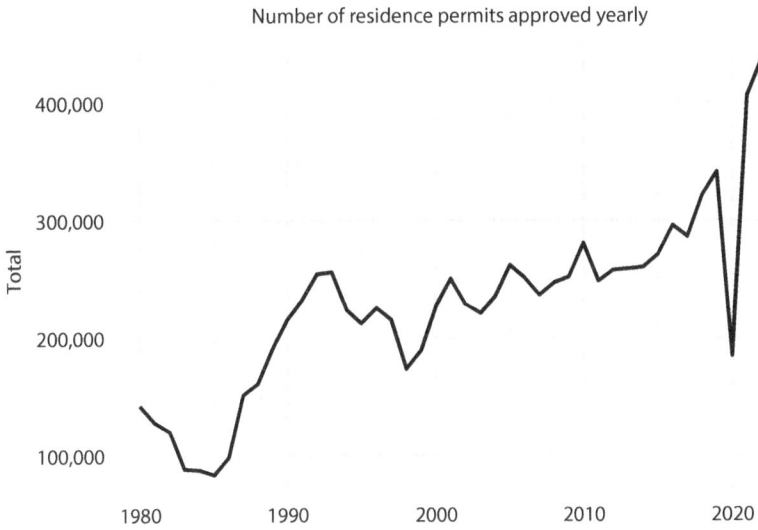

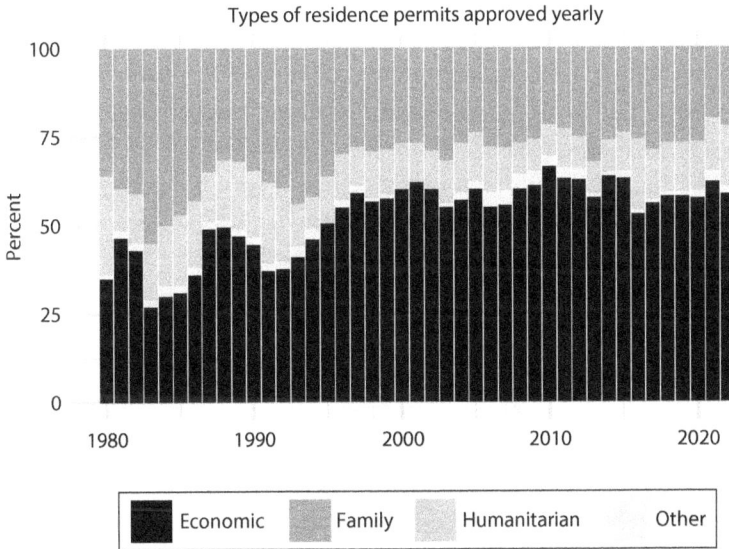

FIGURE 8.1 Canada's permanent resident admission flows, 1980–2022.

Source: Government of Canada (IRCC) data.

initial day-to-day selection practices of immigration bureaucrats and the eventual regulations codified in the law were likely shaped as much by bureaucrats' own perceptions of the ideal Canadian citizen as by an objective assessment of Canada's economic needs or public opinion.[23]

Despite their political insulation and a dose of idealism, however, the Canadian immigration bureaucrats have been well aware of the importance of maintaining legitimacy in immigration policymaking among the broader public. As a result, they have consistently and pragmatically implemented various measures and adjusted the policy to increase public support for the country's expansive immigration system.[24] According to most possible metrics, postwar Canadian attitudes toward immigration just before the reforms took place were as negative as everywhere else.[25] Since then, however, despite occasional setbacks, Canadian attitudes have evolved to become among the most positive globally, particularly in terms of highly positive assessments of the economic impact of immigration and satisfaction with how the government handles the issue.[26]

These changes in public opinion did not occur overnight. In fact, one of the country's biggest pro-immigration leaps in attitude did not occur until the early 2000s—more than two decades after the policy reforms had been implemented.[27] Thus, it took several decades for the Canadian public to accept and embrace the country's new immigration policies (figure 8.2).

There is no doubt that this change has been the result of various factors, from changing domestic political coalitions to the global context. For instance, it was also in the twenty-first century that Canada's largest ever anti-immigration Reform Party joined the Conservative Party to avoid splitting the right vote in national elections. Once they merged, however, the Conservatives instead found it more beneficial to appeal to immigrants than to demonize them to win votes given the concentration of immigrants in large metropolitan areas and the relative ease of their naturalization.[28] Still, partisan politics aside, it is hard to imagine how the exceptional positivity among regular Canadian citizens could have been possible without the demonstrable prioritization of national interest in immigration policymaking.

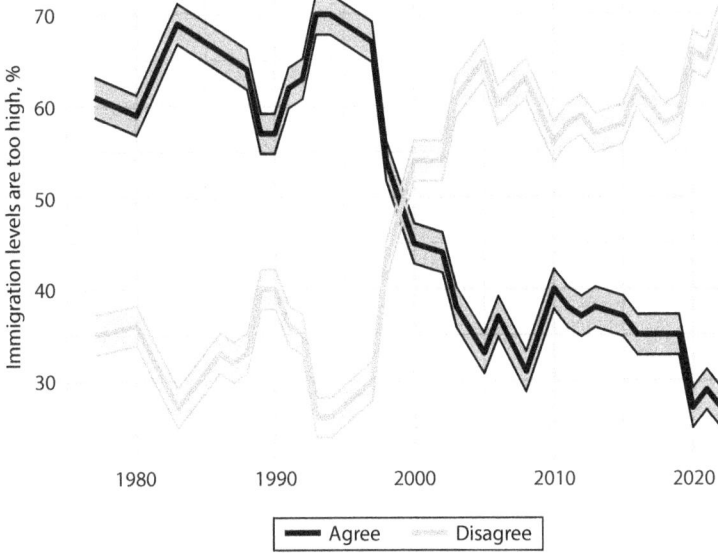

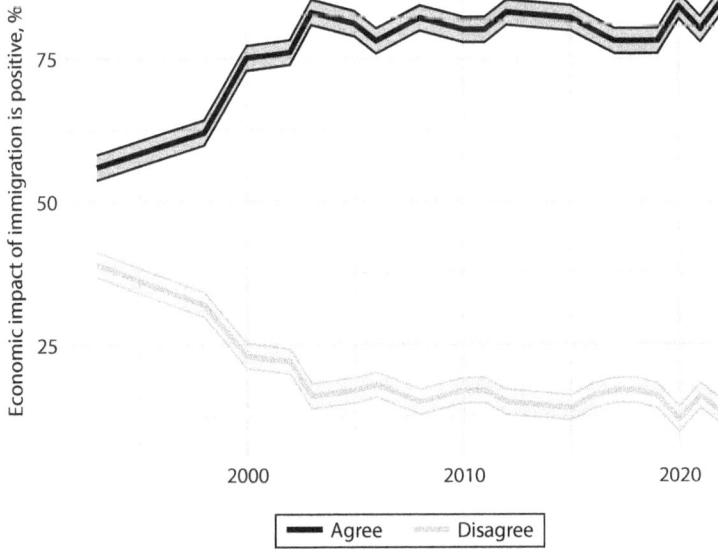

FIGURE 8.2 Canadian immigration attitudes, 1977–2022.

Source: Environics survey data.

EVEN IN CANADA, IMMIGRATION POLICYMAKING
IS CHALLENGING

Despite its advantages over the U.S. and other immigration systems, the Canadian system is not perfect. Most prominently, many scholars document that the point-based system that generally rewards education at the expense of labor market needs has led to disproportional unemployment and persistent overeducation among its immigrant workers,[29] creating what is commonly known as the "immigrants with PhDs driving taxis" problem. Immigrant skill mismatch, however, is not confined to Canada or to selective immigration systems more generally.[30] Further, the government has tried to address the issue by incorporating employer and regional labor demand into the system, as well as by improving skill certification and validation processes.[31]

But despite the well-deserved praise for the efficiency and effectiveness of Canadian immigration governance, the system is not immune to occasional glitches and mistakes. Processing times for immigration applications and visas, for example, have often been quite lengthy (though still better than in the United States and many other countries). More recently, the COVID-19 pandemic created a significant backlog in the system, the consequences of which the government is still struggling with today in 2024. At the same time, the admission of a large number of students following the pandemic amid significant housing strains has led to significant public dissatisfaction, prompting the government to impose a cap on international student numbers.[32] None of these problems, however, appears to be particularly exceptional or insurmountable. As noted in the OECD report mentioned earlier, what distinguishes the Canadian immigration system is its adaptability to new challenges and changing contexts.

Another set of common of humanitarian-oriented criticisms highlights the general restrictiveness of the system, its increasing reliance on temporary as opposed to permanent visas for less skilled workers, the tough approach to (rare) unauthorized immigration, and equity-related concerns.[33] It is true that, for most workers from the Global South without a university degree, Canada provides very few legal paths for permanent immigration. It is also true that the immigrants selected disproportionally come from middle-class or affluent backgrounds;

they also come from certain regions and have certain ethnic and racial origins.[34] However, it is still unclear whether any other immigration systems do better on any of these accounts from a global humanitarian perspective, especially when considering the sheer number of permanent immigrants that Canada admits every year.

Finally, while freer immigration is much more popular in Canada than in other countries, it still does not yield overwhelming public support. Canada has had its own anti-immigration voters, advocates, politicians, and parties.[35] In addition, the country has been experiencing growing partisan polarization on immigration attitudes, which means that immigration critics are now disproportionally concentrated in the Conservative Party.[36] But it is unknown whether that rise is a result of Canada's immigration policies or other often external factors. After all, with the rise of immigration issue salience over the last two decades, the United States and other countries have experienced similar trends in immigration-related polarization by party.[37] Further, it is possible that greater political polarization in itself may not be a problem for policy success.[38]

Ultimately, it is striking that even the harshest critics of Canadian immigration, which come from members of the Conservative Party (and formerly also the Reform Party), almost never question the country's utilitarian skill-selective system itself but merely suggest making it even more selective. The same goes for today's (not particularly successful) People's Party of Canada, whose most extreme proposal—capping Canadian immigration at 150,000 permanent permits per year—would still make Canada relatively more open to immigration than the United States and most other countries.

HOW SWEDISH IMMIGRATION POLICIES FAILED TO GENERATE THEIR OWN SUPPORT

THE RISE OF A MORAL SUPERPOWER

When I first started writing about the importance of advancing national interest through immigration policy, some of my colleagues were skeptical. Surely, they said, this was something that all countries did or at least said they did. There is some truth to that, as we saw earlier, so I did start having doubts about the existing variation in the extent to which immigration policies prioritize national interest. Everything changed when I dove into the decidedly humanitarian-oriented immigration policy in Sweden. While I had previously written about Sweden and worked with public opinion data from that country, I did not realize just how radically humanitarian the Swedish approach to immigration was until much later.

At the beginning of this book, I noted that my focus was on regular immigration admission policies, not on the related but typically distinct issues of humanitarian migration and integration. However, it is impossible to discuss immigration policy in Sweden without considering these other issues. Over the last half-century, refugees, asylum seekers, and their families have become the main source of permanent immigration in Sweden, while their successful integration into society has become the main political issue during elections. At the same time, Sweden is perhaps the only country that decided not to prioritize skilled immigration in its policies.

According to the official website of the (currently right-wing) Swedish government, "The objective for migration and asylum policy is to ensure a long-term sustainable migration policy that safeguards the right of asylum . . . , facilitates mobility across borders, promotes needs-based labour migration, harnesses and takes into account the effects of migration on development, and deepens European and international cooperation." Apart from a somewhat tautological use of legal jargon, the most striking feature of this quote, written in the aftermath of the 2015–2016 refugee crisis, is that it lacks any even merely rhetorical allusion to the national interest. According to the current mission statement of the Swedish Migration Agency, it is "the UN's Declaration of Human Rights [that] is a cornerstone in the Swedish migration policy."[39]

This is not just rhetoric. For instance, Sweden routinely ranks first in the category of migration in the Commitment to Development Index (CDI) based on purely objective indicators. According to experts from the Center for Global Development, Sweden "hosts the second highest number of refugees relative to its population (24.7 per 1,000 population, compared to a CDI average of 4.5) and it ranks within the top ten countries for the number of migrants it welcomes per head of population when weighted by migrants' origin countries' incomes." It also "demonstrates stronger policy efforts to integrate migrants into its economy and society than any other CDI country."[40]

Traditionally, Sweden had been an emigrant-sending, not an immigrant-receiving, country. Though it invited tens of thousands of guest workers in the aftermath of World War II, its immigration policies were initially relatively restrictive. Because of strong opposition from labor unions and concerns about "cheap labor," in 1972 the government restricted economic immigration further by effectively ending most available legal immigration pathways from non-Nordic countries. As a result, until very recently Sweden issued only a few thousand work migration permits per year, accounting for only a few percent of permanent immigration. Most of the country's de facto economic immigration has likely come from other European countries as part of the free movement agreement after Sweden joined the European Union in 1995.[41]

In 1951, like many other Western democracies, Sweden signed the UN Convention Relating to the Status of Refugees (and later signed the 1967 Protocol). Initially, this commitment amounted to no more than a few thousand humanitarian immigrants each year. Despite its increasingly restrictive labor immigration policies, with the increase of people fleeing conflict in the 1970s, Sweden started to take in more refugees and asylum seekers from non-European countries. However, unlike those of other countries, the Swedish government decided to grant expansive social and political rights to its noncitizen residents. In fact, until recently, all migrants who were anticipated to stay in Sweden for at least a year had the same access to health care, social security, and other welfare benefits as did Swedish citizens, regardless of the purpose of their stay.

In 1975, the Swedish Parliament formulated a new multiculturalist policy of integration breaking with the previously dominant idea of assimilation and giving immigrants the possibility of maintaining their cultures.[42] A few years later, the government also dropped a financial support requirement for the immigration of family members, making Sweden's family reunification policies among the most liberal in the world.[43] These developments cemented the predominance of humanitarian and noneconomic immigration in Sweden (figure 8.3). Sweden's immigration policies have also secured the country's

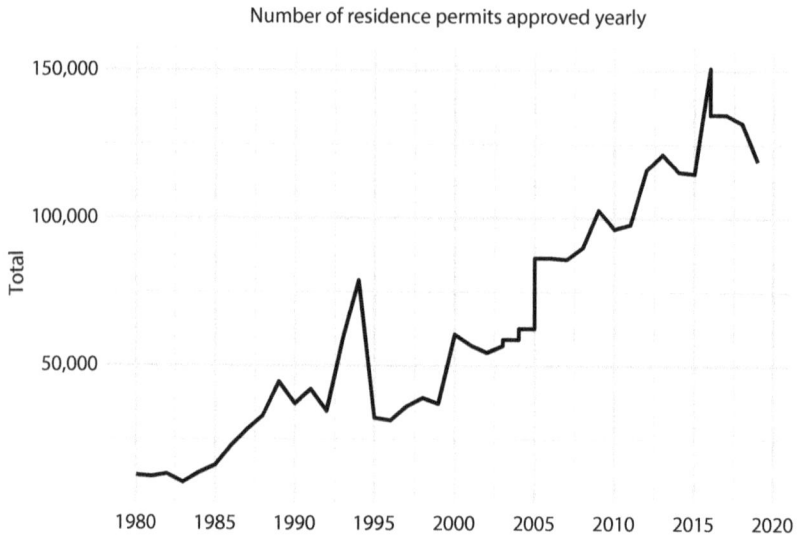

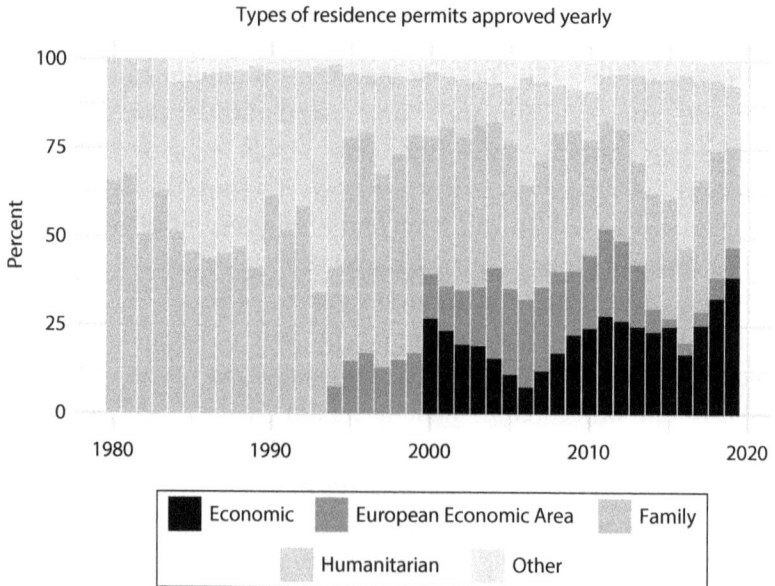

FIGURE 8.3 Sweden's permanent resident admission flows, 1980–2020.

Source: Swedish Migration Agency data.

reputation as a moral superpower owing to their remarkable openness and generosity to those fleeing violence and poverty globally.[44] It
is interesting, if not indicative of the Swedish approach more generally, that the government did not even have a separate category for
economic immigration until 2000 (as shown in figure 8.3).

This is not to say that the Swedish government lacks pragmatism
or has not tried to reform its policies in a more utilitarian direction.[45]
For instance, unlike many other European countries, Sweden has
long allowed refugees and asylum seekers to work upon arrival. The
idea of adopting a more selective, labor-based, Canadian approach to
immigration has also been circulating among Swedish policymakers
who have made many trips to Canada to discuss immigration policy
over the past several decades.[46] Unfortunately, Sweden's labor unions
have historically required employers to hire foreign workers in com-
pliance with prevailing industry standards as determined by collective agreements. As a result, few potential immigrants outside the
European Union could get a job offer and come to Sweden despite its
otherwise relatively open immigration admission policies.[47]

New immigration legislation introduced in 2008, spurred by an
unlikely coalition of the center-right Alliance with the Green Party,
has perhaps been the most ambitious effort of the Swedish government to reform its convoluted labor immigration policies and
increase economic immigration. Upon its introduction, the reforms
were called "the most liberal labor immigration legislation among
the OECD countries" and "a slight revolution."[48] The idea was to
create a flexible employer-driven system that would make it much
easier for employers to hire foreigners by abolishing the previously
required labor market needs assessment and reducing the role of
trade unions. Despite some skepticism, many immigration observers
have been particularly excited about the prospects of the new legislation to transform immigration in Sweden and elsewhere.[49]

THE RISE OF POPULISM AND THE END OF OPENNESS

Over the last few years, however, the headlines have been telling a
very different story about Sweden's immigration realities.[50] Once
deemed a success story of open immigration, Sweden today is viewed

as a cautionary tale for naive if not reckless policy even among some of its earlier pro-immigration enthusiasts. The biggest reason for this change in image is the somewhat unexpected rise of the Sweden Democrats, a radical right-wing populist party. Previously marginalized and deemed unacceptable by mainstream parties in Swedish politics before 2010, the party received 17.5 percent of the vote in the 2018 parliamentary election and 20.5 percent in 2022, at which point it became a partner in the government coalition for the first time in history. After coming to power, the new government expectedly announced a variety of new immigration restrictions, a corresponding reduction of immigration admission targets, and a new international campaign to discourage people from seeking asylum in Sweden.[51] The official website of the Swedish government now quotes its new immigration minister, Maria Malmer Stenergard, who is blunt about the meaning of the recent policy changes: "To bring order to integration, we must reduce immigration."[52]

However, despite all the initial hopes and intentions, the 2008 immigration reform has not been particularly successful in terms of attracting wanted workers or legitimizing immigration in the electorate. One possible reason for this failure was that, in contrast to most existing labor immigration policies (and most arguments made in this book), the law made no distinction between low- and high-skilled workers. That is, it had no selection criteria, requirements, or quotas to prioritize those with higher education, needed occupations, or other favorable characteristics. As summarized in a recent evaluation of the reform, "Attempts to create a one-size-fits-all system have led to longer waiting times and more bureaucracy for highly qualified workers, while the number of low-skilled labour migrants has increased, in particular in professions and branches of the economy where Sweden has a surplus of labour. . . . Because labour immigration to Sweden is supposed to be entirely employer-driven, employers can no longer count on state support to identify, recruit and relocate attractive labour to Sweden. . . . Since controls on working conditions have proven both inefficient and insufficient in this employer-driven system, abuse of labour immigrants has increased."[53]

For many progressives across the Atlantic, what is at stake here is not only the feasibility of liberal immigration policies but also

Sweden's famously strong welfare state, which has recently been in decline.[54] The exact role of immigration in the ongoing retrenchment is debated, especially compared to other economic factors. Still, it is clear that Milton Friedman's famous libertarian mantra, "You cannot simultaneously have free immigration and a welfare state," sounds much less hypothetical in Sweden than in the United States or Canada. While the Swedish government has sometimes attempted to gain support for increasing immigration by alluding to its potential national interest benefits, such as addressing concerns over the aging population and public finances, in practice, the extent of such benefits depends on how much immigrants consume in social benefits and how much they contribute to taxes. According to a review of such estimates, immigration to the country, which has so far consisted primarily of refugees and their families, has not been fiscally beneficial to the Swedish state, even before the 2015 surge in arrivals. This is largely due to high unemployment rates among immigrants and the country's generous social benefits system available to all regardless of their status.[55]

A common way for these issues to be framed in Swedish politics has been as a problem of integration rather than immigration. However, according to the famous Migrant Integration Policy Index (MIPEX) and the Commitment to Development Index, Sweden has the most elaborate integration policies of all OECD countries.[56] The Center for Global Development acknowledges this paradox and specifies that it is integration policy *efforts* that Sweden excels at, not integration *outcomes*.[57] Indeed, according to all economic metrics from labor participation to unemployment, immigrants' integration outcomes are disappointing compared to both native-born citizens and peer countries despite Sweden's integration efforts and the benefits they provide to immigrants.[58]

In Canada, as in the United States, immigrants commit far less crime per capita than do native-born citizens. Given that most data and analyses on immigration come from North America, many observers simply assume that immigrants' law-abidingness must be a universal trait. However, this assumption is demonstrably untrue in many European countries and across the world. While research does not show that immigration generally increases crime, it may be true for the rapid immigration of young, unskilled males facing labor market discrimination. Given the demographic realities of Swedish immigration admissions, it is thus not surprising that foreign-born individuals in Sweden are disproportionately represented in the prison population.[59]

Even those sympathetic to the Swedish immigration system acknowledge the stark gaps between native-born citizens and immigrants in employment and incarceration, as well as in important housing and processing capacity issues. As argued in an otherwise enthusiastic report published in the midst of the refugee crisis, "If the Swedish municipalities, the central government, civil society and economic actors . . . fail to overcome today's difficulties, and if the rise in support for the xenophobic Sweden Democrats continues as it has for similar parties in neighboring Denmark and Norway, fair immigration policies in Sweden might give way to a much more restrictive and less idealistic approach, and some open doors might be closed."[60] Now we know that this is exactly what happened.

Of course, one can reasonably argue that the Swedish immigration model has failed only because of an enormous exogenous shock related to the Syrian civil war and the resultant unprecedented wave of asylum seekers. One can also point out the insufficient responses by the other EU countries, which has strained the preparedness of the Swedish system even further.[61] One could even argue that the rise of the Sweden Democrats and the country's subsequent U-turn on immigration has been facilitated by far-right misinformation campaigns from abroad.[62]

Although all of these things may be true to an extent, the fact that the Swedish immigration system has failed in response to a shock is an indication of its initial faulty design. Despite taking a similar share of refugees in 2015–2016 and facing a similar subsequent rise of the radical right, for instance, Germany has not altered its immigration policies as drastically. Further, the cracks in the Swedish system were evident before the refugee crisis. The Sweden Democrats have been present on the national stage since 2010, and immigrant outcomes themselves have never been encouraging.[63]

Most importantly, however, the high number of asylum seekers Sweden accepted in 2015–2016 was not an inevitable outcome. While Sweden's even relatively isolated geographical position within

Europe still allowed for rapid movement of migrants, the country's generous policies and initially welcoming rhetoric played a significant role. Sweden's approach also differed notably from neighboring countries like Denmark, which experienced much lower immigration numbers during the same period. The pro-asylum decisions made (and the possible restrictive choices *not* made) by the acting government at the time have undoubtedly provided safety and a new home to hundreds of thousands of people fleeing violence and persecution in Syria and other countries. Still, from the perspective of sustaining public legitimacy and the long-term functioning of immigration policy, the Swedish approach has certainly backfired by galvanizing voters' preexisting grievances toward their immigration system, which does not provide tangible benefits to citizens or their communities.

WHY COSMOPOLITAN SWEDES OPPOSE FREER IMMIGRATION

While assessments of the merits of Sweden's immigration policy may vary, it is clear that the government has not been able to build an immigration system that can maintain its own support.[64] The growing success of the anti-immigration populist party there is especially striking when one considers that Sweden has consistently been rated one of the most tolerant and cosmopolitan countries in the world.[65]

On the surface, Swedish immigration attitudes have been and are still among the most positive in the world, often even more so than in Canada.[66] In 2013, 94 percent of Swedes said that immigration was a good thing—more than any other country in the world. Similarly, 68 percent of respondents saw immigration as an opportunity—again, more than in any other studied country.[67] These perspectives have held, even in the aftermath of the refugee crisis. According to many attitudinal indicators, despite a sizable decrease in positivity in 2015, attitudes in 2022 partially reverted back to their 2011 levels.[68] One can be forgiven for thinking that, despite some challenges, Sweden has remained a success story, at least when it comes to public support for its immigration policies.

Looking deeper, however, a very different picture emerges. Even before the 2015 refugee crisis, in the same 2013 survey where vast majority thought immigration was an opportunity, a majority of Swedish respondents (61 percent) thought that the government was doing a poor job at handling immigration. Further, only 34 percent believed that immigrants were integrating well.[69] Similarly, according to a 2018 Eurobarometer survey, 73 percent of Swedish respondents thought that integration was not successful, and 58 percent thought that migrants were a burden on the welfare system.[70] In one cross-national 2021 survey, while 65 percent of Swedish respondents said immigration is positive for their country, 55 percent also believed that immigration policies should be more restrictive, much more so than in Canada or other countries.[71] Finally, according to another 2017 survey, more than 55 percent of Swedish respondents reported believing that "immigration increases crime."[72]

Unfortunately, very few of these important metrics are consistently available across time. However, according to the only comprehensive time-series polling data, gathered by the SOM Institute, a Swedish survey research organisation, immigration-related "integration" and "crime" have consistently been mentioned as important political issues by significant swaths of the electorate at least since the 1990s.[73] Similarly, since 2016, the majority of the population has been consistently in favor of accepting fewer refugees, and this figure is yet to show any sign of recovery (figure 8.4). Incidentally, it is

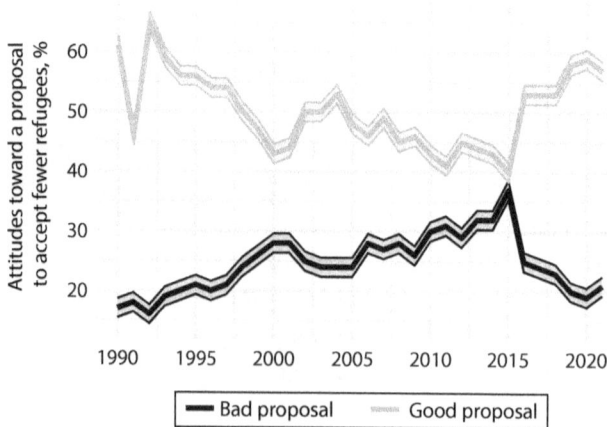

FIGURE 8.4 Swedish (humanitarian) immigration attitudes, 1990–2021.

Source: SOM Institute survey data.

quite telling that Sweden's longest-running national survey is asking people about only refugee admissions, not economic admissions or even immigration admissions in general.

What all these survey data show is that Swedish voters often combine an unusually positive stated outlook on immigration (as may be expected from their comparatively strong humanitarian predispositions) with much more skeptical specific positions and revealed behaviors (as may be expected from the actual policies of their government). This long-standing tension has become even more apparent in the aftermath of the refugee crisis, leading to the previously unimaginable electoral rise of right-wing populists. This situation illustrates that public support for government policies, even among cosmopolitain citizens, cannot be sustained when those policies *demonstrably* go against the national interest.

One does not have to study the meticulously assembled reports of the Center for Global Development to see how Sweden's immigration policies have benefited vulnerable immigrants from other countries. The benefits of these policies to the country itself and its native-born citizens, however, arc much less clear, especially compared to the costs. These benefits are also evidently contestable in politics and contingent on diverse noneconomic understandings of national interest among Sweden's citizens.

CONTRASTING CANADIAN AND SWEDISH IMMIGRATION

Over the last century, the political choice for advanced democracies in which many voters are skeptical of immigration has often been between closed borders and almost closed borders. That is why it is remarkable that some governments have been able to consistently welcome immigrants with the enthusiastic endorsement of their citizens. Until recently, many analysts would have pointed to Canada and Sweden as distinct yet successful examples of the possibility of such relatively open immigration admission policies.

Despite their differences, both Canada and Sweden have often been rightfully praised for focusing on the successful integration of

196 PERSUASION BY DESIGN

large numbers of permanent immigrants as opposed to recruiting temporary guest workers or relying on cheap, undocumented labor. It is thus not surprising that the countries have often been bundled together as potential models for immigration reform in the United States and elsewhere.[74] After all, both countries have also been seen as the quintessential examples of functioning liberal democracies with educated, cosmopolitan voters ready to embrace immigration.

Government policies, including those related to immigration, can be successful in democracies only when they generate and maintain their own support in the electorate. Throughout the last several chapters, I have argued that selective immigration policies that demonstrably benefit citizens are a necessary and significant contributory condition for freer immigration to become robustly popular. Of course, I cannot claim that it is a sufficient condition, and other factors, such as particular political institutions or electorate qualities, may also be important. Still, to the best of my knowledge, no single major democracy has been able to make freer immigration popular without adopting highly selective policies. The increasing political divergence between Canada and Sweden in terms of the popularity and success of their relatively open immigration admission policies provides a vivid illustration of my argument.

International migration has enormous potential to benefit both individuals and states. This is especially true in the case of immigration from lower-productivity countries to highly desirable and well-governed countries like Canada and Sweden. In any domain of human activity, such demand would rightly be viewed as an asset. That so many people around the world are willing to abandon their roots and move to a foreign country, often far away, is testament to the fact that immigrant-receiving countries are doing many important things right. Unlike Sweden, Canada has taken full advantage of that immigration demand by prioritizing and encouraging the immigration of those who are most likely to benefit its economy and integrate into its society.

Despite having a fairly small population until the twentieth century, Canada grew to be more than three times larger than Sweden by the twenty-first century *because* of high immigration. The Canadian government has consistently pursued the idea of population and economic growth by actively attracting willing workers and their families from abroad. These policies have not always been supported by majorities or initiated by citizens, but neither have they been actively opposed by many voters. The exact amount of economic and noneconomic surplus to native-born Canadians from immigration can be debated and is likely modest.[75] But there is no doubt that, without relatively open immigration, Canada would have been a much smaller, less developed, and less influential country than it is today.

As noted by Michael Donnelly, "Canadian exceptionalism, to the extent that it exists, is an elite institutional phenomenon, not a mass attitude one."[76] In all likelihood, Sweden could have similarly become an undeniable model of immigration openness and success. It could even have been larger, more prosperous, and more influential on the world stage under more long-standing, skill-selective immigration policies. Like Canada, Sweden has experienced an elite-led liberalization and deracialization of its immigration policies since the 1970s and has attracted an approximately similar share of permanent immigrants since the early 2000s. But, unlike Canada, Sweden's political elites have decided to take a more humanitarian approach to immigrant selection. This chapter argues that the evident disregard for national interest in Sweden's recent immigration policymaking is the main reason that relatively open immigration admission policies have failed to maintain popular support among (otherwise cosmopolitan) Swedish voters.

One prominent (left-wing) academic critique of Canada's expansive immigration policy is that it is too focused on benefiting Canada, spurring economic growth, and providing selected workers for big businesses instead of advancing equality, human rights, and social justice.[77] In a way, Swedish immigration over the last several decades has addressed most of these critiques by admitting many of the least privileged immigrants and providing them with full social support. Scholars disagree about the exact economic impacts of immigration, but it would be surprising if the actual costs and benefits were similar in both countries despite the stark differences in their approaches. In this respect, while some rightly argue that the economic burdens of immigration are often socially constructed by anti-immigration populists,[78] it is much easier to convincingly "construct" those burdens in Sweden than in Canada.

Sweden is a successful, open country, and it can still reemerge as an immigration success story if the new government decides to prioritize national interest and selection over restrictions. According to a recent OECD report, based on quality of life and related characteristics, Sweden ranks as a top country in terms of its capacity to attract and retain talented immigrants, beating both Canada and the United States.[79] But even if Sweden drastically reformed its immigration policy by successfully attracting skilled or otherwise wanted workers now, the issue would likely remain politically controversial for years to come. As we have seen, it takes time to transform the composition of existing immigrant populations, and it takes time for voters to notice such changes.

Further, it is important to consider the demand factor. For instance, some scholars estimate that the United States is much better than Canada at attracting high-skilled immigrants[80] despite the Canadian policy efforts described here and despite the fact that the U.S. immigration system prioritizes family-based immigration. For various economic and cultural reasons, the United States is still the most desired destination for international migrants of all skill levels, but especially top talent, despite its convoluted immigration system.[81]

In this respect, recruiting skilled immigrants may be an especially uphill battle for otherwise attractive Sweden even if there is political will for such policies simply because many immigrants want to go to the United States instead. But it should be possible; demand can also be influenced by policymaking. For example, the relative desirability of the United States over Canada has been significantly reduced over the past several decades because of the inability of the United States to streamline its increasingly antiquated policies and Canada's deliberate efforts to exploit the U.S. system's problems. Many high-skilled specialists from large immigrant-sending countries like China and India who are unable to acquire permanent residency in the United States owing to obscure per-country cap limits have been consistently and successfully encouraged by the Canadian government to relocate up north.[82]

Similarly, Sweden has both the capacity and interest to compete with Canada and the United States for talent by creating policies that would make immigration there attractive and feasible for foreign professionals from across the world. If successful, such policies and the resultant gradual change in the immigrant population could encourage currently skeptical Swedish voters to try to embrace immigration again.

* * *

Policymaking is hard. Immigration policymaking is doubly so. Thus, one may reasonably wonder what other countries can really learn from Canada's or Sweden's experiences given their distinct histories and institutions. My hope is that the comparison of their divergent approaches to the goals of immigration policy and the eventual political outcomes can still shed light on the necessity of demonstrable national interest in immigration policymaking.

While Canada exemplifies the robustly legitimate "open but selective" approach to immigration, it is not alone. Similar policies have been successfully adopted in Australia and New Zealand where, not coincidentally, immigration is also relatively open and popular. Although these countries have made their immigration policies primarily employer-oriented to ensure that immigrant supply meets demand (a decision that subsequently influenced Canada's policies), the core principle of prioritizing and encouraging skilled and otherwise wanted economic immigration remains the same.[83] Many other countries, including Germany and Denmark, have recently implemented or announced their resolve to implement a point-based system inspired by the successful experience of Canada or Australia.

Point-based systems are increasingly popular among policymakers because they are easy to understand, but policy success is not just about allocating points. In fact, point-based systems can and often do fail.[84] Hopefully, governments can find other ways to adjust their immigration systems to ensure that international labor mobility is beneficial and that voters can understand that. As discussed throughout this book, such policies can include anything from streamlined student immigration to bilateral partnerships and targeted policies attracting less skilled workers to fill specific vacancies.

It is only when governments have sufficient voter support for nationally beneficial immigration that they can consider expanding noneconomic and humanitarian admissions. Sweden, with its prevailing refugee admissions and egalitarian admission rules for skilled and unskilled workers, is an extreme example. But policymakers and advocates in many other countries also deliberately prioritize noneconomic immigration flows, including the United States, which quite fittingly has been grouped with Sweden as a "humanitarian immigration regime" in a recent policy typology.[85] Meanwhile, ever since the refugee crisis, Canada has been admitting more refugees and asylum seekers than Sweden in terms of absolute numbers and as a share of the total population. And over the last several decades, Canada has also almost always admitted more humanitarian immigrants than the United States as a share of the total population.[86]

CONCLUSION

How to Make Immigration Popular

*The economics of labor mobility are simple. . . . The difficult part
is political: How can development-friendly labor mobility
policies that are politically acceptable to voters in rich countries
be devised?*

Lant Pritchett, "Let Their People Come"

LTHOUGH SEVERE government restrictions on international
migration adopted over the last century have substantial human
costs, most voters and politicians in high-income countries do
not want to relax those restrictions. This dissonance is peculiar and
unfortunate because a number of alternative—more open—policy
arrangements could significantly benefit everyone over the long term.
Given the recent humanitarian crises of displaced people and the
related need for novel democratic solutions, it is important to better
understand the motivational bases of widespread anti-immigration
attitudes. However, it is also imperative to know whether the motivations behind those attitudes can be channeled into the pro-immigration direction.

As of now, it is common to explain anti-immigration preferences
by alluding to voters' ignorance and deep-seated racial animus. There
is much truth to these factors, but racism alone cannot explain widespread opposition to freer immigration. To understand why even educated and socially liberal people often support welfare-diminishing
immigration restrictions, scholars and policymakers alike must
move beyond the idea of inherently prejudiced voters and consider
alternative accounts.

The current emphasis on racial prejudice among scholars and advocates in explanations of public immigration skepticism is also not very practical since it does little to change the reality of the situation. Indeed, branding those who oppose immigration as racists or xenophobes rarely changes minds, which is understandable given the well-known rigidity of such predispositions. While the related emphasis on correcting widespread misperceptions of immigration issues is certainly a more viable approach, it is still largely vulnerable to politicized counterinformation in any competitive democratic environment. As a result, despite all the efforts to combat xenophobia, the public in most high-income countries is almost as opposed to open immigration now as it has always been, and the borders of those countries are almost as closed as ever.

Considering the reality of robust popular opposition to immigration in general, this book offers a path forward for responsive and responsible democratic governments: adopting new, more *demonstrably beneficial* pro-immigration policies that explicitly and straightforwardly benefit countries' national economies and regular voters. Importantly, policies showcasing national benefits could extend beyond attracting top talent—from filling shortages and boosting regions to facilitating education and reuniting families. To that end, my research highlights the unlikely role of genuine altruism in both popular resistance to and the popular embrace of immigration.

In particular, I argue that resistance to immigration stems from the well-documented fact that most people, including those who are highly educated and socially liberal, care about others but prioritize their compatriots' interests. Given the persistent public perceptions of the national risks of mass immigration, widespread altruistic motivations toward compatriots are generally not conducive to popular support for international mobility. But I also argue that these motivations could be channeled into support for freer immigration under alternative policies that are explicitly and straightforwardly beneficial to the national interest.

In chapter 1, I contrasted my theory with competing prejudice-based accounts and specified appropriate empirical analyses to test it. Using existing survey data from around the world, I first provided evidence that altruistic voters are generally opposed to immigration, often much more so than those who are not altruistic (chapter 2). To address social desirability concerns, I then conducted a new study with a real-stake charity raffle to measure people's revealed nationalistic and humanitarian commitments and the connection of those commitments to people's attitudes toward immigration (chapter 3). As a part of this study, I also ran an experiment presenting respondents with hypothetical policy choices to understand how people's perceptions of whether immigration is good for them and their countries impact their attitudes causally (chapter 4). Overall, I found that most voters, especially those who are altruistic and nationalistic, can and do support freer immigration when they genuinely believe it will benefit their fellow citizens. My results also showed that those who want to open borders unconditionally for humanitarian reasons and those who want to stop migration because of racial prejudice are both in the minority.

One of the most immediate practical implications of my argument and these findings is that emphasizing and informing voters about the tangible economic and noneconomic benefits of immigration is a very good idea. But why would voters ever truly believe that increasing immigration is in their national interest? After all, various attempts to change people's anti-immigration attitudes by providing facts have generally not been successful.

Indeed, one key reason that even politicians who are well aware of the enormous benefits of immigration to receiving countries rarely campaign on expanding immigration is that they are also well aware of the robust public skepticism on the issue. Given these anti-immigration sentiments, any campaign emphasis on the issue may increase its salience among voters, which is unlikely to be a winning electoral strategy for most mainstream politicians and parties.

The overlooked alternative is for incumbent responsible governments to change the policy environment itself, which does not always have to be electorally risky. If my research on *altruistic nationalists* is correct and if the currently widespread opposition to immigration is not categorical, voters should be willing to compromise their *general* anti-immigration sentiments and support *specific* pro-immigration reforms when they are confident in the favorable national consequences of those reforms. However, the presumed national benefits of certain immigration policies must be demonstrated by policymakers and must be straightforward enough for voters to understand.

Thus, chapter 5 introduced a framework of *durable persuasion by policy design* and showed that changing voters' attitudes toward immigration is not just a matter of framing, rhetoric, or any other form of policy communication. My overview of actual electoral responses to past pro-immigration policy changes showed that they did not cause voter backlash. In fact, chapter 6 showed that broad labor-friendly pro-immigration reforms largely resonate with the public. While this evidence cannot say whether it is ever a good idea for politicians to campaign on pro-immigration policies compared with other possible issues, it does suggest that at least some pro-immigration reforms could be popular and sustainable. Chapter 7 then showed that only *demonstrably beneficial* immigration policies in line with the perceived national interest can generate their own support among voters.

Finally, chapter 8 illustrated this dynamic using an in-depth comparison of modern immigration policy and politics in Canada and Sweden. While both countries have had their immigration highs and lows since opening up to the world in the 1960s, Canada's unabashedly nationalistic approach to selecting immigrants based on their ability to contribute to the economy has clearly been more politically successful and sustainable than the otherwise admirable humanitarian approach of Sweden. My research in this area made me conclude that the best way to persuade voters that freer immigration is desirable is to *show* them by adopting *selective* pro-immigration reforms that open legal pathways for skilled or otherwise needed foreign workers.

IMPLICATIONS FOR UNDERSTANDING PUBLIC OPINION AND POLICYMAKING

Stepping aside from the immigration debate for a moment, in this book, I have also advanced a novel theoretical framework of *nationalism as parochial altruism* and provided new evidence about what motivates people's political decision-making. Building on the previously disparate literatures in political psychology and behavioral economics, I showed that many voters respond to national interest incentives even when they are against their own interest. In prioritizing the costs and benefits to their compatriots, however, voters often disregard the well-being of people in general—in immigration, international relations, and even domestic politics. The related individual differences in parochial altruism systematically predict people's political choices (in addition to other personal characteristics and identities).

As a result, the idea that genuine altruistic motivations may often be in conflict appears to be useful in explaining political behavior across a variety of outcomes and contexts, providing a more nuanced psychological basis for the increasingly salient globalization divides across the world. Overall, I showed that voters in rich democracies make political decision based on what they think is good for themselves and their compatriots but pay little regard to other interests.[1]

The proposed distinction among altruist types should be especially important in political as opposed to economic behavior since people are often uncertain about the personal impacts of various political alternatives and because their choices are rarely personally consequential.[2] The notion of this division can also complement a prominent, but often less analytically useful, juxtaposition of economic or material and cultural or symbolic behavioral causes. For instance, the current debate over the rise of populism, which often relies on economic and cultural concerns as exhaustive explanations, may be overlooking an important preference variation in the electorate.[3]

In distinguishing between more and less parochial altruism, this book also informs the long-standing debate over how individuals prioritize their identities and interests in a competitive political environment.[4] For example, though my results are not consistent with accounts of pure or predominant self-interest in political preferences,[5] they also counter the widespread idea that self-interest matters only in exceptional circumstances.[6] Further, contrary to the conventional wisdom that "all politics is local," the fact that voters generally care more about their national rather than local interests is in line with the growing evidence of greater nationalization in politics.[7] As opposed to existing sociotropic accounts, however, my research also clarifies that voters would generally *not* choose a policy that is beneficial to their compatriots at great expense to themselves or everyone else.

Using experimental and revealed preference evidence rather than self-reported attitudes, this book corroborates the idea of nationality as a defining political category in the contemporary world.[8] Both the Brexit vote in the United Kingdom and the 2016 and 2024 elections of Donald Trump in the United States have often been described as exemplifying the growing electoral divide between *communitarian nationalists*, or "somewheres," and *cosmopolitan globalists*, or "any-wheres."[9] However, since most people today say they love their country and care about the world, it may be more instructive to ask to what extent voters are willing to sacrifice their own well-being for the sake of national or global interests. In other words, *altruism* is what gives motivational power to nationalism, globalism, and other competing social identities.

The book also speaks to the long-standing question of finding the right balance between responsible and responsive policymaking,[10] and it highlights the necessity of both in any successful policy persuasion effort. Most existing initiatives to persuade voters to support immigration and other issues have been concerned primarily with what to say (information), how to say it (framing), and who should say it (source).[11] While insightful, these approaches overlook the fact that politicians and governments can and routinely do *lead* public opinion by enacting new policies.[12] The legitimation of proposed policies does not happen automatically, and backlash to even responsible reforms is always possible when they do not align with what voters want. But legitimation is possible when voters can understand and see for themselves that the reforms proposed and implemented by their government are evidently in their own and in their country's interests. It is important to remember, however, that even policies that provide tangible personal benefits may not necessarily generate their own support.[13]

Of course, the evidence presented here also raises a number of important questions for future research. For instance, what about the role of other prosocial motivations like fairness or reciprocity[14] in general and vis-à-vis (parochial) altruism in particular? There is ample evidence that such other preferences are also politically consequential but often parochial.[15] There is also some indication that those who are more averse to inequality and unfairness are generally less anti-immigration,[16] but how those motivations interact with parochialism and how much influence they have relative to altruism are still unclear. Given the well-documented popularity of "welfare chauvinism" among voters,[17] one may suspect that voters' application of their fairness and inequity concerns to immigration issues is rather limited. Though more research is certainly warranted, it is unlikely that such concerns can be channeled into significant immigration support. Still, there is some evidence that bilateral and multilateral migration agreements may be quite popular because of their explicit reciprocity.[18]

Regardless of whether one believes that nationalism, parochial altruism, or any other individual predisposition is normatively desirable, it is important to agree on the empirical reality of what motivates people's political decision-making.[19] After all, the evidence for widespread parochialism implies that, under certain conditions, sincere altruistic motivations can not only promote cooperation, such as solving problems of collective action, but also exacerbate conflict, as in the cases of immigration and other global issues like climate change mitigation. Prosocial motivations and preferences are relatively stable, so it is highly unlikely that people can be made more altruistic or less parochial by any government or nongovernment intervention. In this respect, the ultimate question is, *What institutional arrangements and policymaking practices can help societies reap the benefits of parochial altruism but also minimize its costs, both domestically and globally?*

WHY MAKING IMMIGRATION POPULAR REQUIRES SMARTER NATIONALISM AND BETTER POLICIES

Going back to the immigration debate, the evidence presented here implies that more open immigration admission policies can be popular and sustainable in a representative democracy only when they are in line with voters' genuine preferences for the common national good.

Many books have addressed the question of whether immigration is beneficial or detrimental to receiving countries. But the quest to find one ultimate answer seems misguided since it clearly depends on the context and policies in question.[20] While immigration—or at least most related policies and the immigrants involved—contributes significantly to the well-being of some countries, like Canada, its impact on other countries, like Sweden, can be more ambiguous or even negative. The more pertinent question is whether and to what extent the observed or anticipated effects of immigration should matter to policymakers.

This book is unabashedly data driven, and so far, I've been careful not to make any judgments about what governments *should* do about immigration. It is notoriously difficult to move from knowing "what is" to knowing what "ought to be." Some readers may agree that voters generally want more selective policies but may disagree that immigration should be more selective on various normative grounds. To make things a bit more interesting and outline some policy recommendations, for the remainder of this chapter, I will openly embrace moral uncertainty[21] and adopt a version of the middle-ground "enlightened national interest" approach with moderate degrees of cosmopolitanism and consequentialism.[22]

Indeed, immigration policy disagreements have often come down to a clash of two major political values: *nationalism* and *cosmopolitanism*. Nationalists believe their government ought to restrict immigration to protect the safety and interests of their fellow citizens. Cosmopolitans and humanitarians demand a much more open immigration system that is mindful of the well-being of vulnerable migrants.

If there is anything that cosmopolitan and nationalist thinkers seem to agree on, it is that there have always been disagreements between these perspectives on immigration. In particular, there is a clear tension between governments' nationalistic commitments to their citizens and freer immigration. My research demonstrates that this tension diminishes when immigration policymaking is demonstrably beneficial to the nation.

Ostensibly, nationalism and cosmopolitanism are polar opposites, but there are known ways to reap the benefits of immigration for the sake of the national interest while also respecting the basic rights of noncitizens. Indeed, economic research has repeatedly demonstrated that most forms of immigration can be positive for receiving countries in the long run.[23] A smarter form of nationalism would recognize that fact and require governments to embrace selective immigration policies that can explicitly and straightforwardly benefit their citizens. I call this type of responsible and responsive democratic governance *demonstrably beneficial policymaking.*

Since Adam Smith, economists have recognized the power of enlightened self-interest. Individuals prioritize their long-term goals over short-term desires by helping and cooperating with others in an informed way. Similarly, a more enlightened form of nationalism would advance national interest over longer time spans by recognizing common human concerns. Those concerns may often demand extensive and well-thought-out international cooperation among national governments and their citizens. For instance, it is clearly in the national interest of the United States to help stop the spread of COVID-19 and prevent future global pandemics, even if doing so would mean significant increases in immediate foreign assistance.

At the same time, cosmopolitans—some of whom might in principle want to reject nationalism in all forms—must recognize that most people *are* nationalists, at least in terms of intuitively and selflessly prioritizing their fellow citizens, and that is unlikely to change in the foreseeable future. Similarly, only governments that are perceived to prioritize their citizens' needs are realistically able to sustain their democratic legitimacy and govern effectively. While it may be important for some people and even some politicians to sometimes transcend their patriotic commitments and consider the interests of humanity as a whole, nationalism is the only game in town for both domestic and global governance.[24]

As with any other human activity, immigration has winners and losers. Immigration and its restrictions are harmful to some people and beneficial to others. The general intention of immigration restrictions is to protect and improve the well-being of a nation's citizens.[25] Unfortunately, however, not only do those restrictions directly impose substantial costs on global productivity and harm potential migrants, they also often come at a price to the national economy and freedoms of native-born citizens.[26]

All things considered, human mobility among countries is neither good nor bad. It is what governments and their policies make of it.[27]

This notion is well illustrated by the divergent impacts of immigration on crime in the United States and Europe.[28] Instead of debating whether immigration is inherently good or bad or whether it should be increased or decreased in the abstract, policymakers should identify concrete ways to improve immigration policy for the benefit of their countries and citizens given the realities and constrainsts they face right now.

Based on the evidence I have presented, I argue that demonstrably beneficial policymaking, which seeks to advance national interest over the long term in responsive and responsible ways, is a more effective and humane guiding principle for designing immigration policies than any alternatives. With demonstrably beneficial policymaking, governments do not need to reconcile the differences between nationalist and cosmopolitan outlooks to move forward on immigration. Under this principle, governments would take those conflicting value differences out of the immigration debate and focus on the actual evidence of immigration costs and benefits to their country. It is a principle that both anti- and pro-immigration advocates can and should embrace.

Immigration stakeholders should stop pairing symbolic, patriotic-sounding, or immigrant-friendly rhetoric with predefined policy conclusions. Instead, they should focus on what regulations will materially advance the national interest in the long run. Cosmopolitan-minded and libertarian supporters of immigration should acknowledge that democratic governments have unique obligations to their citizens, making some level of immigrant selection necessary to serve the country's long-term interests. Patriotism-driven immigration skeptics should recognize that prioritizing citizens does not imply that foreign lives have no value or that the opportunity costs of immigration restrictions can be ignored.

Understood this way, it is possible that a more open immigration admission system may in fact be more nationalistic relative to other values currently guiding immigration policy (e.g., tradition, partisanship, empathy, or antipathy for select groups). Immigration is contentious because of polarizing slogans like "America First" from nationalists and purist rejections of nationalism from cosmopolitans. That does not have to be the norm. The most important immigration question, according to my findings regarding demonstrably beneficial policymaking, is whether significantly restricting certain types of immigration is, in fact, a prudent thing to do. Does it actually benefit our national interest to prohibit most foreigners from willingly joining our country? Or, conversely, would it make more sense to encourage the immigration of people who are clearly wanted by our citizens and communities?

However, I do not argue that immigration policymaking should simply be more evidence-based or responsible because such a thesis would still be vulnerable to disagreement over the responsibilities of individual citizens and their democratic governments. It is important to separate often empty and sometimes destructive nationalist rhetoric from truly nationalistic policies that demonstrably benefit citizens. In other words, simply having politicians on the left and across the political spectrum embrace patriotism or nationalism is not enough. What responsible governance under any political ideology in power requires is demonstrably beneficial policymaking in the country's interest, and that is especially true in the case of immigration today.

BREAKING THE CATCH-22 OF MAKING IMMIGRATION POPULAR THROUGH DEMONSTRABLY BENEFICIAL POLICIES

At this point, you may wonder whether making immigration popular is a catch-22. How can governments—that generally want to stay in power—enact meaningful pro-immigration reforms when voters are so hostile to immigration? And how can they do that when it seems like it is always in the interest of some politicians to demonize immigrants and stoke anti-immigration views?

Making immigration popular is undoubtedly an uphill battle. Voters tend to be uninformed and hold negative views of the issue.[29] Populists often exploit this lack of knowledge and negativity for political gain by using divisive rhetoric about immigration to attract voters.[30] Journalists further contribute to negative public perceptions by focusing on attention-grabbing stories about poor government

performance at the border rather than the "boring" stories of successful immigrant integration throughout the country.[31] As a result,
voters consistently receive the signal that their government lacks
control over immigration,[32] and few responsible politicians are willing to make an affirmative case for freer immigration in this context.

But immigration is not unique in this regard. Voters are similarly
ill informed about many important technical issues for which they
lack personal incentives to seek accurate information.[33] Voters also
tend to show loss aversion and care more about potential threats
rather than benefits when it comes to politics more generally.[34] Journalists want their stories to be read, so this negativity bias then shows
up in media coverage everywhere.[35] Ultimately, the restrictive status
quo generally prevails, even when evidence suggests that liberal policy reforms would have net positive effects on society.

Despite these challenges in making pro-immigration politics, there
are also reasons for optimism. As documented throughout this book,
many forms of immigration are already popular or at least conditionally popular among the public. Journalists do report positive stories,
and politicians are always eager to take credit for favorable policy outcomes. These facts suggests that the vicious cycle of anti-immigration
politics and opinion can be broken by responsible governments making programmatic pro-immigration reforms that align with people's
underlying preferences and that have tangible positive results.

After all, real-world policies and objective indicators still matter,
even if many voters do not understand them well and if many journalists do not report them accurately.[36] When immigration policies
are not demonstrably beneficial, it is easier for voters to hold negative
views and for politicians to exploit such views, regardless of policy
communication efforts. The divergent experiences of immigration
politics in Canada and Sweden illustrate this point clearly.

As Larry Bartels has documented, democratic institutions develop
and erode from the top, not the bottom.[37] Similarly, the success or
failure of immigration reforms depends on the actions of those in
power. While advocates, experts, and nongovernmental organizations can help identify responsible and responsive policies, run pilot
programs, and provide examples of successful immigration initiatives, governments are the key actors in making this change happen

in a world of nationalism, representative democracy, and state-run immigration regulations.

To break the catch-22, governments must recognize that though public opinion is important, it is not an absolute constraint on policy-making.[38] Governments can change policies even in the face of prevailing public sentiment. By demonstrating responsiveness to people's concerns, governments can earn greater trust from voters, allowing them to implement policies that may not be immediately popular but are ultimately beneficial.[39]

When liberal governments overreach with overly generous pro-immigration policies, they may face voter backlash. However, when they align their policies with people's underlying motivations, such as concern for their compatriots, those policies can generate their own support and improve the public's attitudes toward related policies. Therefore, opening new legal pathways for demonstrably beneficial immigration should be the first step in sustaining public support for more open immigration admission policies.

The successful passage of Germany's Skilled Immigration Act is a particularly promising example of breaking the anti-immigration catch-22 and making immigration popular through demonstrably beneficial policymaking. German lawmakers navigated numerous political compromises but faced no voter backlash despite the country's otherwise contentious immigration politics. The new "opportunity card" visa recently cleared in both Houses of Parliament should make it easier for most professionals from non-EU countries to immigrate to Germany even when they do not have a university degree or a job offer.[40] Similar to the Canadian point-based system, the new policy rewards one's qualifications, experience, age, and language proficiency but also allows some flexibility with regard to the fulfillment of those criteria. Although it remains to be seen whether the reform will ultimately be successful at attracting skilled workers, it has great potential to make freer immigration more popular in the long run.

There are no easy solutions to the challenge of making immigration popular. This is particularly true in the United States given its majoritarian institutions, weak political parties, and large border regions. As Daniel Hopkins rightly notes in his exploration of a similar ordeal in the case of U.S. health care reform, even well-designed programmatic policies are unlikely to build meaningful political support within a few electoral cycles in today's polarized environment. Therefore, responsible policymakers should focus on designing policies that accomplish their goals while minimizing the risk of *sustained* political backlash.[41]

In sum, overcoming the catch-22 of making immigration popular in the face of public skepticism, negative media coverage, and perverse political incentives is undoubtedly difficult but possible. Whether helped by pro-immigration advocates or not, any feasible solution requires those in power to responsibly design and implement demonstrably beneficial policies. By capitalizing on the conditional popularity of many forms of immigration and focusing on policies that address citizens' concerns, it should be possible to gradually shift public opinion and build trust in a freer immigration system. While this process may be time-consuming and involve numerous trade-offs, it is essential for creating a more sustainable and politically viable approach to immigration in the long run.

MAKING IMMIGRATION POPULAR BEYOND CONSIDERATION OF SKILLS AND POINTS

Demonstrably beneficial immigration policymaking works. Governments must look after their own citizens first, and research has demonstrated that immigration is a useful tool for policymakers to improve conditions for both native-born citizens and immigrants. Canada, whose selective point-based immigration system is perhaps the system most aligned with the principles listed here, has been successful for more than fifty years, experiencing little political conflict—despite having some of the largest labor and humanitarian immigration flows among Western democracies.

Of course, immigration policy and public opinion do not end with more or less selective and demonstrably beneficial admissions.[42] While a detailed discussion of related issues is beyond the scope of this book, it is clear that more open immigration admission policies also need a set of sound integration and border security policies in line with the national interest to be durably popular.

While some may scoff at the idea of immigrant assimilation in a liberal democracy, some form of adoption of the mainstream culture of receiving countries by immigrants is evidently important. This point is crucial from the perspectives of voters, who usually have a specific conception of a "good citizen"; their governments, which have a set of naturalization rules; and immigrants themselves, who want to succeed in their new countries.[43] Fortunately, there is little evidence to suggest that most voters want immigrants to completely shed their culture and all connections to their origin country. Instead, voters want immigrants to speak the language and adhere to the civic norms of the host nation.[44] Ultimately, successful integration is about both native-born citizens and immigrants having the knowledge and capacity to achieve success in the society they live in.[45]

Similarly, freer immigration can arguably be popular only when voters are confident that their country's borders are secured and their government is in full control of immigration flows.[46] Populist politicians are always eager to exploit anxieties about the need for order and to exaggerate stories of chaos at borders, perhaps even more so than the alleged lack of immigrant integration. This is especially true for countries like the United States with large border regions where it is always possible to come up with a credible story of some unauthorized activity. Fortunately, people's perceptions are grounded in reality, at least to some extent, so incumbent governments can actually do something about those perceptions by implementing more secure border policies.[47]

At the same time, high immigration flows cannot be achieved without sound housing, transportation, occupational licensing, and other social and local policies on the ground.[48] People's concerns about overcrowding and fiscal burdens in their communities are reasonable and stem from genuine prosocial motivations, not just selfishness or prejudice. Obviously, there is only so much immigration agencies can do about these localized burden concerns, especially in federal states, but it is also paramount for local governments to consider immigration's demonstrable benefits and harms. The recent 2022–2023 asylum crisis in New York City is a testament to the dysfunctional local and federal immigration policies that brought havoc to one of the most immigrant-friendly cities in the world.[49]

It is notable that even Canada, despite its openness and long tradition of multiculturalism, has relatively tough border security and numerous policies in place to encourage immigrants' language and job integration. It is also notable that Canada's immigration success has recently come under pressure because of the dysfunctional housing policies so common in Anglophone countries.[50]

Still, Canada's point-based system has come to exemplify the idea of selective immigration and its political success. The country's positive immigration experience and the relative simplicity of the idea have motivated many governments and other stakeholders to adopt or at least advocate for this approach: more than a dozen countries have recently implemented or proposed legislation to implement a point-based immigration system. In the United States alone, many legislative attempts have been made to implement a "merit-based" immigration reform with some type of point system. One of the largest, yet still somewhat underappreciated, benefits of a Canadian-style point-based system is that it provides a clear signal from the government to its citizens that immigrants are selected based on their ability to benefit the nation.

Nonetheless, the United Kingdom's convoluted immigration politics of the last two decades, alongside a bizarre experience of repeatedly (re)introducing, modifying, and removing points tests in their immigration system, should serve as a cautionary tale for all policymakers looking for easy solutions.[51] Point-based systems may sound objective and efficient, which may rhetorically convince some voters to trust their government on immigration, but there is nothing magical about them. The trick is for governments to not just claim but also *demonstrate* that their immigration policies and the immigrants they bring actually benefit voters.

Demonstrably beneficial immigration is not just about selecting skilled workers by allocating points. Historically, many types of immigrant selection have been successful, including employer-driven and locally sponsored admission policies that include a wide range of migrant skills and backgrounds.[52] Policies can also attract international students, small businesses, and foreign investors.[53] Put simply, demonstrably beneficial immigration is not necessarily *exclusive* immigration (e.g., of highly skilled professionals) but *wanted* immigration:

wanted by families, society, employers, local and national governments, or nonprofits.

In this respect, though there is limited survey evidence on the
matter, it is likely that voters would be naturally supportive of global
skill partnership programs that are increasingly gaining traction
among experts. These bilateral agreements facilitate the movement
of workers from developing to developed countries to fill particular
labor market shortages while also investing in training programs in
the sending countries, creating a win-win-win situation for migrants,
sending countries, and receiving countries by design.[54] One particularly fruitful application of these programs could be in "green-skilled"
migration, in which the idea is not only to meet the burgeoning labor
demands in renewable energy sectors of receiving countries but also
to promote environmental progress globally.[55]

Of course, such programs are not without ethical challenges related
to their temporary nature and the difficulty of achieving fair democratic representation of all sides.[56] Still, in line with my argument, by
clearly demonstrating the mutual benefits for all parties involved,
these programs have enormous potential to garner widespread public
support for expanding immigration.

Similarly, regional agreements that allow citizens of member
states to live and work in other member states without permits have
the potential for strong popular support. Despite various crises like
Brexit, COVID-19, and the rise of anti-immigration and Eurosceptic
politics in recent decades, the European Union's free movement policies have not only survived but prospered.[57] This enduring legitimacy
and popularity among the vast majority of Europeans against all odds
demonstrates the power of such agreements to generate and sustain their own support. While the EU experience is unique in many
ways, its success in fostering popular support for free migration can
serve as a model for other regions.[58] By establishing and empower-
ing similar regional agreements that emphasize the mutual benefits
of free movement and increased opportunities for all citizens, other
parts of the world can also reap the rewards of enhanced mobility.
For example, some recent evidence suggests that a similar bilateral
agreement between the United States and Canada to allow for common residency and work rights in both countries would be popular.[59]

Importantly, to make freer immigration durably popular, it is crucial that the benefits of immigration policies are easily understandable to the average person without requiring extensive education or specialized knowledge. In this respect, one particularly promising, although still untried, policy alternative—which is even simpler than a point-based system—is the auctioning of immigration visas.[60] In such a system, prospective immigrants would bid for visas, with entry granted to the highest bidders who meet basic eligibility criteria. This market-based approach could efficiently allocate visas, generate government revenue, and incentivize economic contributions from immigrants. To ensure access for skilled but less affluent individuals, the government could offer loans or financing options to help them participate in the bidding process.

Another promising proposal is the use of place-based visas, which would attract new immigrants to economically stagnant regions, helping distribute immigration benefits more evenly. This policy aims to revitalize struggling areas by bringing skilled migrants to fill labor shortages, start businesses, and boost local economies. By tying visas to specific regions that choose to participate in this program, this approach ensures that immigrants settle where their contributions can have the greatest impact, maximizing immigrations' demonstrable benefits.[61]

Demonstrably beneficial immigration policies for receiving countries do not have to be limited to governmental actions. While most pro-immigration organizations understandably focus on helping immigrants already living in their new countries, opportunities exist for both the private sector and nonprofits to enhance their efforts on the immigration admissions front. One innovative example of a potentially demonstrably beneficial initiative is Malengo (https://malengo. org/), a nonprofit organization that facilitates the movement of students from low-income to high-income countries for higher education.[62] Malengo provides comprehensive support to selected students, including assistance with the application process, funding for living expenses and travel costs, and guidance in finding part-time jobs to support themselves after their first year of studies. In return, students agree to contribute a share of their earnings after graduation through an income share agreement to help fund the program for future generations of students.

By designing a program that benefits both the students and the sending countries, while also creating a sustainable funding model with no apparent downside for receiving countries, Malengo provides a model for creating politically viable solutions that promote international mobility. For the program to be scaled up, however, it would have to develop a tangible way to provide explicit and straightforward benefits to receiving countries *and* emphasize those benefits to the public to avoid politicization and backlash. Similar to the idea of global skill partnerships mentioned earlier, this process could involve developing partnerships with local businesses and industries to ensure that the skills and expertise of graduates directly contribute to the host economy.

Meanwhile, the increasingly popular idea of private refugee sponsorship, which allows individuals and communities to financially support the resettlement of migrants from certain affected regions in their communities, is a good example of a humanitarian policy consistent with demonstrable national benefit.[63] When refugees are directly invited and supported by willing citizens, especially when they are encouraged and eager to work,[64] it is hard to argue that they are unwanted or a social burden. At this point, it should be no surprise that such programs—which combine real-world humanitarian impact with a healthy dose of pragmatism—originated in Canada, not Sweden.

When it comes to the United States, it is worth noting that some also reasonably argue that adopting a more skill-selective system would not work as well there because of the institutions and high demand for lower-skilled immigrants in that country.[65] Some also worry that a "merit-based" overhaul of the U.S. system could undermine its relatively successful and long-standing family-based immigration policy.[66] As others rightly point out, however, some form of point-based system, as well as visa auctions or place-based visas for that matter, could be added seamlessly to the current system if only Congress would decide to do so.[67]

Indeed, unless there is an unlikely political opportunity for (re) writing immigration laws from scratch altogether, U.S. immigration policy proposals might benefit from being more targeted so that their national benefits are incontrovertible. Though an exploration of the legislative process of immigration reform and its context-dependent complexities is beyond the scope of this book, my evidence indicates that the more narrow and specific pro-immigration policy tweaks are, the more likely they are to succeed in the court of public opinion compared to more broad and comprehensive attempts at reform, which necessarily invoke more controversial aspects such as border control. Examples of potentially succesful, incremental reforms include increasing caps for particular categories of skilled visas, allowing international students to stay in their new country to work after graduation, and simplifying administrative processing for existing uncapped categories.[68] Ultimately, it is difficult to see how the United States can expand immigration, even to Canadian levels—which some argue it must do urgently[69]—without explicitly and straightforwardly prioritizing national interest in its immigration policies.

PRINCIPLES OF DEMONSTRABLY BENEFICIAL IMMIGRATION POLICYMAKING

If my research findings on altruistic nationalism and demonstrably beneficial immigration policies are correct, the current widespread opposition to immigration is not rooted only in prejudice, and voters should be willing to support new pro-immigration policies when they are confident that those policies are good for their countries. This is not just a matter of elite messaging: presumed national benefits of immigration policies must be demonstrated by policymakers and be straightforward enough to be understood by voters.

As a result, the principles of demonstrably beneficial immigration policymaking imply a much more open but selective immigration admission system for most affluent democracies where people actually want to immigrate. As we have seen throughout this book, what this often means in practice is the prioritization or even active encouragement of high-skilled or otherwise wanted immigration in government policies. While I do not aim to advocate for any specific policy solutions here since what is best for a country is often contingent on the particular national and political context, it is important to examine what demonstrably beneficial immigration looks like in practice.

Governments, stakeholders, and advocates aiming for demonstrably beneficial immigration policymaking should do the following:

1. *Determine which immigration policies are actually better for the country.*

In a system of representative democratic government, a truly responsible immigration policy furthers the national interest over the long term. It is important for every anti-immigration and pro-immigration stakeholder to concede that democratic immigration policy should constitute a national public good and leave plenty of room for compromise.

The principle that governments should prioritize their citizens while recognizing the legitimate interests of foreigners requires a cost–benefit analysis. Since even nationalists can disagree about what constitutes national interest, this analysis should involve a consideration of the potential economic trade-offs of immigration and its restriction for the country. In other words, the national interest in limiting immigration (or expanding it for that matter) cannot be assumed; it must be demonstrated.

2. *Acknowledge but not get sidetracked by isolated costs.*

Like any government activity, immigration policymaking involves considerable trade-offs that should not be ignored. Cosmopolitan-minded stakeholders are often dismissive about any possible downsides of immigration, including its well-documented negative impacts on the wages of similarly skilled citizens. However, nationalists make the mistake of disproportionately focusing on the costs of immigration that occur to some native-born citizens some of the time while ignoring the benefits that immigration brings to others most of the time.

For example, though empirical research indicates that immigrants to the United States are on average less prone to crime than native-born citizens, some nationalist skeptics argue that even one crime committed by an immigrant is too much since it could have been prevented by harsher immigration restrictions. Unfortunately, such reasoning omits all the benefits to citizens that would be unrealized if harsher restrictions were imposed, and it is those benefits that are of utmost importance for evidence-based policymaking.

3. Question seemingly restrictive public opinion.

Demonstrably beneficial policymaking must be responsive, not just responsible. Cost–benefit analyses and subsequent policy changes must be done in the face of public opinion surveys that say most voters want to reduce immigration. But although many people are skeptical about immigration when considered in isolation, my research shows that public preferences are much more nuanced.

Very few people support reducing immigration no matter what. The majority's view may better be described as a desire for immigration policies that economically benefit the average citizen, even when those policies lead to significant increases in immigration. Simply slowing down immigration to appease those who currently oppose it or vote for populist parties—an increasingly popular idea among the center-right—will not work without addressing people's underlying concerns and desires for better policies.

4. Ensure policy benefits are clear to all citizens.

To be popular, immigration must advance the national interest in a way that is demonstrable to citizens across political and demographic divides. This means that pro-immigration policies must always be explicit about their goal of benefiting the nation. Those benefits also need to be straightforward enough to be understood by most voters. Put simply, one should not have to have a PhD to understand why aspects of immigration policy are beneficial for oneself and one's country.

That is why greater skill selection should be considered among the legitimate policy tools of pro-immigration advocates. This is especially true when the selection criteria are transparent and attainable, such as language fluency or skill match, and the only politically feasible alternative is less immigration. The same applies to other pro-immigration policies likely to have greater popular appeal, such as those that emphasize immigrant integration. However, it is worth noting that while the benefit of high-skilled immigration to the national interest is straightforward and tends not to be controversial among voters, lower-skilled immigration can be as valuable. An immigration system that promotes the national interest is also one that respects the familial and cultural ties of citizens with people from around the world.

5. Avoid policies and rhetoric that undermine special obligations to compatriots.

While most people are willing to help foreigners in need during a crisis, my research shows that there are important limits to this generosity. Similarly, although immigration is often a mutually beneficial interaction from which all parties can benefit, it can also be a zero-sum game under certain circumstances. As a result, even when policymakers have some political autonomy, they should refrain from enacting policies that can be credibly viewed as detrimental to the interests of receiving countries and local communities. Prioritizing or even rhetorically emphasizing the humanitarian aspects of immigration at the expense of the national interest will never win support among the majority in a democracy.

In other words, proposing that taxpayers' money should be used to help foreigners outside emergency situations is politically challenging, and for good reason. For example, policies like New York City's "right to shelter" clearly pit the interests of existing residents against newcomers, which makes the policies unsustainable. Similarly, even when designed with the best humanitarian intentions, employment bans for refugees and asylum seekers are usually counterproductive. After all, these policies prevent economic integration and understandably increase public perceptions of foreign-born individuals as freeloaders. Given the robust presence of anti-immigration parties and politicians across most democracies today, any policy decision that can be viewed as demonstrably harmful to one's country or local community will likely be exploited by these actors.

6. Be ready to compromise and meet voters where they are.

While responsible policymakers should generally strive to create immigration policies with clear benefits for the nation, there will always be some disagreement about what constitutes the national interest or how important it is compared to other competing values. This may be especially true when it comes to the noneconomic impacts of immigration, which may be difficult to quantify precisely. For example, while many experts, voters, and politicians believe that long-term economic growth should be a key consideration when setting immigration policy, others may prioritize social solidarity, a sense of control, and national sovereignty.

Responsive policymakers must recognize the natural differences in public opinion related to people's personalities and motivations and be ready to find common ground and compromise when necessary. Doing so may involve acknowledging the concerns and priorities of various stakeholders, even if they do not align perfectly with the policymakers' ideal policy. By being open to compromise and meeting voters where they are by acknowledging and addressing their existing concerns about immigration, policymakers can build trust and create a more sustainable and politically viable immigration system that benefits the nation as a whole.

7. Leave room to help foreigners in need.

Demonstrably beneficial policymaking recognizes that citizens have other values besides nationalism. A sole focus on how individual immigrants benefit the country would violate other societal ideals such as personal autonomy and egalitarianism. Indeed, while nationalism by definition demands the prioritization of compatriots over foreigners, a more nuanced understanding of nationalism recognizes that such prioritization is never absolute. It also requires paying attention to opportunities abroad, which can often be used for national advantage.

Indeed, demonstrably beneficial policymaking leaves extensive room for humanitarian policies that aid refugees. According to my research, most people—including self-proclaimed nationalists—are not completely indifferent to the plight of foreigners and are ready to support certain humanitarian immigration policies. Of course, my research also suggests that such policies are much more popular with the public when they are orderly and present tangible benefits—not just costs—to the receiving country. Scaling up private refugee sponsorship by willing citizens in host countries is a good example of a politically viable approach to increasing humanitarian admissions.

8. Think of better policies, not the worth of particular migrants or categories of migrants.

While skilled immigration is generally viewed by voters as straightforwardly beneficial, all types of immigration can be made more demonstrably beneficial depending on the policies in place.

Importantly, demonstrable benefit is about not only the intrinsic value of individual migrants but also how effectively the immigration system leverages their potential. For example, overly stringent licensing requirements can prevent highly skilled immigrants, such as PhD holders, from using their qualifications, thus negating the benefits of prioritizing skilled immigration.

Similarly, creating structured legal pathways for immigrants with fewer formal qualifications through mechanisms like global skill partnerships and sponsorships, rather than relegating them to unauthorized or unregulated channels of immigration, can enhance both their contributions to receiving countries and the visibility of those contributions. The challenge is to develop immigration policies that are flexible and responsive to the changing needs of the economy and society. By reducing bureaucratic barriers and tailoring legal pathways to fit various skill sets, governments can ensure that most immigrants—regardless of their skill level—can contribute effectively. This approach not only boosts economic output but also improves public perception of immigration, fostering a supportive consensus among the populace.

9. Get help from nonprofits, businesses, and researchers.

Demonstrably beneficial policymaking is most effective when executed in a top-down manner by national and local governments. Without effective regulations in place, even the most vigorous advocacy efforts are unlikely to convince voters of the benefits of immigration. However, this does not mean that actions by other stakeholders are unnecessary. Government policies are not designed in a vacuum, and it is essential to include nongovernmental actors such as academic researchers, think tanks, immigration-oriented nonprofits, and businesses. Their insights and innovative ideas can critically enhance the effectiveness and public acceptance of immigration policies.

Responsible governments should actively engage with these diverse stakeholders to draw on a broad range of experiences, both successful and otherwise. This type of collaboration allows for the continuous refinement and adaptation of policies, making them more responsive to actual needs and challenges. By integrating evidence-based strategies and real-world feedback into policymaking, governments can develop robust, balanced immigration policies that are more likely to gain widespread support and withstand political pressures. This process not only adapts to evolving circumstances but also fosters public trust, reducing the risk of backlash and ensuring the sustainability of pro-immigration reforms.

10. *Aim to build public trust in the immigration system as a whole.*

From the perspective of responsible policymakers, it would be desirable for voters to consider the regulation of legal immigration on its own merits in isolation from all other related issues. However, in reality, people's views on immigration admissions are often influenced by their broader concerns about law enforcement, cultural integration, and more distant issues like housing and social benefits. To build public trust in the immigration system as a whole, policymakers must address those concerns through programmatic policies that align with the principles outlined here.

Some politicians will always seek to exploit anxieties around immigration for political gain. The principles of demonstrably beneficial policymaking require governments to take proactive steps and strengthen public confidence in the immigration system to minimize the political incentives for anti-immigration politics. Doing so may involve investing in effective immigration enforcement and implementing other responsive policies that provide a credible signal that immigration is in a country's national interest, even if those policies are not necessarily pro-immigrant.

Ultimately, given the enormous costs of current restrictions and the potential opportunities for mutual benefit, a more popular and sustainable freer immigration system requires neither charity nor much cosmopolitanism. To be successful, freer immigration requires demonstrably beneficial policies made by our representative democratic governments in *our* national interest.

ACKNOWLEDGMENTS

I WOULD LIKE TO THANK MY EDITOR, Caelyn Cobb, who has been enthusiastic about my book from the get-go. I am grateful to my longtime advisor, Grigo Pop-Eleches, and all the mentors I have had throughout my academic career, who have provided valuable guidance and extensive feedback on my research: Sabine Carey, Rafaela Dancygier, Marty Gilens, Ron Inglehart, Tali Mendelberg, Ed Ponarin, Frances Rosenbluth, Ian Shapiro, Jim Walsh, and Beth Whitaker. I am greatly indebted to them for their helpful advice and many years of support.

I would also like to thank all my colleagues who have read and provided extensive comments on previous drafts of the book and its parts, including Jon Baron, Randy Besco, Michael Donnelly, Sara Goodman, Ron Inglehart, David Laitin, Rahsaan Maxwell, and Diana Mutz. I also wish to extend much gratitude to everyone who patiently listened to my ideas, shared their feedback, and invariably pushed me toward better reasoning in my work, including Chris Achen, Claire Adida, Hannah Alarian, Andreas Asplén Lundstedt, Mark Beissinger, Bryan Caplan, Charlotte Cavaille, Helen Dempster, James Dennison, Lenka Dražanová, Michael Ewers, Jeremy Ferwerda, Verena Fetscher, Nick Fraser, Andrew Geddes, Justin Gest, Matt Graham, Marc Helbling, Simon Hix, Dan Hopkins, Becky Johnson, Amanda

Kennard, Michael Kenwick, Jae Yeon Kim, Dillon Laaker, Michelangelo Landgrave, Morris Levy, Gabriel Magni, Elif Naz Kayran Meier, Alex Nowrasteh, Mireille Paquet, Giuli Pardelli, Maggie Peters, Stephanie Potochnick, Marcel Roman, Martin Ruhs, Tim Ryan, Jake Shapiro, Miranda Simon, Josh Smith, Omer Solodoch, Grigory Tovbis, Anna Triandafyllidou, Kris-Stella Trump, Ali Valenzuela, Kurt Weyland, Andreas Wimmer, Chris Wlezien, and Matthew Wright.

It is hard to overstate the importance of my participation in various workshops and conferences. Various parts of the project that informed this book were presented at annual meetings of the American Political Science Association, the International Studies Association, the Midwest Political Science Association, the Public Choice Society, the Southern Political Science Association, and World Bank's Migration and Development Group. I have also benefited from presenting my work at numerous research seminars at Princeton University, the University of North Carolina, and Yale University, as well as the City University of New York, Cornell University, Duke University, the European University Institute, George Mason University, Harvard University, the London School of Economics, Louisiana State University, New York University, Toronto Metropolitan University, the University of Houston, the University of Michigan, the University of Pennsylvania, and the University of Toronto.

I am grateful to the Mamdouha S. Bobst Center for Peace and Justice and Princeton Research in Experimental Social Science for their financial support. Parts of chapters 4 and 5 were published in 2021 as "Borders of Compassion: Immigration Preferences and Parochial Altruism" (see *Comparative Political Studies* 54 [3–4]: 445–81). Parts of chapter 7 were published in 2022 as "Testing the Backlash Argument: Voter Responses to (Pro-)immigration Reforms" (see *Journal of European Public Policy* 30 [6]: 1183–1203). Some of the ideas discussed in the book have also appeared in blog posts for the European University Institute's Migration Policy Center and the Center for Growth and Opportunity.

No person is an island. This book would not have been possible without a number of great people and particularly their parochial altruism toward me. I have been incredibly lucky to have such caring, smart, and fun friends and colleagues as Elizabeth Baisley, Yaoyao Dai, Sharan

Grewal, Angelina Grigoryeva, Egor Lazarev, Candace Miller, Isabelle Nilsson, DongWon Oh, Denis Orlov, Giuli Pardelli, InYoung Park, Andrea Placidi, Tom Povone, Kristina Puzarina, Ben Redford, Anna Smirnova, Jim Walsh, and Beth Whitaker. I have learned so much from their wit and wisdom. They were always there for me, whether it was getting through tough times or having a blast together.

Finally, I would like to thank my extended family from across the Atlantic: Nina, Alex, Nancy, Marian, Steve, and Sue. They have supported me, encouraged me, and cherished with me every great moment throughout the years, even when at a distance. But my biggest debt is to my better half, Sam, who has taught me that two people can be far stronger and happier together than they ever could be by themselves. I also cannot imagine what my book—or life—would look like without Sam's invaluable advice and unceasing inspiration to use the best available evidence to advance social good.

APPENDIX A

DATA

CHAPTER 3

GALLUP WORLD POLL

The Gallup World Poll consists of representative samples from the following countries: Austria (2013), Belgium (2013), Canada (2014), Denmark (2013), Finland (2013), France (2013), Germany (2013), Greece (2013), Hungary (2013), Iceland (2013), Ireland (2013), Italy (2013), Japan (2013), the Netherlands (2013), New Zealand (2013), Poland (2013), South Korea (2014), Spain (2013), Sweden (2013), the United Kingdom (2013), and the United States (2013).

1. Outcomes of interest (scale 0–1 or binary):
   - Contacting politicians (WP111): "Have you done any of the following in the past month? How about voiced your opinion to a public official?"
   - Immigration attitudes (WP1328): "In your view, should immigration from this country be kept at its present level, increased, or decreased?"

2. Explanatory variables (scale 0–1 or binary):
   - Education (WP3117): "What is your highest completed level of education?"
   - Altruism index: an average of three items
     - Donating (WP108): "Have you done any of the following in the past month? How about donated money to a charity?"
     - Volunteering (WP109): "Have you done any of the following in the past month? How about volunteered your time to an organization?"
     - Helping (WP110): "Have you done any of the following in the past month? How about helped a stranger or someone you didn't know who needed help?"
   - Control variables: Gender (WP1219), Age (WP1220), Marital Status (WP1223), Urban/Rural Status (WP14), Nativity (WP4657), Income Quintile (INCOME5), Employment Status (EMP2010), Religiosity (WP119)

U.S. GENERAL SOCIAL SURVEY

1. Data: General Social Survey (GSS) 2014, [variable name]
2. Outcomes of interest (policy preferences, scale 0–1 or binary):
   - Immigration
     - Admission policy: *"Do you think the number of immigrants from foreign countries who are permitted to come to the United States to live should be increased a lot, increased a little, left the same as it is now, decreased a little, or decreased a lot?"* [letin]
     - Illegal immigration (exclusion): *"America should take stronger measures to exclude illegal immigrants"* (5-item Likert scale, reverse coded) [excldimm]
     - Legal immigration (education): *"Legal immigrants should have equal access to public education as American citizens."* (5-item Likert scale) [immeduc]
     - Legal immigration (rights): *"Legal immigrants to America who are not citizens should have the same rights as American citizens."* (5-item Likert scale) [immrghts]

- Foreign aid (nataid)
- Domestic redistribution
  - Government spending: Childcare [natchld], Social security [natsoc], Welfare [natfare)
  - Government help: Aid to the poor [helppoor], Aid to the sick [helpsick], Income redistribution [eqwlth]
  - Race-targeted policy: Racial spending [natrace], Aid to Blacks [helpblk]
3. Explanatory variables (scale 0–1):
   - **Prosocial motivations**
     - **Altruism**, 7-item index (e.g., *"People should be willing to help others who are less fortunate."*) [othshelp, careself, peoptrbl, selffrst, selfless, accptoth]
   - **National favoritism**, 2-item index:
     - *"People should support their country even it is in the wrong."* [ifwrong]
     - *"America should follow its own interests, even if this leads to conflicts with other nations."* [amownway]
   - Control variables:
     - Age [age], Gender (Female == 1) [sex], Race/ethnicity (Non-Hispanic white == 1) [race, hispanic], Immigration background (Generation 3+ == 1) [born, parborn], Education (College+ == 1) [degree], Partisanship (Republican or Independent, Democrat == baseline) [partyid], Ideology (7 point Liberal–Conservative scale) [polviews], Religiosity [reliten]
     - Racial prejudice: Relative favorability of White (versus Black, Asian, and Hispanic): *"What about having a close relative marry [x] person? Would you be very in favor of it happening, somewhat in favor, neither in favor nor opposed to it happening, somewhat opposed, or very opposed to it happening?"* [marwht, marblk, marasian, marhisp]
     - Racial prejudice (alternative operationalization): Relative favorability of White (versus Black): *"Do people in these groups tend to be unintelligent (lazy) or tend to be intelligent (hardworking)? Where would you rate [x] in general on this scale?"* [workwhts, intlwhts, workblks, intlblks]

CHAPTERS 4 AND 5

ORIGINAL ENGLAND SURVEY (QUALTRICS)

Survey Items

1. Outcomes of interest (political preferences, scale 0–1 or binary):
   - Pro-immigration index: an average of two items
     - *"Do you think immigration to Britain should be increased a lot, increased a little, left the same as it is now, decreased a little, or decreased a lot?"*
     - *"Britain should make it much easier for people from other countries to come and live here regardless of their contribution to our economy."* (Strongly agree, Somewhat agree, Neither agree or disagree, Somewhat disagree, Strongly disagree)
   - Pro-immigration attitudes by national impact
     - Unconditional: *"Britain should make it much easier for people from other countries to come and live here regardless of their contribution to our economy."* (coded as 1 if "agreed")
     - Conditional: *"Britain should make it much easier for people from other countries who would contribute to our economy to come and live here."* (coded as 1 if "agreed")
   - Political participation index: an average of seven items
     - *"Here are some different forms of political and social action that people can take. Please indicate, for each one, whether you have done any of these things in the past, whether you have not done it but might do it or have not done it and would never, under any circumstances, do it."* (Signed a petition; Boycotted, or deliberately bought, certain products for political, ethical or environmental reasons; Took part in a demonstration; Attended a political meeting or rally; Contacted, or attempted to contact, a politician or a civil servant to express your views; Voted in the last UK general election in June 2017, Voted in the EU Referendum in June 2016)
   - Pro-redistribution index: an average of two items
     - *"We are faced with many problems in this country, none of which can be solved easily or inexpensively. Should the government increase or decrease its spending on . . . Housing for low-income*

families; Aid to the poor." (Significantly increase, Slightly increase, Keep at the current level, Slightly decrease, Significantly decrease)

- Foreign aid and military spending attitudes
  - *"We are faced with many problems in this country, none of which can be solved easily or inexpensively. Should the government increase or decrease its spending on . . . Military and defense; Humanitarian foreign aid."* (Significantly increase, Slightly increase, Keep at the current level, Slightly decrease, Significantly decrease)
- Brexit vote
  - *"Did you vote in the EU Referendum in June 2016?"* (Yes, No, Not eligible)
  - *"How did you vote?"* (Remain, Leave)
- Social attitudes:
  - *"How much do you agree or disagree with the following statement? Homosexual couples should be able to adopt children."* (Strongly agree, Somewhat agree, Neither agree or disagree, Somewhat disagree, Strongly disagree)

2. Parochial altruism (revealed preference, categorical or continuous):
   - Altruist's dilemma task: *"Independent of your compensation for the survey, we raffle off £100 among all respondents. If you are selected, you can decide to keep this money as a bonus or donate any or all of it to top charities that are committed to helping British citizens or people around the world. The winner will be contacted and the money will be distributed within five working days. First, please select one or more options for the contribution."* Respondents then choose from a randomized list of top charities and allocate money between them and their own account. The list is made of the following UK charities: British Red Cross; International Committee of the Red Cross; International Rescue Committee; National Society for the Prevention of Cruelty to Children; Shelter, the housing and homelessness charity; Save the Children International; Other (please specify). Those who made a greater or equal (lesser) donation to global than national charities are coded as universal (parochial) altruist type. The winnings were distributed according to the preference of a randomly selected respondent after the survey.

3. Other covariates (categorical or binary):

- Ideology (0–10 scale): *"In politics people sometimes talk of 'left' and 'right.' Using this scale, where would you place yourself on this scale, where 0 means the left and 10 means the right?"* (coded as "left-leaning" if < 5 or "right-leaning" if > 5)

- Religiosity (0–10 scale): *"Regardless of whether you belong to a particular religion, how religious would you say you are?"* ("religious" if > 5)

- Racial prejudice (0–100 scale): *"We'd like to get your feelings toward a number of groups on a feeling thermometer. A rating of 0 means you feel as cold and negatively as possible toward the group. A rating of 100 means you feel as warm and positively as possible toward the group. You would rate the group at 50 if you feel neither positively nor negatively toward the group. How do you feel toward . . . Whites, Blacks, Asians, Arabs?"* (constructed as the relative preference for one's own group as in the ethnocentrism index in Kinder and Kam 2010)

- Diversity preferences: *"Suppose you were choosing where to live. Which of the three types of area would you ideally wish to live in? [An area where almost nobody was of a different race or ethnic group from most British people; Some people were of a different race or ethnic group from most British people; Many people were of a different race or ethnic group; It would make no difference]"* (coded as "anti-diversity preferences" if the respondent chose either of the first two options)

- Immigration impact beliefs: *"Do you think making legal immigration to Britain easier, in the long run, would be positive or negative for you and other people and groups [You and your family; Britain; World as a whole]?"* (Clearly negative, Rather negative, Neither negative or positive, Rather positive, Clearly positive)

CONJOINT EXPERIMENT

Vignette

All respondents were provided with the following instructions prior to the conjoint tasks: *"Immigration control policies have a significant but different impact on the well-being of each particular individual, their community and sometimes even the world as a whole (including the effects on prices, jobs, wages, and taxes). Now, suppose Britain is hold-ing a popular vote about two competing policy proposals concerning the regulation of immigration from different regions. In each case, suppose that the experts estimate with a good degree of precision that the policy choice will affect some overall measure of economic well-being over the next decade (but has no other effects that matter). Please examine each table carefully before answering the questions that follow."*

Treatments

1. *Number of immigrants*: allow almost none, allow some, allow many, allow almost all
2. *Sending region*: Western Europe, Eastern Europe, Asia, Middle East, Africa
3. *Your household wealth*: decreased by 5–6 percent, decreased by 1–2 percent, no change, increased by 1–2 percent, increased by 5–6 percent
4. *Your city or town's wealth*: decreased by 5–6 percent, decreased by 1–2 percent, no change, increased by 1–2 percent, increased by 5–6 percent
5. *British wealth*: decreased by 5–6 percent, decreased by 1–2 percent, no change, increased by 1–2 percent, increased by 5–6 percent
6. *Global wealth*: decreased by 5–6 percent, decreased by 1–2 percent, no change, increased by 1–2 percent, increased by 5–6 percent

Variables

1. Main outcome (binary): "If you had to choose, which of these two policy proposals should be enacted?"
2. Supplementary outcome (ordinal): "On a scale from 1 to 7, where 1 indicates that the United Kingdom should absolutely not enact the policy and 7 indicates that the United Kingdom should definitely enact the policy, how would you rate Proposal 1? Proposal 2?"
3. Personal gain condition includes only the policies that are benefi-cial or inconsequential for one's wealth

4. Personal loss condition includes only the policies that are detrimental or inconsequential for one's wealth
5. Self-, local, national, global interest (continuous): recoded from 0–decreased by 5–6 percent to 1–increased by 5–6 percent
6. Collective interests treatment is calculated as the mean of the continuous measures for local, national, global interest

U.S. SURVEY (MTurk)

Survey Items

1. Outcomes of interest (political preferences, scale 0–1):
   - Pro-immigration index: an average of three items
     - *"Do you think the number of immigrants from foreign countries who are permitted to come to the United States to live should be increased a lot, increased a little, left the same as it is now, decreased a little, or decreased a lot?"*
     - *"Anyone should be able to move freely between countries and work anywhere in the world, including the United States, regardless of the potential impact."* (Strongly agree, Somewhat agree, Neither agree or disagree, Somewhat disagree, Strongly disagree)
     - *"The U.S. government should regulate and restrict the number of immigrants who are allowed to live and work in the country."* (Strongly agree, Somewhat agree, Neither agree or disagree, Somewhat disagree, Strongly disagree)
   - Political participation index: an average of three items
     - *"Here are some different forms of social action that people can take. Please indicate, for each one, whether you have done any of these things in the past, whether you have not done it but might do it or have not done it and would never, under any circumstances, do it."* (Contact or visited someone in government to seek public action on important issues; Signed a petition for an important domestic cause; Signed a petition for an important global cause)
   - Pro-redistribution index: an average of three items
     - *"We are faced with many problems in this country, none of which can be solved easily or inexpensively. Should the federal*

government increase or decrease its spending on . . . Education, Health care, Pensions?" (Significantly increase, Slightly increase, Keep at the current level, Slightly decrease, Significantly decrease)

2. Parochial altruism (revealed preference, categorical):
   - Altruist's dilemma task: *"Independent of your compensation for the survey, we raffle off $100 among all respondents. If you are selected, you can decide to add this money to your Amazon account as a bonus. You can also decide to donate any or all of it to top national or global charities that are committed to helping fellow citizens in the United States or people around the world. The winner will be contacted and the money will be distributed within five working days. Please select one or more options for the contribution."* Respondents then choose from a randomized list of top charities and allocate money between them and their own account. The list is made of the following U.S. charities: Family Promise; Project Sunshine; Ent. Community Partners; Direct Relief; Child Aid; GlobalGiving. Those who made a greater or equal (lesser) donation to global than national charities are coded as universal (parochial) altruist type. The winnings were distributed according to the preference of a randomly selected respondent after the survey.

3. Other covariates (categorical or binary):
   - High (low) self-monitoring subgroup includes the respondents who scored above (below) the median on the agreement with following three items (on a Likert 5-point scale):
     - *"I put on a show to impress or entertain others."*
     - *"I would probably make a good actor."*
     - *"In a group of people, I am rarely the center of attention."* (Reverse-coded)

CONJOINT EXPERIMENT

Vignette

All respondents were provided with a following instruction prior to the conjoint tasks: *"Immigration control policies have a significant but different impact on the well-being of each particular individual, local community, country, or the world as a whole (including the effects on jobs, wages, and taxes). Now, suppose the U.S. is holding a referendum about two competing policy proposals concerning the regulation of immigration from different regions. In each case, suppose that the experts estimate with a good degree of precision that the policy choice will affect some over-all measure of economic well-being over the next decade (but has no other effects that matter). Please examine each table carefully before answering the questions that follow."*

Treatments

1. *Number of immigrants*: decreased a lot, decreased a little, increased a little, increased a lot
2. *Sending region*: Europe, Asia, Africa, Latin America, Middle East
3. *Your household wealth*: decreased by 10 percent, decreased by 2 percent, no change, increased by 2 percent, increased by 10 percent
4. *Your local community's wealth*: decreased by 10 percent, decreased by 2 percent, no change, increased by 2 percent, increased by 10 percent
5. *U.S. wealth*: decreased by 10 percent, decreased by 2 percent, no change, increased by 2 percent, increased by 10 percent
6. *Global wealth*: decreased by 10 percent, decreased by 2 percent, no change, increased by 2 percent, increased by 10 percent

Variables

1. Main outcome (binary): "If you had to choose, which of these two policy proposals should be enacted?"
2. Supplementary outcome (ordinal): "On a scale from 1 to 7, where 1 indicates that the United Kingdom should absolutely not enact the policy and 7 indicates that the United Kingdom should definitely enact the policy, how would you rate Proposal 1? Proposal 2?"
3. Self-, local, national, global interest (continuous): recoded from 0–decreased by 10 percent to 1–increased by 10 percent
4. Collective interests treatment is calculated as the mean of the continuous measures for local, national, global interest

CHAPTER 7

MAJOR VARIABLES

- *Immigration openness (IMPIC) index* is calculated as the (reverse coded) average of IMPIC's labor (*AvgSRegA*) and family (*AvgSRegB*) immigration (restrictiveness) summary scores for a particular country-year
- *Change in immigration openness (IMPIC)* is calculated as the difference between *Immigration openness (IMPIC) index* at year t and $t-1$ for a particular country-year
- *Right-wing populist vote, %* is based on the Timbro Authoritarian Populism Index, which measures the share of votes cast for (right-wing) "authoritarian populist" parties (in each country-year since the last elections in a national legislature)
- *Far-right populist seats, %* indicates the share of seats won by "far-right populist" parties in each country-year since the last elections in a national legislature as coded by PopuList (Rooduijn et al. 2019).
- *Anti-immigration attitudes* are based on the "immigration conservatism" index compiled by Caughey et al. (2019). Derived as the aggregation of major public opinion survey questions regarding immigration (e.g., "Do you think immigration should be decreased?"), this index indicates the general restrictiveness of the electorate in a given country-year.
- *Immigration stocks*, *unemployment rate*, and *GDP per capita (PPP)* are taken from the World Bank

EXAMPLES OF IMMIGRATION REFORMS

Among the most pro-immigration reforms identified by both datasets is Ireland's Employment Permits Act of 2006, which significantly simplified and facilitated the immigration and permanent residency processes for a range of skilled workers and their families. Among the most anti-immigration reforms identified is Italy's "Bossi-Fini" law (Act 189) of 2002, which regularized many undocumented workers but also made future labor migration to the country much more difficult by imposing a strict job contract requirement and reducing the duration of available work permits (for details about these laws and regulations, the detailed Determinants of International Migration [DEMIG] country datasets can be accessed from the International Migration Institute at https://www.migrationinstitute.org/data/demig-data/demig-policy-1/download-the-data/demig-policy-data-downloads).

CHAPTER 8

CROSS-NATIONAL SURVEY DATA

The survey data are based on the Ipsos 2017 Global Trends survey with 17,903 interviews conducted from June 24 to July 8, 2017, among adults in twenty-five countries, conducted via the Ipsos Online Panel system (Skinner and Gottfried 2017).

- *Immigration is good for the economy* (net perceptions): "Please tell whether you agree or disagree with the following statement—'Immigration is good for the economy of your country'" (Strongly disagree, Tend to disagree, Neither agree nor disagree, Tend to Agree, Strongly Agree) [recoded as −1, −0.5, 0, 0.5, 1]
- *Perceived immigration impact* (net perceptions): an average of six items with similar coding
  - *"Immigration is good for the economy of your country."*
  - *"Immigrants in your country have made it more difficult for people of your nationality to get jobs."*
  - *"Immigration has placed too much pressure on public services in your country."*
  - *"Immigrants make your country a more interesting place to live."*
  - *"Immigration is causing my country to change in ways that I don't like."*
  - *"Would you say that immigration has generally had a positive or negative impact on your country?"*

CROSS-NATIONAL ADMINISTRATIVE DATA

- *"High-educated among foreign-born, %"* (OECD foreign-born population data)
- *"Low-educated among foreign-born, %"* (OECD foreign-born population data)
- *"Unemployment among foreign-born, %"* (OECD foreign-born population data)
- *"Work-related immigration flows, % (of total flows)"* indicates the number of both new temporary and permanent work immigrants divided by the total immigration flow in 2011 using the data from Boucher and Gest (2018)
- *Admission skill selectivity index* (0–100) indicates how much governments prioritize high-skilled workers over low-skilled workers in their labor immigration admission policies (in terms of labor market tests, job offer requirements, and points tests) [average score across 2000–2010] (Kolbe and Kayran 2019)
- *Demonstrably beneficial immigration index*: a simple average of the five items above

APPENDIX B

TABLES

TABLE B.1 Descriptive statistics: 2018 Original England Qualtrics sample (N = 1,963)

STATISTIC	MEAN	ST. DEV.	MIN	MAX
Female	0.58	0.49	0	1
Age	48.92	16.13	18	86
Nonwhite	0.07	0.25	0	1
Has university degree	0.31	0.46	0	1
Makes more than £50,000/year	0.14	0.35	0	1
Has a religious affiliation	0.38	0.49	0	1
General elections, 2017				
Voted Conservative	0.42	0.49	0	1
Voted Labour	0.43	0.49	0	1
Voted Liberal Democrat	0.07	0.26	0	1
EU referendum, 2016				
Voted Remain	0.46	0.50	0	1
Voted Leave	0.54	0.50	0	1

TABLE B.2 The relationship between parochial altruism and political behavior (U.S. General Social Survey)

	INCREASE IMMIGRATION LEVELS			INCLUDE ILLEGAL IMMIGRANTS	INCLUDE LEGAL IMMIGRANTS	INCREASE GOVERNMENT SPENDING	INCREASE GOVERNMENT HELP
	[1]	[2]	[3]	[4]	[5]	[6]	[7]
National favoritism	0.464***	0.446***	0.522***	0.399**	0.114	0.161	0.156
	(0.145)	(0.140)	(0.150)	(0.183)	(0.149)	(0.155)	(0.156)
Altruism	0.586***	0.611***	0.533***	0.620***	0.366***	0.275*	0.388***
	(0.129)	(0.126)	(0.134)	(0.162)	(0.133)	(0.137)	(0.139)
National favoritism ×	−1.058***	−0.982***	−0.974***	−1.007***	−0.259	−0.292	−0.294
Altruism	(0.231)	(0.224)	(0.238)	(0.289)	(0.236)	(0.245)	(0.249)
Demographic control variables	No	Yes	Yes	Yes	Yes	Yes	Yes
Political control variables	No	No	Yes	Yes	Yes	Yes	Yes
Observations	1,090	1,085	715	703	715	658	709
Adjusted R^2	0.041	0.111	0.223	0.211	0.069	0.169	0.365

Source: U.S. General Social Survey data, 2014.

Note: This table shows the interaction effect of self-reported altruism and national favoritism on immigration (1–5) and redistribution (6–7) preferences. All models were ordinary least squares (OLS) regressions. Demographic controls include education, age, gender, race, ethnicity, and immigration status. Political controls include partisanship, ideology, religiosity, and racial bias. Standard errors are given in parentheses.

$*p < .05$; $**p < .01$; $***p < .001$

TABLE B.3 The relationship between parochial altruism and political behavior (with and without adjusting for sociodemographic characteristics)

	POLITICAL PARTICIPATION		PRO-REDISTRIBUTION ATTITUDES		PRO-IMMIGRATION ATTITUDES	
	(1)	(2)	(3)	(4)	(5)	(6)
Preference type (reference: egoist)						
Parochial altruist	0.041*** (0.011)	0.032** (0.010)	0.039*** (0.011)	0.041*** (0.010)	0.009 (0.012)	0.020 (0.011)
Universal altruist	0.061*** (0.016)	0.032* (0.015)	0.052*** (0.016)	0.038* (0.015)	0.166*** (0.018)	0.119*** (0.016)
Age (reference: 18 to 29 y)						
30 to 44 y		0.052*** (0.015)		−0.017 (0.015)		−0.068*** (0.016)
45 to 64 y		0.099*** (0.015)		−0.032* (0.015)		−0.148*** (0.015)
65 y and up		0.107*** (0.017)		−0.031 (0.017)		−0.123*** (0.018)
Female		−0.001 (0.010)		0.009 (0.010)		−0.028** (0.010)
Nonwhite		−0.074*** (0.020)		−0.001 (0.020)		0.030 (0.021)
Education (reference: secondary)						
Postsecondary degree		−0.046** (0.018)		0.025 (0.018)		−0.078*** (0.019)
Undergraduate degree		−0.131*** (0.019)		0.046* (0.019)		−0.087*** (0.020)
Postgraduate degree		−0.022 (0.018)		0.004 (0.018)		−0.026 (0.019)
Income (80th percentile or higher)		0.001 (0.011)		−0.041*** (0.011)		0.002 (0.012)
Ideology (reference: center)						
Left-leaning		0.152*** (0.011)		0.095*** (0.011)		0.122*** (0.012)
Right-leaning		0.086*** (0.012)		−0.067*** (0.012)		−0.038** (0.012)
Religious		0.041*** (0.011)		0.039*** (0.011)		0.038** (0.012)
Racially prejudiced		−0.027** (0.010)		−0.044*** (0.010)		−0.108*** (0.011)
Observations	1,967	1,917	1,967	1,917	1,967	1,917
Adjusted R^2	0.010	0.182	0.009	0.128	0.043	0.285

Source: Original England Qualtrics survey data, 2018.
Note: All models were ordinary least squares (OLS) regressions. Standard errors are given in parentheses, *$p < .05$; **$p < .01$; ***$p < .001$

TABLE B.4 The effects of policy consequences on policy selection and rating

	SELECTION		RATING	
	(1)	(2)	(3)	(4)
Immigration (reference: allow almost none)				
Allow some	−0.017	−0.019	−0.104***	−0.100*
	(0.011)	(0.041)	(0.014)	(0.043)
Allow many	−0.116***	−0.132**	−0.411***	−0.420***
	(0.011)	(0.045)	(0.014)	(0.047)
Allow almost all	−0.158***	−0.183***	−0.465***	−0.496***
	(0.011)	(0.045)	(0.014)	(0.046)
Sending region (reference: Western Europe)				
Eastern Europe	−0.047***	−0.054	−0.223***	−0.232***
	(0.012)	(0.044)	(0.014)	(0.040)
Asia	−0.066***	−0.072 +	−0.211***	−0.234***
	(0.012)	(0.043)	(0.014)	(0.041)
Africa	−0.098***	−0.110*	−0.257***	−0.323***
	(0.012)	(0.043)	(0.014)	(0.041)
Middle East	−0.113***	−0.125**	−0.292***	−0.310***
	(0.012)	(0.044)	(0.014)	(0.041)
Self-interest (reference: no change)				
Decreased by 1–2%	−0.177***	−0.198***	−0.397***	−0.429***
	(0.012)	(0.043)	(0.014)	(0.040)
Increased by 1–2%	−0.080***	−0.089*	−0.234***	−0.256***
	(0.012)	(0.043)	(0.014)	(0.040)
Decreased by 5–6%	0.045***	0.055	0.155***	0.165***
	(0.012)	(0.045)	(0.014)	(0.041)
Increased by 5–6%	0.103***	0.118**	0.324***	0.325***
	(0.012)	(0.045)	(0.014)	(0.042)
Local interest (reference: no change)				
Decreased by 1–2%	−0.084***	−0.097*	−0.229***	−0.264***
	(0.012)	(0.043)	(0.015)	(0.040)
Increased by 1–2%	−0.044***	−0.052	−0.143***	−0.151***
	(0.012)	(0.042)	(0.015)	(0.040)
Decreased by 5–6%	0.029*	0.033	0.113***	0.139***
	(0.012)	(0.042)	(0.014)	(0.040)
Increased by 5–6%	0.054***	0.060	0.198***	0.198***
	(0.012)	(0.044)	(0.015)	(0.042)

National interest (reference: no change)

Decreased by 1–2%	−0.110***	−0.123**	−0.226***	−0.289***
	(0.012)	(0.042)	(0.014)	(0.038)
Increased by 1–2%	−0.056***	−0.063	−0.161***	−0.203***
	(0.012)	(0.043)	(0.014)	(0.039)
Decreased by 5–6%	0.043***	0.049	0.137***	0.135***
	(0.012)	(0.043)	(0.014)	(0.039)
Increased by 5–6%	0.080***	0.091*	0.248***	0.252***
	(0.012)	(0.044)	(0.014)	(0.040)

Global interest (reference: no change)

Decreased by 1–2%	−0.067***	−0.079 +	−0.133***	−0.138***
	(0.012)	(0.043)	(0.014)	(0.038)
Increased by 1–2%	−0.026*	−0.031	−0.038**	−0.086*
	(0.012)	(0.043)	(0.014)	(0.040)
Decreased by 5–6%	0.025*	0.027	0.191***	0.127**
	(0.012)	(0.043)	(0.014)	(0.040)
Increased by 5–6%	0.038**	0.041	0.128***	0.117**
	(0.012)	(0.043)	(0.014)	(0.040)
Respondent fixed effects	No	Yes	No	Yes
Vignette fixed effects	No	Yes	No	Yes
Observations	16,650	16,650	16,650	16,650
Adjusted R^2	0.094	−0.008	0.056	0.376

Source: Original England Qualtrics survey data, 2018.
Note: All models are OLS regressions based on the 2018 England Qualtrics survey data. Standard errors clustered by respondent are given in parentheses, $^+p < .1$; $^*p < .05$; $^{**}p < .01$; $^{***}p < .001$

NOTES

PREFACE

1. National Academies of Sciences, Engineering, and Medicine 2022; Esterline 2023.
2. For some of the best-detailed accounts, see Weiner 2013; Kamarck and Stenglein 2019; and Chishti and Hipsman 2014.
3. Ruhs 2013; Cerna 2016.
4. Radford and Connor 2019.

INTRODUCTION: IS FREER IMMIGRATION IN OUR INTEREST?

1. United Nations 2018.
2. Esipova et al. 2011.
3. See the U.S. State Department statistics, available at https://travel.state.gov/content/visas/en/immigrate/diversity-visa/diversity-visa-program-statistics.html.
4. For U.S. interstate numbers, see Molloy et al. 2011.
5. Nowrasteh and Powell 2020.
6. For the most recent statistics, see the UN Population Division data, available at https://www.un.org/development/desa/pd/data/international-migration-flows.
7. Ruhs 2013.
8. Pritchett 2006; Margalit and Solodoch 2022.

9. David Miller 2016; Kaufmann 2019.

10. Cornelius and Rosenblum 2005; Czaika and De Haas 2013; Ortega and Peri 2013.

11. R. Jones 2016; Peters 2017.

12. Clemens 2011.

13. Clemens et al. 2019.

14. Clemens and Pritchett 2019; Nowrasteh and Powell 2020. Carens 2013; Kukathas 2021.

15. Clemens et al. 2018; Kerr 2018; Kane 2021; Hernandez 2024.

16. Pritchett 2018.

17. Abizadeh 2012; Song 2018.

18. Ruedin 2015; Wlezien and Soroka 2016; O'Grady and Abou-Chadi 2019.

19. Peters 2017.

20. Alonso and da Fonseca 2011; Levy et al. 2016.

21. Ford et al. 2015; Ruhs 2022.

22. Gonzalez-Barrera and Connor 2019; Inglehart and Welzel 2023.

23. Banai et al. 2022; Ollerenshaw and Jardina 2023.

24. Kustov 2022a; Kustov 2024c. See also Saad 2023. For the latest Gallup immigration polls, see https://news.gallup.com/poll/1660/immigration.aspx.

25. German Marshall Fund 2014; Skinner and Gottfried 2017.

26. Hopkins et al. 2019.

27. Freeman 1995.

28. Kustov 2023a.

29. Levy et al. 2016; Böhmelt 2021; Ruhs 2022.

30. Skinner and Gottfried 2017.

31. Chan 2015.

32. Dawes et al. 2011; Gilens and Thal 2018.

33. Hainmueller and Hopkins 2014.

34. Brubaker 2015; vom Hau et al. 2023.

35. See Pulse of the Nation, November 2017, accessed at https://thepulseofthe nation.com/downloads/201711-CAH_PulseOfTheNation_Crosstabs.pdf.

36. Clemens et al. 2018.

37. Ruhs 2013.

38. Golash-Boza 2009; Nowrasteh 2022; Heinrich et al. 2024.

39. Markowitz 2020.

40. Hainmueller and Hiscox 2010; Naumann and Stoetzer 2018; Ford and Mellon 2020.

41. Mazzolari and Neumark 2012.

42. Solodoch 2021; Dennison and Geddes 2021b.

43. Gest 2016; Kaufmann 2019.

44. Donnelly 2017; Boucher and Gest 2018.

45. Ruhs 2013; Inglehart and Welzel 2023.

1. NATIONALISM AS PAROCHIAL ALTRUISM: A THEORY OF CONDITIONAL SUPPORT FOR IMMIGRATION

1. For some of the best accounts, see Triandafyllidou 2001; Kunovich 2009; Schildkraut 2014; and Bonikowski 2016.
2. For some of the best accounts, see Burns and Gimpel 2000; Pérez 2010; Kinder and Kam 2010; and A. Rosenberg 2022. For a critical review of these group-centric accounts, see Wright and Levy 2020b.
3. Stolcke 1995; Wimmer 1997.
4. Hopkins et al. 2019; Kustov et al. 2021.
5. Talaska et al. 2008; Vala et al. 2009; Pereira et al. 2010; Hartman et al. 2014; Bahns 2017.
6. Malhotra et al. 2013, 394.
7. Kaufmann 2019; Gest 2022.
8. Stenner 2005; Thomsen et al. 2008; Cohrs and Stelzl 2010.
9. Tetlock 2003; Ryan and Hall 2019; Hix et al. 2021. Despite the prominent hypothesis that increasing ethnic diversity per se can be detrimental to social cooperation and economic outcomes, there is a growing literature that either questions (e.g., Gisselquist 2014; Kustov 2017) or disregards this relationship as largely spurious (e.g., Abascal and Baldassarri 2015; Kustov and Pardelli 2018; Pardelli and Kustov 2022; Kustov and Pardelli 2024).
10. Elkins and Kemp 2021.
11. Duffy 2023.
12. Wright and Levy 2020a.
13. Helbling et al. 2024.
14. For the related concept of adaptive preferences in the context of refugees' resettlement preferences when refugees prefer to remain where they are only when relocating to another country is not an option, see Gerver et al. 2024.
15. See Downs 1957. For a comprehensive review, see Schnellenbach and Schubert 2015.
16. Edlin et al. 2007; Dawes et al. 2011.
17. Fehr and Fischbacher 2002; Fehr and Schmidt 2006.
18. Gilens and Thal 2018, 213.
19. Oliner and Oliner 1988; Monroe 1998.
20. Titmuss 1997; Marsh et al. 2014.
21. Simler and Hanson 2018.
22. Singer 2015.
23. Marwell 1982; Monroe 1998; Fong 2001; Dawes et al. 2011; Gilens and Thal 2018; Bechtel et al. 2019.
24. Newman 2013; Dinesen et al. 2016; O. Hansen and Legge 2016; Fraser and Murakami 2022.

25. Sen 1977; Tajfel and Turner 1986; Bernhard et al. 2006; Chen and Li 2009; Shayo 2009; Everett et al. 2015; Rueda 2017.
26. Schildkraut 2014, 443.
27. Billig 1995; Brubaker et al. 2004; Goode and Stroup 2015; Schildkraut 2014. Note that people need not be aware of the relative importance of their identities for these identities to be objectively or even subjectively important (Stryker and Serpe 1994).
28. Gellner 1983.
29. Wimmer 2018.
30. Mylonas and Tudor 2023.
31. Billig 1995; Wimmer and Schiller 2003; Kochenov 2019.
32. Milanovic 2015.
33. Chandra 2006; Goode and Stroup 2015.
34. Brubaker 2015.
35. Tankard and Paluck 2016.
36. Mutz and Kim 2017; Choi et al. 2019; Magni 2021.
37. For example, see Nowrasteh and Somin 2024.
38. B. Anderson 1983; R. Hansen 2009; Wimmer 2018; vom Hau et al. 2023.
39. Beitz 1999; U. Beck 2002.
40. Newman et al. 2013; Fraser and Murakami 2022.
41. Oliner and Oliner 1988; Monroe 1998; S. Schwartz 2007; Singer 2015.
42. Schueth and O'Loughlin 2008; Buchan et al. 2011; Maxwell 2019.
43. Bayram 2015.
44. Straume and Odèen 2010; Singer 2015.
45. Sen 1977; Hardin 1982; Schwartz-Shea and Simmons 1991; Wit and Kerr 2002; De Dreu et al. 2014; Böhm et al. 2020.
46. Brewer 1999; Rusch et al. 2016; Böhm et al. 2020; Pisor and Ross 2024.
47. See Kustov 2021. For an alternative formalization of in-group favoritism and altruism in a unified framework, see Robalo et al. 2017. For a review of general altruism models, see Rotemberg 2014.
48. Blau and Mackie 2016; Muste 2013; Skinner and Gottfried 2017.
49. van Lange et al. 2014; Miller and Ali 2014.
50. For existing evidence on this point, see Margalit and Solodoch 2022.
51. Penner et al. 2005; Pisor and Ross 2024.
52. See Alexander and Christia 2011 and Falk et al. 2018. Although of great interest, a detailed examination of why some people and societies are more nationalistic and parochially altruistic than others is beyond the scope of this book. Future studies could examine the contextual variation of parochial altruism in a population, as well as the rules that constrain or encourage nationalistic and parochially altruistic motivations across time and space (see Hruschka and Henrich 2013 and Pisor and Ross 2024). It may be especially informative to gauge the manifestations of parochial altruism and how they relate to immigration attitudes in low-income countries, where the political salience

---

of national identities is much lower than in the high-income countries studied in this book (e.g., Barber et al. 2013; Lutz 2024).

53. Gellner 1983; Wimmer 2018; Mylonas and Tudor 2023.

54. Hopkins 2010.

55. Esipova et al. 2011

56. Franzen and Pointner 2012; Carlsson et al. 2014; Gilens and Thal 2018.

57. Gest 2016; Sobolewska and Ford 2020.

58. Mutz 2018; Reny et al. 2019.

59. See McCrone 2002. As specified in the pre-analysis plan, the sample was
obtained from an initial pool of 2,050 respondents after excluding noncitizens and applying standard quality control measures such as attention checks and survey completion criteria. However, including all 2,050
respondents in the analysis does not affect the results.

60. The sample was obtained from the initial 647 respondents after accounting
for response quality and excluding noncitizens.

61. For a detailed review, see Kustov 2019a.

62. Tajfel and Turner 1986; Brewer 1991.

63. Huddy and Khatib 2007; Kunovich 2009; Schildkraut 2011; Yogeeswaran
and Dasgupta 2014; Bonikowski 2016.

64. Kosterman and Feshbach 1989; Theiss-Morse 2009; Transue 2007; Wright et
al. 2012.

65. Esses et al. 2005; Sniderman and Theriault 2004; Kunovich 2009; Wagner et
al. 2012.

66. Shulman 2002.

67. For one recent exception, see Mutz and Kim 2017.

68. Brewer 1999; Transue 2007; Charnysh, Lucas, and Singh 2015; Wimmer 2018;
Gest 2022.

69. Hewstone et al. 2002; Spinner-Halev and Theiss-Morse 2003; Cikara and
Bavel 2014.

70. Baron et al. 2013; Pratto and Glasford 2008; Mutz and Kim 2017.

71. For a comprehensive review, see Careja and Harris 2022.

72. Kiewiet and Lewis-Beck 2011; Schaffer and Spilker 2019; van der Duin et al.
2023.

73. Kramer 1983; Kiewiet and Lewis-Beck 2011; Weeden and Kurzban 2017; Simler and Hanson 2018; Donnelly 2021b.

74. Kramer 1983; Dawson 1994; T. Lee 2008; Yamagishi and Mifune 2008.

75. For an overview, see Hainmueller and Hopkins 2014.

76. Baron 1997.

77. For a review, see Guryan and Charles 2013.

78. Kinder and Kiewiet 1981; Lewin 1991; van der Duin et al. 2023.

79. Citrin and Green 1990; Sears and Funk 1991; Caplan 2007; Hainmueller and
Hopkins 2014.

80. Hainmueller et al. 2015.

81. Ceobanu and Escandell 2010; Hopkins 2010; Enos and Gidron 2016; Kustov 2022c. For a review of group threat theories, see Oliver and Mendelberg 2000; Riek et al. 2006; and Stephan et al. 2009. For the application of group threat theories to immigration, see Quillian 1995 and Pottie-Sherman and Wilkes 2017.
82. Harell et al. 2017; Solodoch 2021; Nowrasteh 2022; Briggs and Solodoch 2023.
83. Malhotra et al. 2013; Dancygier and Donnelly 2013. Although some scholars also differentiate between more universalistic "sociotropic" and more parochial, group-based (Mutz and Mondak 1997) or "communotropic" (Rogers 2014) preferences, the literature remains largely oblivious to the fact that national interest is by definition parochial (Baron et al. 2013). When thinking about immigration policy, people may also consider the perceived interest of their other group categories such as ethnicity (Gay 2006) or partisanship (Mayda et al. 2016).
84. Kiewiet and Lewis-Beck 2011; van der Duin et al. 2023.

2. THE ALTRUIST'S DILEMMA IN THE DATA: WHY DON'T ALTRUISTS SUPPORT IMMIGRATION?

1. T. Smith 2009.

3. ALTRUISTIC NATIONALISM REVEALED: WHY DO MOST VOTERS OPPOSE IMMIGRATION?

1. Manski 2004.
2. Simler and Hanson 2018.
3. For a discussion of similar results, see Straume and Odèen 2010 and Buntaine and Prather 2018.
4. Micklewright and Wright 2004.
5. Giving USA Foundation 2021.
6. Dawes et al. 2011; Gilens and Thal 2018.
7. Kustov 2021.
8. Bayram 2017.
9. Herrmann 2017.

4. NATIONAL INTEREST RANDOMIZED: WHEN WOULD MOST VOTERS SUPPORT IMMIGRATION?

1. For examples, see Uhlmann et al. 2009; Hertel and Kerr 2001; Hassin et al. 2007; and Lacetera et al. 2012. For a critical account, see Kahneman 2012.

2. Baron 2012; Mutz and Kim 2017; Hainmueller et al. 2014; Hainmueller and Hopkins 2015.
3. Hainmueller et al. 2014.
4. Hainmueller et al. 2015.
5. Iyengar et al. 2013.
6. Hainmueller and Hangartner 2013; Hainmueller et al. 2015.
7. Kahan 2016.
8. Yamagishi and Mifune 2008.
9. Kaufmann 2019.
10. Hainmueller et al. 2014.
11. Leeper et al. 2020.
12. The registration for this study can be found in EGAP registry: https://doi.org/10.17605/OSF.IO/Z8V7Y (registration ID 20180529AB).
13. Kustov 2021.
14. Despite the discreteness of all policy attributes, this variable transformation (from discrete to continuous) can be justified given the evidently linear nature of most observed effects in figure 4.2.
15. Dickert et al. 2015.
16. Mercer 2005.
17. Kustov 2021.
18. Kustov 2019a; Kustov 2021.
19. Ruhs 2013; Hainmueller and Hopkins 2014; Helbling et al. 2024.
20. Abramson et al. 2022.
21. Donnelly 2013; Donnelly 2021b.
22. Berinsky and Lavine 2011.
23. Dale Miller 1999.

5. MAKING IMMIGRATION POPULAR: FROM FRAMING TO POLICYMAKING

1. Kustov 2021.
2. Kustov 2023b.
3. Kustov et al. 2021.
4. For a more academic overview of the argument and the evidence, see Kustov 2023b and Kustov and Roman 2024.
5. Kustov et al. 2021.
6. Dennison et al. 2023.
7. Hainmueller and Hiscox 2010; Hainmueller and Hopkins 2015; Naumann and Stoetzer 2018; Hedegaard and Larsen 2023.
8. Gilliam 2010; Dennison 2020; Gest 2020.
9. Gest 2022.
10. Djourelova 2023.
11. Ruhs 2013; Boucher and Gest 2018.

12. Abu-Ladan and Gabriel 2002; Gordon 2010.
13. DeLaet 2000; Bloemraad et al. 2016; Voss et al. 2020.
14. Yukich 2013.
15. Cook 2010; Bloemraad et al. 2016; Voss et al. 2020.
16. van de Wardt et al. 2014; Hutter and Kriesi 2021.
17. Sides et al. 2018; Dennison and Geddes 2019; Claassen and McLaren 2021; Kustov 2023a.
18. Dai and Kustov 2023.
19. Slothuus and Bisgaard 2021; Barber and Pope 2024.
20. Kustov 2023a.
21. Reny and Gest 2023.
22. Coppock 2022; Haaland et al. 2023.
23. Hopkins et al. 2019; Lutz and Bitschnau 2023.
24. Kustov and Landgrave 2023; Thorson and Abdelaaty 2023; Thorson 2024.
25. Dennison and Geddes 2021a; Cattaneo and Grieco 2021; Facchini et al. 2022.
26. Abascal et al. 2021; Alesina et al. 2023; Grigorieff et al. 2020; Hopkins et al. 2019.
27. Gest 2022.
28. Allen 2024.
29. Kustov 2024a.
30. Kustov et al. 2021; Porter and Wood 2019; Coppock 2022.
31. Caplan 2007; Somin 2015; Achen and Bartels 2016; Mercier 2020.
32. Donnelly 2017.
33. Kustov and Landgrave 2023; Thorson 2024.
34. Gordon 2010.
35. For some of the best recent accounts of anti-immigrant discrimination as group prejudice, see Kinder and Kam 2010; Choi et al. 2022; and A. Rosenberg 2022. For some of the best qualifications to and criticisms of these accounts, see Hainmueller and Hopkins 2014; Kaufmann 2019; and Wright and Levy 2020b.
36. Zhou and Lyall 2024.
37. Paluck et al. 2021; Littman et al. 2023.
38. Choi et al. 2022.
39. Adida et al. 2018; Kalla and Broockman 2023; Williamson et al. 2021.
40. Berinsky et al. 2023.
41. Peters 2022.
42. Kinder and Kam 2010.
43. Rydgren 2008; Dempster et al. 2020.
44. Margalit and Solodoch 2022.
45. Mair 2009; Rosenbluth and Shapiro 2018.
46. Bartels 2005.
47. See Martin and Ruhs 2011. For a general argument, see G. Jones 2020.
48. Rothstein 1998.

49. Pierson 1993; Lenz 2012; Ura 2014; Béland et al. 2022.
50. Linde and Peters 2020.
51. Mercier 2020; Norris 2023; Devine 2024.
52. Freeman 1995; Levy et al. 2016.
53. Hicken 2011.
54. Blau and Mackie 2016; OECD 2021; Nowrasteh et al. 2023; Colas and Sachs 2024.
55. S. Lee 2023.
56. For a critical discussion of existing policies, see Collier and Betts 2017.
57. Marbach et al. 2018; Ginn et al. 2022.
58. Cornelius 2001; Massey et al. 2016.
59. Béland et al. 2022; Larsen 2019.
60. Wlezien 1995; Atkinson et al. 2021; Van Hauwaert 2023.
61. Hopkins 2023.

6. BACKLASH VERSUS LEGITIMATION: DO PROGRAMMATIC PRO-IMMIGRATION REFORMS BACKFIRE?

1. Prokop 2016.
2. Wintour 2018.
3. Pevnick 2024; Kapelner 2024.
4. Ruhs 2013.
5. Powell 2015.
6. OECD 2020.
7. Thomas 2008; Bishin et al. 2015; Abrajano and Hajnal 2015; Norris and Inglehart 2019; Patashnik 2023.
8. Pottie-Sherman and Wilkes 2017; Kaufmann and Goodwin 2018.
9. Dinas et al. 2019; Van Hauwaert 2023; Claassen and McLaren 2022.
10. Solodoch 2021.
11. Czaika and De Haas 2013.
12. For notable recent papers, see R. Flores 2017; Abou-Chadi and Helbling 2018; Vrânceanu and Lachat 2021; Solodoch 2021.
13. To learn more about CANZUK, visit https://www.canzukinternational.com/.
14. Pierson 1993; Weldon 2006; Lenz 2012; Ura 2014; Béland et al. 2022.
15. Bishin et al. 2015; Flores and Barclay 2016; Abou-Chadi and Finnigan 2019; Aksoy et al. 2020.
16. Kustov et al. 2021; Dennison and Kustov 2023.
17. Kaufmann 2019.
18. Vrânceanu and Lachat 2021; Abou-Chadi and Finnigan 2019.
19. Kropko and Kubinec 2020; Imai and Kim 2021.
20. Caughey et al. 2019.
21. Heinö 2016.

22. Rooduijn et al. 2019; Claassen and McLaren 2022.
23. Helbling et al. 2017.
24. Caughey, O'Grady, and Warshaw 2019; Claassen and McLaren 2022.
25. For various robustness tests, see Kustov 2023b.
26. Dancygier and Margalit 2020; Lutz 2019.
27. Sommer et al. 2023.
28. Wlezien 1995.
29. Van Hauwaert 2023; Solodoch 2021.
30. Collingwood et al. 2018; Schwartz et al. 2021.
31. Dennison and Kustov 2023.
32. Vrânceanu and Lachat 2021.
33. Kustov and Roman 2024.
34. Jardina and Ollerenshaw 2022.
35. McHugh 2018.
36. Margalit and Solodoch 2022.
37. Pritchett 2006; Clemens 2011; Caplan 2019.
38. Pevnick 2024; Kapelner 2024.
39. For more general evidence of such a dynamic beyond immigration, see Patashnik 2023.
40. Chou et al. 2021.
41. Claassen and McLaren 2022.
42. Dennison and Kustov 2023.
43. Jardina and Ollerenshaw 2022.

7. THERE IS NO SHORTCUT: WHY DOES IMMIGRATION HAVE TO BE DEMONSTRABLY BENEFICIAL TO BE POPULAR?

1. Cerna and Chou 2023.
2. This is not to say that people never engage in collective violence against high-status ethnic minorities, including those of immigrant origin.
3. Kennedy 2019; Malhotra et al. 2013.
4. J. Rosenberg 2020.
5. Hainmueller and Hiscox 2010; Hainmueller and Hopkins 2015.
6. Naumann et al. 2018; Ford and Mellon 2020; Hedegaard and Larsen 2023.
7. Mortimore 2017; Brown and Gitis 2023.
8. Mortimore 2017; Connor and Ruiz 2019; Ford and Mellon 2020; Brown and Gitis 2023; Lettieri and O'Brien 2024.
9. Igarashi et al. 2022.
10. Newman and Malhotra 2019; Kustov 2019b; Ellermann and Goenaga 2019; A. Rosenberg 2022.

11. Ford and Mellon 2020.
12. Cattaneo 2007; Macaluso 2022.
13. van de Beek et al. 2023.
14. For a general discussion and evidence of stereotype (in)accuracy in ethnic and demographic contexts, see Jussim et al. 2015. In this respect, it is worth noting that a common finding about the relative preference for refugees over economic migrants is contingent on the widespread belief that those economic migrants are necessarily "unskilled" and would be a "fiscal burden." Available experimental data that allow for an explicit comparison of humanitarian migrants with skilled economic migrants indicate a popular preference for the latter; see Arias and Blair 2021 and Kustov 2022b.
15. Park et al. 2012; Ford 2024.
16. Katwala et al. 2014.
17. Helms and Spreitzer 2021.
18. Igarashi et al. 2022.
19. Kootstra 2016; Magni 2024.
20. Borwein and Donnelly 2021.
21. Cepla 2021.
22. Kustov and Landgrave 2023.
23. Ford 2024.
24. Helbling et al. 2024; Briggs and Solodoch 2023.
25. Markowitz 2020; Choi et al. 2022.
26. Wright and Levy 2020b.
27. Margalit and Solodoch 2022.
28. Clemens et al. 2018.
29. R. Hansen 2014; van de Beek et al. 2023.
30. Lu and Hou 2020; Cepla 2021.
31. Kerr 2018; Charnysh 2022.
32. Skinner and Gottfried 2017.
33. Boucher and Gest 2018.
34. Kerr 2018.
35. Kolbe and Kayran 2019.
36. Liao et al. 2020.
37. Hager et al. 2024.
38. Cerna 2016.
39. Clemens 2016.
40. Boucher and Gest 2018.
41. Freeman 1995; Kaufmann 2019.
42. Levy et al. 2016; Böhmelt 2021; Van Hauwaert 2023.
43. Kennedy 2019.

8. HOW (NOT) TO DESIGN POPULAR IMMIGRATION POLICIES: COMPARING REFORMS IN CANADA AND SWEDEN

1. Picot and Sweetman 2011; Bevelander and Pendakur 2014; Koning 2019. For a recent comparison of refugee selection in Canada and Sweden, see Asplén Lundstedt 2024.
2. Inglehart and Welzel 2023.
3. Esipova et al. 2013.
4. For an overview of Quebec's unique role in Canadian immigration policy and opinion, see Beauregard et al. 2021 and Kaufman 2019. Quebec has historically had a more restrictive stance on immigration than the rest of Canada, especially with regard to linguistic integration. However, given that Quebec's policies have never challenged the broader economic selection model, an exploration of this issue is beyond the scope of this chapter.
5. Taylor 2021.
6. McConnell 2010.
7. OECD 2019b.
8. Kaufmann 2019.
9. Banting 2010; Reitz 2011; Bloemraad 2012; Hiebert 2016; Triadafilopoulos 2022.
10. Reitz 2011.
11. Wallace et al. 2021.
12. R. Hansen 2017; Wright et al. 2017; Poushter et al. 2019; Donnelly 2021a; Besco 2021.
13. Connor and Passel 2019.
14. Boyd and Ly 2021.
15. Donnelly 2017.
16. Banting 2010.
17. Borwein and Donnelly 2021.
18. Marchand 1966, 6–7.
19. Triadafilopoulos 2013.
20. Troper 1993; Ramón and Downs 2020.
21. Troper 1993; Paquet 2021; Elrick 2022.
22. Ellermann 2021.
23. Elrick 2022.
24. Simmons and Keohane 1992.
25. Troper 1993; Reitz 2011.
26. German Marshall Fund 2014; Gonzalez-Barrera and Connor 2019.
27. Besco 2021; Environics 2022; Aytac et al. 2024.
28. Taylor 2021.
29. Cornelissen and Turcotte 2020; Lu and Hou 2020.
30. Joona et al. 2014; Visintin, Tijdens, and van Klaveren 2015.
31. Papademetriou and Sumption 2011.

32. For example, see Schemitsch 2022 and Kustov 2024b.
33. Abu-Ladan and Gabriel 2002; Triadafilopoulos 2021.
34. Elrick 2022.
35. For some notable examples, see Kaufmann 2019.
36. Besco 2021.
37. Baker and Edmonds 2021; Gonzalez-Barrera and Connor 2019.
38. For a general argument, see McCarthy 2019; Klein 2020.
39. See "The Mission of the Swedish Migration Agency," Migrationsverket, accessed February 18, 2023, https://www.migrationsverket.se/English/About-the-Migration-Agency/Our-mission.html.
40. Center for Global Development 2023.
41. Westin 2006.
42. Ericsson 2020.
43. Borevi 2015.
44. Dahl 2006.
45. Borevi 2015.
46. Hojem and Ådahl 2011; Ugland 2014.
47. Ruhs 2013.
48. Boräng and Cerna 2019.
49. Ruhs 2013.
50. Erlanger 2018; Wooldridge 2022.
51. "In Numbers" 2023.
52. See "Maria Malmer Stenergard," Government Offices of Sweden, accessed February 14, 2023, https://www.government.se/government-of-sweden/ministry-of-justice/maria-malmer-stenergard/.
53. Pelling 2020, 6.
54. Burström 2015; Koning 2019.
55. Ruist 2015.
56. MIPEX 2020.
57. Robinson and Käppeli 2018.
58. Wiesbrock 2011.
59. Marie and Pinotti 2024.
60. Parusel 2015, 151.
61. Parusel 2016.
62. Becker 2019.
63. Wiesbrock 2011; Fredlund-Blomst 2014; Parusel 2015; Sanandaji 2020.
64. For contrasting perspectives, see Parusel 2015 and Sanandaji 2020.
65. Inglehart and Welzel 2023.
66. Donnelly 2017.
67. German Marshall Fund 2013.
68. Munobwa, Ahmadi, and Darvishpour 2021.
69. German Marshall Fund 2013.
70. Directorate-General for Communication 2018.

71. German Marshall Fund 2021.
72. Marie and Pinotti 2024.
73. Martinsson and Andersson 2021.
74. For example, see Rodriguez 2022.
75. Carey 2018.
76. Donnelly 2021a, 182.
77. Abu-Ladan and Gabriel 2002.
78. Koning 2019.
79. OECD 2019a.
80. Kerr 2018.
81. Esipova et al. 2011; Agarwal 2022.
82. National Academies of Science, Engineering, and Medicine 2022.
83. Koslowski 2014.
84. Sumption and Walsh 2022.
85. Boucher and Gest 2018.
86. For the official statistics for Canada, see https://irb.gc.ca/en/statistics/pages/index.aspx; for Sweden, see https://www.migrationsverket.se/English/About-the-Migration-Agency/Statistics/; and for the United States, see https://www.dhs.gov/immigration-statistics/refugees-asylees.

CONCLUSION: HOW TO MAKE IMMIGRATION POPULAR

1. Kustov 2019a.
2. Schnellenbach and Schubert 2015.
3. Norris and Inglehart 2019.
4. Chong 2000; Smith 2004; Wong 2010; Druckman and Lupia 2016; Donnelly 2021b.
5. Weeden and Kurzban 2017.
6. Sears and Funk 1990; Citrin and Green 1990.
7. Hopkins 2018.
8. Schildkraut 2014.
9. Haidt 2016; Goodhart 2017.
10. Mair 2009; Rosenbluth and Shapiro 2018.
11. Coppock 2022.
12. Lenz 2012; Béland et al. 2022.
13. Hopkins 2023.
14. Fehr and Schmidt 2006; Cavaille and Trump 2015.
15. Romano et al. 2017; Mironova and Whitt 2021.
16. Rothmund et al. 2020; Kerschbamer and Müller 2020.
17. Hjorth 2016; Magni 2021.
18. Landgrave 2020.
19. Caplan 2007; Achen and Bartels 2016.

20. Clemens et al. 2018.
21. Macaskill et al. 2020.
22. Ruhs 2013.
23. Legrain 2007.
24. Wimmer 2018; Tamir 2020.
25. Borjas 2016.
26. Pritchett 2006.
27. Clemens et al. 2018.
28. Marie and Pinotti 2024.
29. Muste 2013; Lutz and Bitschnau 2023.
30. Golash-Boza 2009; Dai and Kustov 2022.
31. Heinrich et al. 2024.
32. Briggs and Solodoch 2023.
33. Caplan 2007; Achen and Bartels 2016.
34. Baumeister et al. 2001; Alesina and Passarelli 2019.
35. Lengauer et al. 2012; Soroka et al. 2019.
36. Dennison and Kriesi 2023.
37. Bartels 2023.
38. Ruhs 2022.
39. Linde and Peters 2020; Norris 2023.
40. Cerna and Chou 2023.
41. Hopkins 2023.
42. Ruhs 2013; Helbling et al. 2024.
43. Citrin, Levy, and Wright 2023; Goodman 2014; Salam 2018.
44. Sobolewska et al. 2017; Ivarsflaten and Sniderman 2022; Choi et al. 2022.
45. Harder et al. 2018; Legrain 2020. However, it is important to note that current citizenship practices in many countries may still be more coercive than expressed by these sentiments; see Kochenov 2019 and Goodman 2023. Further, it is unclear whether even demonstrably beneficial integration requirements can effectively assuage people's concerns about immigration more generally; see Alarian and Neureiter 2021.
46. Harell et al. 2017; Nowrasteh 2022; Briggs and Solodoch 2023.
47. Solodoch 2021.
48. Yglesias 2020.
49. Ketcham and Martino 2023; Demsas 2024.
50. Gravelle 2023.
51. Sumption and Walsh 2022.
52. Koslowski 2014.
53. Liao et al. 2020.
54. Clemens 2015.
55. Huckstep and Dempster 2024.
56. Bauböck and Ruhs 2022.
57. Vasilopoulou and Talving 2019.

58. Bauböck 2024.
59. Landgrave 2020.
60. Zavodny 2023.
61. Ozimek et al. 2019.
62. Haushofer 2022.
63. Fratzke et al. 2019.
64. Hager et al. 2024.
65. C. Anderson 2010.
66. Zavodny 2023.
67. Yale-Loehr and Eason 2020.
68. Stapp and Neufeld 2022; Martino 2022.
69. Yglesias 2020.

REFERENCES

Abascal, Maria, and Delia Baldassarri. 2015. "Love Thy Neighbor? Ethnoracial Diversity and Trust Reexamined." *American Journal of Sociology* 121 (3): 722–82.

Abascal, Maria, Tiffany J. Huang, and Van C. Tran. 2021. "Intervening in Anti-immigrant Sentiments: The Causal Effects of Factual Information on Attitudes Toward Immigration." *Annals of the American Academy of Political and Social Science* 697 (1): 174–91.

Abizadeh, Arash. 2012. "On the Demos and Its Kin: Nationalism, Democracy, and the Boundary Problem." *American Political Science Review* 106 (4): 867–82.

Abou-Chadi, Tarik, and Ryan Finnigan. 2019. "Rights for Same-Sex Couples and Public Attitudes Toward Gays and Lesbians in Europe." *Comparative Political Studies* 52 (6): 868–95.

Abou-Chadi, Tarik, and Marc Helbling. 2018. "How Immigration Reforms Affect Voting Behavior." *Political Studies* 66 (3): 687–717.

Abrajano, Marisa, and Zoltan L. Hajnal. 2015. *White Backlash: Immigration, Race, and American Politics*. Princeton, NJ: Princeton University Press.

Abramson, Scott F., Korhan Kocak, and Asya Magazinnik. 2022. "What Do We Learn About Voter Preferences from Conjoint Experiments?" *American Journal of Political Science* 66 (4): 1008–20.

Abu-Ladan, Yasemeen, and Christina Gabriel. 2002. *Selling Diversity: Immigration, Multiculturalism, Employment Equity, and Globalization*. Peterborough, ON: Broadview.

Achen, Christopher H., and Larry M. Bartels. 2016. *Democracy for Realists: Why Elections Do Not Produce Responsive Government*. Princeton, NJ: Princeton University Press.

Adida, Claire L., Adeline Lo, and Melina R. Platas. 2018. "Perspective Taking Can Promote Short-Term Inclusionary Behavior Toward Syrian Refugees." *Proceedings of the National Academy of Sciences of the United States of America* 115 (38): 9521–26.

Agarwal, Ruchir. 2022. "Strengthening U.K. Foreign Talent Policy." Testimony submitted to the British parliament (written evidence PSU0013). https://committees.parliament.uk/writtenevidence/111132/pdf/.

Aksoy, Cevat G., Christopher S. Carpenter, Ralph De Haas, and Kevin D. Tran. 2020. "Do Laws Shape Attitudes? Evidence from Same-Sex Relationship Recognition Policies in Europe." *European Economic Review* 124: 103399.

Alarian, Hannah M., and Michael Neureiter. 2021. "Values or Origin? Mandatory Immigrant Integration and Immigration Attitudes in Europe." *Journal of Ethnic and Migration Studies* 47 (5): 1006–27.

Alesina, Alberto, Armando Miano, and Stefanie Stantcheva. 2023. "Immigration and Redistribution." *Review of Economic Studies* 90 (1): 1–39.

Alesina, Alberto, and Francesco Passarelli. 2019. "Loss Aversion in Politics." *American Journal of Political Science* 63 (4): 936–47.

Alexander, Marcus, and Fotini Christia. 2011. "Context Modularity of Human Altruism." *Science* 334 (6061): 1392–94.

Allen, William L. 2024. "Communicating Economic Evidence About Immigration Changes Attitudes and Policy Preferences." *International Migration Review* 58 (1): 266–95.

Alonso, Sonia, and Saro Claro da Fonseca. 2011. "Immigration, Left and Right." *Party Politics* 18 (6): 865–84.

Anderson, Benedict. 1983. *Imagined Communities: Reflections on the Origin and Spread of Nationalism*. London: Verso.

Anderson, Cameron. 2010. "Regional Heterogeneity and Policy Preferences in Canada: 1979–2006." *Regional & Federal Studies* 20 (4–5): 447–68.

Asplén Lundstedt, Andreas. 2024. *Desirable Victims: Systems of Refugee Selection in Swedish and Canadian Migration Governing*. PhD Diss. University of Gothenburg.

Arias, Sabrina B., and Christopher W. Blair. 2021. "Changing Tides: Public Attitudes on Climate Migration." *Journal of Politics* 84 (1): 560–67.

Atkinson, Mary Layton, K. Elizabeth Coggins, James A. Stimson, and Frank R. Baumgartner. 2021. *The Dynamics of Public Opinion*. New York: Cambridge University Press.

Aytac, Seyda Ece, Andrew Parkin, and Anna Triandafyllidou. 2024. "Why Are Public Attitudes Towards Immigration in Canada Becoming Increasingly Positive? Exploring the Factors Behind the Changes in Attitudes Towards Immigration (1998–2021)." *Canadian Review of American Studies* 54 (1): 50–74.

Bahns, Angela J. 2017. "Threat as Justification of Prejudice." *Group Processes & Intergroup Relations* 20 (1): 52–74.

Baker, Joseph O., and Amy E. Edmonds. 2021. "Immigration, Presidential Politics, and Partisan Polarization Among the American Public, 1992–2018." *Sociological Spectrum* 41 (4): 287–303.

Banai, Ayelet, Fabio Votta, and Rosa Seitz. 2022. "The Polls—Trends: Trends in Public Opinion Toward Immigration Among EU Member States." *Public Opinion Quarterly* 86 (1): 191–215.

Banting, Keith G. 2010. "Is There a Progressive's Dilemma in Canada? Immigration, Multiculturalism and the Welfare State." *Canadian Journal of Political Science* 43 (4): 797–820.

Barber, Carolyn, Katherine Fennelly, and Judith Torney-Purta. 2013. "Nationalism and Support for Immigrants' Rights Among Adolescents in 25 Countries." *Applied Developmental Science* 17 (2): 60–75.

Barber, Michael, and Jeremy C. Pope. 2024. "Does Issue Importance Attenuate Partisan Cue-Taking?" *Political Science Research and Methods* 12 (2): 435–43.

Baron, Jonathan. 1997. "The Illusion of Morality as Self-Interest: A Reason to Cooperate in Social Dilemmas." *Psychological Science* 8 (4): 330–35.

——. 2012. "Parochialism as a Result of Cognitive Biases." In *Understanding Social Action, Promoting Human Rights*, ed. Ryan Goodman, Derek Jinks, and Andrew K. Woods, 203–43. New York: Oxford University Press.

Baron, Jonathan, Ilana Ritov, and Joshua D. Greene. 2013. "The Duty to Support Nationalistic Policies." *Journal of Behavioral Decision Making* 26: 128–38.

Bartels, Larry M. 2005. "Homer Gets a Tax Cut: Inequality and Public Policy in the American Mind." *Perspectives on Politics* 3 (1): 15–31.

——. 2023. *Democracy Erodes from the Top: Leaders, Citizens, and the Challenge of Populism in Europe*. Princeton, NJ: Princeton University Press.

Bauböck, Rainer. 2024. "Free Movement Regimes: Is the EU Experience Exportable?" In *Handbook of Human Mobility and Migration*, ed. Ettore Recchi and Mirna Safi, 242–56. Cheltenham: Edward Elgar.

Bauböck, Rainer, and Martin Ruhs. 2022. "The Elusive Triple Win: Can Temporary Labour Migration Dilemmas Be Settled Through Fair Representation?" *Migration Studies* 10 (3): 528–52.

Baumeister, Roy F., Ellen Bratslavsky, Catrin Finkenauer, and Kathleen D. Vohs. 2001. "Bad Is Stronger Than Good." *Review of General Psychology* 5 (4): 323–70.

Bayram, A. Burcu. 2015. "What Drives Modern Diogenes? Individual Values and Cosmopolitan Allegiance." *European Journal of International Relations* 21 (2): 451–79.

——. 2017. "Due Deference: Cosmopolitan Social Identity and the Psychology of Legal Obligation in International Politics." *International Organization* 71 (S1): S137–63.

Beauregard, Pierre-Loup, Alain-G. Gagnon, and Jean-Denis Garon. 2021. "Managing Immigration in the Canadian Federation: The Case of Quebec." In *International Affairs and Canadian Migration Policy*, ed. Yiagadeesen Samy and Howard Duncan, 227–45. Cham: Palgrave Macmillan.

Bechtel, Michael M., Federica Genovese, and Kenneth F. Scheve. 2019. "Interests, Norms, and Attitudes Toward Global Public Goods: The Case of Climate Cooperation." *British Journal of Political Science* 49 (4): 1–23.

Beck, Ulrich. 2002. "The Cosmopolitan Society and Its Enemies." *Theory, Culture & Society* 19 (1–2): 17–44.

Becker, Jo. 2019. "The Global Machine Behind the Rise of Far-Right Nationalism." *New York Times*, August 10. https://www.nytimes.com/2019/08/10/world/europe/sweden-immigration-nationalism.html.

Beitz, Charles R. 1999. *Political Theory and International Relations*. Cambridge: Cambridge University Press.

Béland, Daniel, Andrea Louise Campbell, and R. Kent Weaver. 2022. *Policy Feedback: How Policies Shape Politics*. New York: Cambridge University Press.

Berinsky, Adam J., Christopher F. Karpowitz, Zeyu Chris Peng, Jonathan A. Rodden, and Cara J. Wong. 2023. "How Social Context Affects Immigration Attitudes." *Journal of Politics* 85 (2): 372–88.

Berinsky, Adam J., and Howard Lavine. 2011. "Self-Monitoring and Political Attitudes." In *Improving Public Opinion Surveys: Interdisciplinary Innovation and the American National Election Studies*, ed. John H. Aldrich and Kathleen M. McGraw, 29–45. Princeton, NJ: Princeton University Press.

Bernhard, Helen, Urs Fischbacher, and Ernst Fehr. 2006. "Parochial Altruism in Humans." *Nature* 442 (7105): 912–15.

Besco, Randy. 2021. "From Stability to Polarization: The Transformation of Canadian Public Opinion on Immigration, 1975–2019." *American Review of Canadian Studies* 51 (1): 143–65.

Bevelander, Pieter, and Ravi Pendakur. 2014. "The Labour Market Integration of Refugee and Family Reunion Immigrants: A Comparison of Outcomes in Canada and Sweden." *Journal of Ethnic and Migration Studies* 40 (5): 689–709.

Billig, Michael. 1995. *Banal Nationalism*. London: Sage.

Bishin, Benjamin G., Thomas J. Hayes, Matthew B. Incantalupo, and Charles Anthony Smith. 2015. "Opinion Backlash and Public Attitudes: Are Political Advances in Gay Rights Counterproductive?" *American Journal of Political Science* 60 (3): 625–48.

Blau, Francine D., and Christopher Mackie. 2016. *The Economic and Fiscal Consequences of Immigration*. Washington, DC: National Academies Press.

Bloemraad, Irene. 2012. *Understanding "Canadian Exceptionalism" in Immigration and Pluralism Policy*. Washington, DC: Migration Policy Institute.

Bloemraad, Irene, Kim Voss, and Fabiana Silva. 2016. "Rights, Economics, or Family? Frame Resonance, Political Ideology, and the Immigrant Rights Movement." *Social Forces* 94 (4): 1647–74.

Böhm, Robert, Hannes Rusch, and Jonathan Baron. 2020. "The Psychology of Intergroup Conflict: A Review of Theories and Measures." *Journal of Economic Behavior and Organization* 178: 947962.

Böhmelt, Tobias. 2021. "How Public Opinion Steers National Immigration Policies." *Migration Studies* 9 (3): 1461–79.

Bonikowski, Bart. 2016. "Nationalism in Settled Times." *Annual Review of Sociology* 19 (1): 1–23.

Boräng, Frida, and Lucie Cerna. 2019. "Constrained Politics: Labour Market Actors, Political Parties and Swedish Labour Immigration Policy." *Government and Opposition* 54 (1): 121–44.

Borevi, Karin. 2015. "Family Migration Policies and Politics: Understanding the Swedish Exception." *Journal of Family Issues* 36 (11): 1490–1508.

Borjas, George J. 2016. *We Wanted Workers: Unraveling the Immigration Narrative.* New York: Norton.

Borwein, Sophie, and Michael J. Donnelly. 2021. "Fiscal Burdens and Knowledge of Immigrant Selection Criteria." *Journal of Ethnic and Migration Studies* 47 (7): 1704–23.

Boucher, Anna, and Justin Gest. 2018. *Crossroads: Comparative Immigration Regimes in a World of Demographic Change.* Cambidge: Cambridge University Press.

Boyd, Monica, and Nathan T. B. Ly. 2021. "Unwanted and Uninvited: Canadian Exceptionalism in Migration and the 2017–2020 Irregular Border Crossings." *American Review of Canadian Studies* 51 (1): 95–121.

Brewer, Marilynn B. 1991. "The Social Self: On Being the Same and Different at the Same Time." *Personality and Social Psychology Bulletin* 17 (5): 475–82.

——. 1999. "The Psychology of Prejudice: Ingroup Love and Outgroup Hate?" *Journal of Social Issues* 55 (3): 429–44.

Briggs, Ryan C., and Omer Solodoch. 2023. "Changes in Perceptions of Border Security Influence Desired Levels of Immigration." *Journal of Conflict Resolution* 68 (6): 1252–75.

Brown, Theresa Cardinal, and Ben Gitis. 2023. *Americans Support High Skilled Immigration, Worry About Waits for Some.* Washington, DC: Bipartisan Policy Center.

Brubaker, Rogers. 2015. *Grounds for Difference.* Cambridge, MA: Harvard University Press.

Brubaker, Rogers, Mara Loveman, and Peter Stamatov. 2004. "Ethnicity as Cognition." *Theory and Society* 33: 31–64.

Buchan, Nancy R., Marilynn B. Brewer, Gianluca Grimalda, Rick K. Wilson, Enrique Fatas, and Margaret Foddy. 2011. "Global Social Identity and Global Cooperation." *Psychological Science* 22 (6): 821–28.

Buntaine, Mark T., and Lauren Prather. 2018. "Preferences for Domestic Action Over International Transfers in Global Climate Policy." *Journal of Experimental Political Science* 5: 1–15.

Burns, Peter, and James G. Gimpel. 2000. "Economic Insecurity, Prejudicial Stereotypes, and Public Opinion on Immigration Policy." *Political Science Quarterly* 115: 201–25.

Burström, Bo. 2015. "Sweden—Recent Changes in Welfare State Arrangements." *International Journal of Health Services* 45 (1): 87–104.

Caplan, Bryan. 2007. *The Myth of the Rational Voter: Why Democracies Choose Bad Policies.* Princeton, NJ: Princeton University Press.

——. 2019. *Open Borders: The Science and Ethics of Immigration.* New York: First Second.

Careja, Romana, and Eloisa Harris. 2022. "Thirty Years of Welfare Chauvinism Research: Findings and Challenges." *Journal of European Social Policy* 32 (2): 212–24.

Carens, Joseph H. 2013. *The Ethics of Immigration.* New York: Oxford University Press.

Carey, David. 2018. *Making the Most of Immigration in Canada.* OECD Economic Department Working Paper No. 1520. Paris: OECD.

Carlsson, Fredrik, Olof Johansson-Stenman, and Pham Khanh Nam. 2014. "Social Preferences Are Stable Over Long Periods of Time." *Journal of Public Economics* 117: 104–14.

Cattaneo, Cristina. 2007. "The Self-Selection in the Migration Process: What Can We Learn?" LIUC Papers in Economics 199. Cattaneo University.

Cattaneo, Cristina, and Daniela Grieco. 2021. "Turning Opposition Into Support to Immigration: The Role of Narratives." *Journal of Economic Behavior and Organization* 190: 785–801.

Caughey, Devin, Tom O'Grady, and Christopher Warshaw. 2019. "Policy Ideology in European Mass Publics, 1981–2016." *American Political Science Review* 113 (3): 674–93.

Cavaille, Charlotte, and Kris-Stella Trump. 2015. "The Two Facets of Social Policy Preferences." *Journal of Politics* 77 (1): 146–60.

Center for Global Development. 2023. "The Commitment to Development Index 2023." https://www.cgdev.org/cdi.

Ceobanu, Alin M., and Xavier Escandell. 2010. "Comparative Analyses of Public Attitudes Toward Immigrants and Immigration Using Multinational Survey Data: A Review of Theories and Research." *Annual Review of Sociology* 36: 309–28.

Cepla, Zuzana. 2021. "Skills Mix: Foreign-Born Workers Bring More Than University Degrees to High-Income Countries," Labor Mobility Partnerships, April 28. https://lampforum.org/2021/04/28/skills-mix-foreign-born-workers-bring-more-than-university-degrees-to-high-income-countries/.

Cerna, Lucie. 2016. *Immigration Policies and the Global Competition for Talent.* London: Palgrave Macmillan.

Cerna, Lucie, and Meng Hsuan Chou. 2023. "Talent Migration Governance and the COVID-19 Pandemic: Comparing Germany and Singapore." *Journal of Immigrant and Refugee Studies* 21 (1): 73–88.

Chan, Gabrielle. 2015. "Tony Abbott Urges Europe to Adopt Australian Policies in Refugee Crisis." *Guardian*, October 27. https://www.theguardian.com/world/2015/oct/28/tony-abbott-urges-europe-to-adopt-australian-border-policies.

Chandra, Kanchan. 2006. "What Is Ethnic Identity and Does It Matter?" *Annual Review of Political Science* 9 (1): 397–424.

Charnysh, Volha. 2022. "Historical Political Economy of Migration." In *The Oxford Handbook of Historical Political Economy*, ed. Jeffery A. Jenkins and Jared Rubin, 747–68. Oxford: Oxford University Press.

Charnysh, Volha, Christopher Lucas, and Prerna Singh. 2015. "The Ties That Bind: National Identity Salience and Pro-social Behavior Toward the Ethnic Other." *Comparative Political Studies* 48 (3): 267–300.

Chen, Yan, and Sherry Xin Li. 2009. "Group Identity and Social Preferences." *American Economic Review* 99 (1): 431–57.

Chishti, Muzaffar, and Faye Hipsman. 2014. "U.S. Immigration Reform Didn't Happen in 2013; Will 2014 Be the Year?" Migration Policy Institute, January 9. https://www.migrationpolicy.org/article/us-immigration-reform-didnt-happen-2013-will-2014-be-year.

Choi, Donghyun Danny, Mathias Poertner, and Nicholas Sambanis. 2019. "Parochialism, Social Norms, and Discrimination Against Immigrants." *Proceedings of the National Academy of Sciences of the United States of America* 116 (33): 16274–79.

Choi, Donghyun Danny, Nicholas Sambanis, and Mathias Poertner. 2022. *Native Bias: Overcoming Discrimination Against Immigrants*. Princeton, NJ: Princeton University Press.

Chong, Dennis. 2000. *Rational Lives: Norms and Values in Politics and Society*. Chicago: University of Chicago Press.

Chou, Winston, Rafaela Dancygier, Naoki Egami, and Amaney A. Jamal. 2021. "Competing for Loyalists? How Party Positioning Affects Populist Radical Right Voting." *Comparative Political Studies* 54 (12): 2226–60.

Cikara, Mina, and Jay J. Van Bavel. 2014. "The Neuroscience of Intergroup Relations: An Integrative Review." *Perspectives on Psychological Science* 9 (3): 245–74.

Citrin, Jack, and Donald P. Green. 1990. "The Self-Interest Motive in American Public Opinion." *Research in Micropolitics* 3: 1–28.

Citrin, Jack, Morris E. Levy, and Matthew Wright. 2023. *Immigration in the Court of Public Opinion*. New York: Polity.

Claassen, Christopher, and Lauren McLaren. 2021. "Do Threats Galvanize Authoritarians or Mobilize Non-authoritarians? Experimental Tests from 19 European Societies." *Political Psychology* 42 (4): 677–94.

——. 2022. "Does Immigration Produce a Public Backlash or Public Acceptance? Time-Series, Cross-Sectional Evidence from Thirty European Democracies." *British Journal of Political Science* 52 (3): 1013–31.

Clemens, Michael A. 2011. "Economics and Emigration: Trillion-Dollar Bills on the Sidewalk?" *Journal of Economic Perspectives* 25 (3): 83–106.

——. 2015. "Global Skill Partnerships: A Proposal for Technical Training in a Mobile World." *IZA Journal of Labor Policy* 4 (2): 1–18.

——. 2016. "Losing Our Minds? New Research Directions on Skilled Emigration and Development." *International Journal of Manpower* 37 (7): 1227–48.

Clemens, Michael, Cindy Huang, Jimmy Graham, and Kate Gough. 2018. *Migration Is What You Make It: Seven Policy Decisions That Turned Challenges Into Opportunities*. Washington, DC: Center for Global Development.

Clemens, Michael A., Claudio E. Montenegro, and Lant Pritchett. 2019. "The Place Premium: Bounding the Price Equivalent of Migration Barriers." *Review of Economics and Statistics* 101 (2): 201–13.

Clemens, Michael A., and Lant Pritchett. 2019. "The New Economic Case for Migration Restrictions: An Assessment." *Journal of Development Economics* 138: 153–64.

Cohrs, J. Christopher, and Monika Stelzl. 2010. "How Ideological Attitudes Predict Host Society Members' Attitudes Toward Immigrants: Exploring Cross-National Differences." *Journal of Social Issues* 66: 673–94.

Colas, Mark, and Dominik Sachs. 2024. "The Indirect Fiscal Benefits of Low-Skilled Immigration." *American Economic Journal: Economic Policy* 16 (2): 515–50.

Collier, Paul, and Alexander Betts. 2017. *Refuge: Rethinking Refugee Policy in a Changing World*. Oxford: Oxford University Press.

Collingwood, Loren, Nazita Lajevardi, and Kassra A. R. Oskooii. 2018. "A Change of Heart? Why Individual-Level Public Opinion Shifted Against Trump's 'Muslim Ban.'" *Political Behavior* 40 (4): 1035–72.

Connor, Phillip, and Jeffrey S. Passel. 2019. *Summary of Findings: Europe's Unauthorized Immigrant Population Peaks in 2016, Then Levels Off*. Washington, DC: Pew Research Center.

Connor, Phillip, and Neil G. Ruiz. 2019. *Majority of U.S. Public Supports High-Skilled Immigration*. Washington, DC: Pew Research Center.

Cook, Maria Lorena. 2010. "The Advocate's Dilemma: Framing Migrant Rights in National Settings." *Studies in Social Justice* 4 (2): 145–64.

Coppock, Alexander. 2022. *Persuasion in Parallel: How Information Changes Minds About Politics*. Chicago: University of Chicago Press.

Cornelissen, Louis, and Martin Turcotte. 2020. *Persistent Overqualification Among Immigrants and Non-immigrants*. Insights on Canadian Society. Catalogue No. 75-006-X. Ottawa: Statistics Canada.

Cornelius, Wayne A. 2001. "Death at the Border: Efficacy and Unintended Consequences of US Immigration Control Policy." *Population and Development Review* 27 (4): 661–85.

Cornelius, Wayne A., and Marc R. Rosenblum. 2005. "Immigration and Politics." *Annual Review of Political Science* 8: 89–119.

Czaika, Mathias, and Hein De Haas. 2013. "The Effectiveness of Immigration Policies." *Population and Development Review* 39 (3): 487–508.

Dahl, Ann-Sofie. 2006. "Sweden: Once a Moral Superpower, Always a Moral Superpower?" *International Journal* 61 (4): 895.

Dai, Yaoyao, and Alexander Kustov. 2022. "When Do Politicians Use Populist Rhetoric? Populism as a Campaign Gamble." *Political Communication* 39 (3): 383–404.

———. 2023. "The (In)effectiveness of Populist Rhetoric: A Conjoint Experiment of Campaign Messaging." *Political Science Research and Methods*, 1–8, https://doi.org/10.1017/psrm.2023.55.

Dancygier, Rafaela M., and Michael J. Donnelly. 2013. "Sectoral Economies, Economic Contexts, and Attitudes Toward Immigration." *Journal of Politics* 75 (1): 17–35.

Dancygier, Rafaela M., and Yotam Margalit. 2020. "The Evolution of the Immigration Debate: A Study of Party Positions Over the Last Half-Century." *Comparative Political Studies* 53 (5): 734–74.

Dawes, Christopher T., Peter John Loewen, and James H. Fowler. 2011. "Social Preferences and Political Participation." *Journal of Politics* 73 (3): 845–56.

Dawson, Michael C. 1994. *Behind the Mule: Race and Class in African-American Politics*. Princeton, NJ: Princeton University Press.

DeLaet, Debra L. 2000. *U.S. Immigration Policy in an Age of Rights*. New York: Praeger.

Dempster, Helen, Amy Leach, and Karen Hargrave. 2020. "Public Attitudes Towards Immigration and Immigrants: What People Think, Why, and How to Influence Them." Working paper. ODI.

Demsas, Jerusalem. 2024. "Something's Fishy About the 'Migrant Crisis.'" *Atlantic*, February 19. https://www.theatlantic.com/ideas/archive/2024/02/asylum-seekers-migrant-crisis/677464/.

Dennison, James. 2020. "A Basic Human Values Approach to Migration Policy Communication." *Data & Policy* 2: e18.

Dennison, James, and Andrew Geddes. 2019. "A Rising Tide? The Salience of Immigration and the Rise of Anti-immigration Political Parties in Western Europe." *Political Quarterly* 90 (1): 107–16.

———. 2021a. "The Centre No Longer Holds: The Lega, Matteo Salvini and the Remaking of Italian Immigration Politics." *Journal of Ethnic and Migration Studies* 48 (2): 441–60.

———. 2021b. "Thinking Globally About Attitudes to Immigration: Concerns About Social Conflict, Economic Competition and Cultural Threat." *Political Quarterly* 92 (3): 541–51.

Dennison, James, and Hanspeter Kriesi. 2023. "Explaining Europe's transformed Electoral Landscape: Structure, Salience, and Agendas." *European Political Science Review* 15 (4): 483–501.

Dennison, James, and Alexander Kustov. 2023. "The Reverse Backlash: How the Success of Populist Radical Right Parties Relates to More Positive Immigration Attitudes." *Public Opinion Quarterly* 87 (4): 1013–24.

Dennison, James, Alexander Kustov, and Andrew Geddes. 2023. "Public Attitudes to Immigration in the Aftermath of COVID-19: Little Change in Policy Preferences, Big Drops in Issue Salience." *International Migration Review* 57 (2): 557–77.

Devine, Daniel. 2024. "Does Political Trust Matter? A Meta-analysis on the Consequences of Trust." *Political Behavior*, https://doi.org/10.1007/s11109-024-09916-y.

Dickert, Stephan, Daniel Västfjäll, Janet Kleber, and Paul Slovic. 2015. "Scope Insensitivity: The Limits of Intuitive Valuation of Human Lives in Public Policy." *Journal of Applied Research in Memory and Cognition* 4 (3): 248–55.

Dinas, Elias, Konstantinos Matakos, Dimitrios Xefteris, and Dominik Hangartner. 2019. "Waking Up the Golden Dawn: Does Exposure to the Refugee Crisis Increase Support for Extreme-Right Parties?" *Political Analysis* 27 (2): 244–54.

Dinesen, Peter Thisted, Robert Klemmensen, and Asbjørn Sonne Nørgaard. 2016. "Attitudes Toward Immigration: The Role of Personal Predispositions." *Political Psychology* 37 (1): 55–72.

Directorate General for Communication. 2018. "Special Eurobarometer 469: Integration of Immigrants in the European Union." European Union. https://data.europa.eu/data/datasets/s2169_88_2_469_eng?locale=en.

Djourelova, Milena. 2023. "Persuasion Through Slanted Language: Evidence from the Media Coverage of Immigration." *American Economic Review* 113 (3): 800–835.

Donnelly, Michael J. 2013. "Identity and Interests: Voter Heuristics and Support for Redistributive Policies." PhD diss., Princeton University.

——. 2017. *Canadian Exceptionalism: Are We Good or Are We Lucky? A Survey of Canadian Attitudes in Comparative Perspective.* Montreal: McGill Institute for the Study of Canada.

——. 2021a. "Discrimination and Multiculturalism in Canada: Exceptional or Incoherent Public Attitudes?" *American Review of Canadian Studies* 51 (1): 166–88.

——. 2021b. *Group Interests, Individual Attitudes: How Group Memberships Shape Attitudes Towards the Welfare State.* New York: Oxford University Press.

Downs, Anthony. 1957. *An Economic Theory of Democracy.* New York: Harper and Row.

Dreu, Carsten K. W. de, Daniel Balliet, and Nir Halevy. 2014. "Parochial Cooperation in Humans: Forms and Functions of Self-Sacrifice in Intergroup Conflict." In *Advances in Motivation Science*, vol. 1, ed. Andrew J. Elliot, 1–47. Waltham, MA: Elsevier.

Druckman, James N., and Arthur Lupia. 2016. "Preference Change in Competitive Political Environments." *Annual Review of Political Science* 19: 13–31.

Duffy, Bobby. 2023. *UK Attitudes to Immigration: How the Public Became More Positive.* London: Policy Institute, King's College London.

Edlin, Aaron, Andrew Gelman, and Noah Kaplan. 2007. "Voting as a Rational Choice: Why and How People Vote to Improve the Well-Being of Others." *Rationality and Society* 19 (3): 293–314.

Elkins, Emily, and David Kemp. 2021. *E Pluribus Unum: Findings from the Cato Institute 2021 Immigration and Identity National Survey.* Technical report. Washington, DC: Cato Institute.

Ellermann, Antje. 2021. *The Comparative Politics of Immigration: Policy Choices in Germany, Canada, Switzerland, and the United States.* Cambridge: Cambridge University Press.

Ellermann, Antje, and Agustín Goenaga. 2019. "Discrimination and Policies of Immigrant Selection in Liberal States." *Politics and Society* 47 (1): 87–116.

Elrick, Jennifer. 2022. "Bureaucratic Implementation Practices and the Making of Canada's Merit-Based Immigration Policy." *Journal of Ethnic and Migration Studies* 48 (1): 110–28.

Enos, Ryan D., and Noam Gidron. 2016. "Intergroup Behavioral Strategies as Contextually Determined: Experimental Evidence from Israel." *Journal of Politics* 78 (3): 851–67.

Environics. 2022. *Focus Canada – Fall 2022: Canadian Public Opinion About Immigration and Refugees*. Toronto: Environics Institute for Survey Research.

Ericsson, Martin. 2020. "Enfranchisement as a Tool for Integration: The 1975 Extension of Voting Rights to Resident Aliens in Sweden." *Immigrants and Minorities* 38 (3): 233–53.

Erlanger, Steven. 2018. "Sweden Was Long Seen as a 'Moral Superpower.' That May Be Changing." *New York Times*, September 3. https://www.nytimes.com /2018/09/03/world/europe/sweden-election-populism. html.

Esipova, Neli, Anita Pugliese, and Julie Ray. 2013. "The Demographics of Global Internal Migration." *Migration Policy Practice* 3 (2): 3–5.

Esipova, Neli, Julie Ray, and Rajesh Srinivasan. 2011. *The World's Potential Migrants: Who They Are, Where They Want to Go, and Why It Matters*. Gallup White Paper. Washington, DC: Gallup.

Esses, Victoria M., John F. Dovidio, Antoinette H. Semenya, and Lynne M. Jackson. 2005. "Attitudes Toward Immigrants and Immigration: The Role of National and International Identity." In *Social Psychology of Inclusion and Exclusion*, ed. Dominic Abrams, Michael A. Hogg, and José M. Marques, 317–37. New York: Psychology.

Esterline, Cecilia. 2023. "Previously Unreported Data: The U.S. Lost 45,000 College Grads to Canada's High-Skill Visa from 2017 to 2021." Niskanen Center, March 14. https://www.niskanencenter.org/previously-unreported-data-the-u -s-lost-45000-college-grads-to-canadas-high-skill-visa-from-2017-to-2021/.

Everett, Jim A. C., Nadira S. Faber, and Molly Crockett. 2015. "Preferences and Beliefs in Ingroup Favoritism." *Frontiers in Behavioral Neuroscience* 9: 1–21.

Facchini, Giovanni, Yotam Margalit, and Hiroyuki Nakata. 2022. "Countering Public Opposition to Immigration: The Impact of Information Campaigns." *European Economic Review* 141: 103959.

Falk, Armin, Anke Becker, Thomas Dohmen, Benjamin Enke, David Huffman, and Uwe Sunde. 2018. "Global Evidence on Economic Preferences." *Quarterly Journal of Economics* 133 (4): 1645–92.

Fehr, Ernst, and Urs Fischbacher. 2002. "Why Social Preferences Matter—The Impact of Non-selfish Motives on Competition, Cooperation and Incentives." *Economic Journal* 112: C1–C33.

Fehr, Ernst, and Klaus M. Schmidt. 2006. "The Economics of Fairness, Reciprocity and Altruism: Experimental Evidence and New Theories." In *Handbook of the Economics of Giving, Altruism and Recipcrocity*, ed. Serge-Christophe Kolm and Jean Mercier Ythier, 615–91. New York: Elsevier.

Flores, Andrew R., and Scott Barclay. 2016. "Backlash, Consensus, Legitimacy, or Polarization: The Effect of Same-Sex Marriage Policy on Mass Attitudes." *Political Research Quarterly* 69 (1): 43–56.

Flores, René D. 2017. "Do Anti-immigrant Laws Shape Public Sentiment? A Study of Arizona's SB 1070 Using Twitter Data." *American Journal of Sociology* 123 (206): 353340.

Fong, Christina. 2001. "Social Preferences, Self-Interest, and the Demand for Redistribution." *Journal of Public Economics* 82 (2): 225–46.

Ford, Rob. 2024. "Immigration: Where Would Voters Cut?" UK in a Changing Europe, March 25. https://ukandeu.ac.uk/immigration-where-would-voters-cut/.

Ford, Robert, Will Jennings, and Will Somerville. 2015. "Public Opinion, Responsiveness and Constraint: Britain's Three Immigration Policy Regimes." *Journal of Ethnic and Migration Studies* 41 (9): 1391–1411.

Ford, Robert, and Jonathan Mellon. 2020. "The Skills Premium and the Ethnic Premium: A Cross-National Experiment on European Attitudes to Immigrants." *Journal of Ethnic and Migration Studies* 46 (3): 512–32.

Franzen, Axel, and Sonja Pointner. 2012. "The External Validity of Giving in the Dictator Game." *Experimental Economics* 16 (2): 155–69.

Fraser, Nicholas A. R., and Go Murakami. 2022. "The Role of Humanitarianism in Shaping Public Attitudes Toward Refugees." *Political Psychology* 43 (2): 255–75.

Fratzke, Susan, Lena Kainz, Hanne Beirens, Emma Dorst, and Jessica Bolter. 2019. "Refugee Sponsorship Programs: A Global State of Play and Opportunities for Investment." *Migration Policy Institute Europe Policy Brief* 15: 1–21.

Fredlund-Blomst, Sofie. 2014. "Assessing Immigrant Integration in Sweden After the May 2013 Riots." Migration Policy Institute, January 16. https://www.migrationpolicy.org/article/assessing-immigrant-integration-sweden-after-may-2013-riots.

Freeman, Gary P. 1995. "Modes of Immigration Politics in Liberal Democratic States." *International Migration Review* 29 (4): 881–913.

Gay, Claudine. 2006. "Seeing Difference: The Effect of Economic Disparity on Black Attitudes Toward Latinos." *American Journal of Political Science* 50 (4): 982–97.

Gellner, Ernest. 1983. *Nations and Nationalism.* Oxford: Basil Blackwell.

German Marshall Fund. 2013. *Transatlantic Trends: Key Findings 2013.* Washington, DC: German Marshall Fund.

——. 2014. *Transatlantic Trends: Mobility, Migration and Integration.* Washington, DC: German Marshall Fund.

——. 2021. *Transatlantic Trends: Transatlantic Opinion on Global Challenges.* Washington, DC: German Marshall Fund.

Gerver, Mollie, Miranda Simon, and Faten Ghosn. 2024. "Refugee Resettlement and Preferences." *Political Studies*, ahead of print, May 24.

Gest, Justin. 2016. *The New Minority: White Working Class Politics in an Age of Immigration and Inequality*. Oxford: Oxford University Press.

——. 2020. *Mass Appeal: Communicating Policy Ideas in Multiple Media*. New York: Oxford University Press.

——. 2022. *Majority Minority*. New York: Oxford University Press.

Gilens, Martin, and Adam Thal. 2018. "Doing Well and Doing Good? How Concern for Others Shapes Policy Preferences and Partisanship Among Affluent Americans." *Public Opinion Quarterly* 82 (2): 209–30.

Gilliam, Franklin D. 2010. *Framing Immigration Reform: A FrameWorks Message Memo*. Technical report. Washington, DC: FrameWorks Institute.

Ginn, Thomas, Reva Resstack, Helen Dempster, Emily Arnold-Fernández, Sarah Miller, Martha Guerrero Ble, and Bahati Kanyamanza. 2022. *2022 Global Refugee Workers Rights Report*. Washington, DC: Center for Global Development.

Gisselquist, Rachel M. 2014. "Ethnic Divisions and Public Goods Provision, Revisited." *Ethnic and Racial Studies* 37 (9): 1605–27.

Giving USA Foundation. 2021. *The Annual Report on Philanthropy for the Year 2020*. Technical report. Indianapolis: Center on Philanthropy at Indiana University.

Golash-Boza, Tanya. 2009. "A Confluence of Interests in Immigration Enforcement: How Politicians, the Media, and Corporations Profit from Immigration Policies Destined to Fail." *Sociology Compass* 3 (2): 283–94.

Gonzalez-Barrera, Ana, and Phillip Connor. 2019. *Around the World, More Say Immigrants Are a Strength Than a Burden*. Washington, DC: Pew Research Center.

Goode, J. Paul, and David R. Stroup. 2015. "Everyday Nationalism: Constructivism for the Masses." *Social Science Quarterly* 96 (3): 717–39.

Goodhart, David. 2017. *The Road to Somewhere: The Populist Revolt and the Future of Politics*. London: Hurst.

Goodman, Sara Wallace. 2014. *Immigration and Membership Politics in Western Europe*. New York: Cambridge University Press.

——. 2023. "Citizenship Studies: Policy Causes and Consequences." *Annual Review of Political Science* 26 (1): 1–18.

Gordon, Jennifer. 2010. "People Are Not Bananas: How Immigration Differs from Trade." *Northwestern University Law Review* 104 (3): 1109–46.

Gravelle, Toni. 2023. *Economic Progress Report: Immigration, Housing and the Outlook for Inflation*. Ottawa: Bank of Canada.

Grigorieff, Alexis, Christopher Roth, and Diego Ubfal. 2020. "Does information Change Attitudes Towards Immigrants?" *Demography* 57: 1117–43.

Guryan, Jonathan, and Kerwin Kofi Charles. 2013. "Taste-Based or Statistical Discrimination: The Economics of Discrimination Returns to Its Roots." *Economic Journal* 123 (572): 417–32.

Haaland, Ingar, Christopher Roth, and Johannes Wohlfart. 2023. "Designing Information Provision Experiments." *Journal of Economic Literature* 61 (1): 3–40.

Hager, Anselm, Hanno Hilbig, and Sascha Riaz. 2024. "Refugee Labor Market Access Increases Support for Immigration." *Comparative Political Studies* 57 (5): 749–77.

Haidt, Jonathan. 2016. "When and why Nationalism Beats Globalism." *Policy: A Journal of Public Policy and Ideas* 32 (3): 46.

Hainmueller, Jens, and Dominik Hangartner. 2013. "Who Gets a Swiss Passport? A Natural Experiment in Immigrant Discrimination." *American Political Science Review* 107: 1–29.

Hainmueller, Jens, Dominik Hangartner, and Teppei Yamamoto. 2015. "Validating Vignette and Conjoint Survey Experiments Against Real-World Behavior." *Proceedings of the National Academy of Sciences of the United States of America* 112 (8): 2395–400.

Hainmueller, Jens, and Michael J. Hiscox. 2010. "Attitudes Toward Highly Skilled and Low-Skilled Immigration: Evidence from a Survey Experiment." *American Political Science Review* 104 (1): 61.

Hainmueller, Jens, Michael J. Hiscox, and Yotam Margalit. 2015. "Do Concerns About Labor Market Competition Shape Attitudes Toward Immigration? New Evidence." *Journal of International Economics* 97 (1): 193–207.

Hainmueller, Jens, and Daniel J. Hopkins. 2014. "Public Attitudes Toward Immigration." *Annual Review of Political Science* 17: 225–49.

——. 2015. "The Hidden American Immigration Consensus: A Conjoint Analysis of Attitudes Toward Immigrants." *American Journal of Political Science* 59 (3): 529–48.

Hainmueller, Jens, Daniel J. Hopkins, and Teppei Yamamoto. 2014. "Causal Inference in Conjoint Analysis: Understanding Multidimensional Choices Via Stated Preference Experiments." *Political Analysis* 22: 1–30.

Hansen, Ole-Petter Moe, and Stefan Legge. 2016. *Drawbridges Down: Altruism and Immigration Preferences.* CESifo Working Paper No. 6204. Center for Economic Studies, IFO Institute.

Hansen, Randall. 2009. "The Poverty of Postnationalism: Citizenship, Immigration, and the New Europe." *Theory and Society* 38 (1): 1–24.

——. 2014. "Making Immigration Work: How Britain and Europe Can Cope with Their Immigration Crises (The Government and Opposition/Leonard Schapiro Lecture, 2015)." *Government and Opposition* 51 (2): 183–208.

——. 2017. "Why Both the Left and the Right Are Wrong: Immigration and Multiculturalism in Canada." *Political Science and Politics* 50 (3): 712–16.

Harder, Niklas, Lucila Figueroa, Rachel M. Gillum, Dominik Hangartner, David D. Laitin, and Jens Hainmueller. 2018. "Multidimensional Measure of Immigrant Integration." *Proceedings of the National Academy of Sciences of the United States of America* 115 (45): 11483–88.

Hardin, Garret. 1982. "Discriminating Altruisms." *Zygon* 17 (2): 163–86.

Harell, Allison, Stuart Soroka, and Shanto Iyengar. 2017. "Locus of Control and Anti-immigrant Sentiment in Canada, the United States, and the United Kingdom." *Political Psychology* 38 (2): 245–60.

Hartman, Todd K., Benjamin J. Newman, and C. Scott Bell. 2014. "Decoding Prejudice Toward Hispanics: Group Cues and Public Reactions to Threatening Immigrant Behavior." *Political Behavior* 36: 143–63.

Hassin, Ran R., Melissa J. Ferguson, Daniella Shidlovski, and Tamar Gross. 2007. "Subliminal Exposure to National Flags Affects Political Thought and Behavior." *Proceedings of the National Academy of Sciences of the United States of America* 104: 19757–61.

Haushofer, Johannes. 2022. "Large-Scale International Educational Migration: A Shallow Investigation." Effective Altruism Forum, August 12. https://forum .effectivealtruism.org/posts/TMjRuTLjQa6z6rdeY/large-scale-international -educational-migration-a-shallow.

Hedegaard, Troels Fage, and Christian Albrekt Larsen. 2023. "The Hidden European Consensus on Migrant Selection: A Conjoint Survey Experiment in the Netherlands, Germany, Sweden, and Denmark." *Acta Politica* 58 (4): 717–36.

Heinö, Andreas Johansson. 2016. *Timbro Authoritarian Populism Index 2016*. Technical report. Stockholm: Timbro.

Heinrich, Tobias, Yoshiharu Kobayashi, and Menevis Cilizoglu. 2024. "Why People Demand Border Restrictions: Journalistic Gate-Keeping, News Consumption, and Border Vetting." Working paper.

Helbling, Marc, Liv Bjerre, Friederike Römer, and Malisa Zobel. 2017. "Measuring Immigration Policies: The IMPIC Database." *European Political Science* 16 (1): 79–98.

Helbling, Marc, Rahsaan Maxwell, and Richard Traunmüller. 2024. "Numbers, Selectivity, and Rights: The Conditional Nature of Immigration Policy Preferences." *Comparative Political Studies* 57 (2): 254–86.

Helms, Robin Matross, and Sarah Spreitzer. 2021. *International Student Inclusion and Success: Public Attitudes, Policy Imperatives, and Practical Strategies*. Washington, DC: American Council on Education.

Hernandez, Zeke. 2024. *The Truth About Immigration: Why Successful Societies Welcome Newcomers*. New York: St. Martin's.

Herrmann, Richard K. 2017. "How Attachments to the Nation Shape Beliefs About the World: A Theory of Motivated Reasoning." *International Organization* 71 (S1): S61–84.

Hertel, Guido, and Norbert L. Kerr. 2001. "Priming In-Group Favoritism: The Impact of Normative Scripts in the Minimal Group Paradigm." *Journal of Experimental Social Psychology* 37 (4): 316–24.

Hewstone, Miles, Mark Rubin, and Hazel Willis. 2002. "Intergroup Bias." *Annual Review of Psychology* 53: 575–604.

Hicken, Allen. 2011. "Clientelism." *Annual Review of Political Science* 14 (1): 289–310.

Hiebert, Daniel. 2016. *What's So Special About Canada? Understanding the Resilience of Immigration and Multiculturalism*. Washington, DC: Migration Policy Institute.

Hix, Simon, Eric Kaufmann, and Thomas J. Leeper. 2021. "Pricing Immigration." *Journal of Experimental Political Science* 8 (1): 63–74.

Hjorth, Frederik. 2016. "Who Benefits? Welfare Chauvinism and National Stereotypes." *European Union Politics* 17 (1): 3–24.

Hojem, Petter, and Martin Ådahl. 2011. *Kanadamodellen: hur invandring leder till jobb.* Stockholm: Fores.

Hopkins, Daniel J. 2010. "Politicized Places: Explaining Where and When Immigrants Provoke Local Opposition." *American Political Science Review* 104: 40–60.

——. 2018. *The Increasingly United States: How and Why American Political Behavior Nationalized.* Chicago: University of Chicago Press.

——. 2023. *Stable Condition: Elites' Limited Influence on Health Care Attitudes.* New York: Russell Sage Foundation.

Hopkins, Daniel J., John Sides, and Jack Citrin. 2019. "The Muted Consequences of Correct Information About Immigration." *Journal of Politics* 81 (1): 315–20.

Hruschka, Daniel J., and Joseph Henrich. 2013. "Economic and Evolutionary Hypotheses for Cross-Population Variation in Parochialism." *Frontiers in Human Neuroscience* 7: 559.

Huckstep, Sam, and Helen Dempster. 2024. *Meeting Skill Needs for the Global Green Transition: A Role for Labour Migration?* Washington, DC: Center for Global Development.

Huddy, Leonie, and Nadia Khatib. 2007. "American Patriotism, National Identity, and Political Involvement." *American Journal of Political Science* 51 (1): 63–77.

Hutter, Swen, and Hanspeter Kriesi. 2021. "Politicising Immigration in Times of Crisis." *Journal of Ethnic and Migration Studies* 48 (2): 341–65.

Igarashi, Akira, Hirofumi Miwa, and Yoshikuni Ono. 2022. "Why Do Citizens Prefer High-Skilled Immigrants to Low-Skilled Immigrants? Identifying Causal Mechanisms of Immigration Preferences with a Survey Experiment." *Research and Politics* 9 (2): 1–6.

Imai, Kosuke, and In Song Kim. 2021. "On the Use of Two-Way Fixed Effects Regression Models for Causal Inference with Panel Data." *Political Analysis* 29 (3): 405–15.

"In Numbers: Swedish Migration Agency Presents New Forecast for 2023." 2023. *The Local Sweden*, February 7. https://www.thelocal.se/20230207/in-numbers -swedish-migration-agency-presents-new-forecast-for-2023.

Inglehart, Ronald F., and Christian Welzel. 2023. "The WVS Cultural Map of the World." World Values Survey, Februry 17. https://www.worldvaluessurvey.org /WVSNewsShow.jsp?ID=467

Ivarsflaten, Elisabeth, and Paul M. Sniderman. 2022. *The Struggle for Inclusion: Muslim Minorities and the Democratic Ethos.* Chicago: University of Chicago Press.

Iyengar, Shanto, Simon Jackman, Solomon Messing, Nicholas Valentino, Toril Aalberg, Raymond Duch, Kyu S. Hahn, Stuart Soroka, Allison Harell, and

Tetsuro Kobayashi. 2013. "Do Attitudes About Immigration Predict Willingness to Admit Individual Immigrants?" *Public Opinion Quarterly* 77: 641–65.

Jardina, Ashley, and Trent Ollerenshaw. 2022. "The Polls—Trends: The Polarization of White Racial Attitudes and Support for Racial Equality in the US." *Public Opinion Quarterly* 86 (S1): 576–87.

Jones, Garett. 2020. *10 Percent Less Democracy: Why You Should Trust Elites a Little More and the Masses a Little Less.* Stanford, CT: Stanford University Press.

Jones, Reece. 2016. *Violent Borders: Refugees and the Right to Move.* New York: Verso.

Joona, Pernilla Andersson, Nabanita Datta Gupta, and Eskil Wadensjö. 2014. "Overeducation Among Immigrants in Sweden: Incidence, Wage Effects and State Dependence." *IZA Journal of Migration* 3 (1): 1–23.

Jussim, Lee, Jarret T. Crawford, and Rachel S. Rubinstein. 2015. "Stereotype (In)accuracy in Perceptions of Groups and Individuals." *Current Directions in Psychological Science* 24 (6): 490–97.

Kahan, Dan M. 2016. "The Politically Motivated Reasoning Paradigm, Part 1: What Politically Motivated Reasoning Is and How to Measure It ." In *Emerging Trends in Social & Behavioral Sciences*, ed. R.A. Scott and S.M. Kosslyn. https://doi.org/10.1002/9781118900772.etrds0417

Kahneman, Daniel. 2012. "A Proposal to Deal with Questions About Priming Effects." *Nature* 490 (2): 1–2.

Kalla, Joshua L., and David E. Broockman. 2023. "Which Narrative Strategies Durably Reduce Prejudice? Evidence from Field and Survey Experiments Supporting the Efficacy of Perspective-Getting." *American Journal of Political Science* 67 (1): 185–204.

Kamarck, Elaine, and Christine Stenglein. 2019. "Can Immigration Reform Happen? A Look Back." Brookings, February 11. https://www.brookings.edu/articles/can-immigration-reform-happen-a-look-back/.

Kane, Timothy. 2021. *The Immigrant Superpower: How Brains, Brawn, and Bravery Make America Stronger.* New York: Oxford University Press.

Kapelner, Zsolt. 2024. "Anti-immigrant Backlash: The Democratic Dilemma for Immigration Policy." *Comparative Migration Studies* 12 (1): 12, https://doi.org/10.1186/s40878-024-00370-7.

Katwala, Sunder, Steve Ballinger, and Matthew Rhodes. 2014. *How to Talk About Immigration.* London: British Future.

Kaufman, Stuart J. 2019. "War as Symbolic Politics." *International Studies Quarterly* 63 (3): 614–25.

Kaufmann, Eric. 2019. *Whiteshift.* New York: Overlook.

Kaufmann, Eric, and Matthew J. Goodwin. 2018. "The Diversity Wave: A Meta-analysis of the Native-Born White Response to Ethnic Diversity." *Social Science Research* 76: 120–31.

Kennedy, Andrew. 2019. "The Politics of Skilled Immigration: Explaining the Ups and Downs of the US H-1B Visa Program." *International Migration Review* 53 (2): 346–70.

Kerr, William R. 2018. *The Gift of Global Talent: How Migration Shapes Business, Economy & Society*. Stanford, CA: Stanford Business Books.

Kerschbamer, Rudolf, and Daniel Müller. 2020. "Social Preferences and Political Attitudes: An Online Experiment on a Large Heterogeneous Sample." *Journal of Public Economics* 182: 104076.

Ketcham, John, and Daniel Di Martino. 2023. *Shelter from the Storm: Better Options for New York City's Asylum-Seeker Crisis*. New York: Manhattan Institute.

Kiewiet, D. Roderick, and Michael S. Lewis-Beck. 2011. "No Man Is an Island: Self-Interest, the Public Interest, and Sociotropic Voting." *Critical Review* 23 (3): 303–19.

Kinder, Donald R., and Cindy D. Kam. 2010. *Us Against Them: Ethnocentric Foundations of American Opinion*. Chicago: University Of Chicago Press.

Kinder, Donald R., and D. Roderick Kiewiet. 1981. "Sociotropic Politics: The American Case." *British Journal of Political Science* 11 (2): 129.

Klein, Ezra. 2020. *Why We're Polarized*. New York: Avid Reader.

Kochenov, Dimitry. 2019. *Citizenship*. Cambridge, MA: MIT Press.

Kolbe, Melanie, and Elif Naz Kayran. 2019. "The Limits of Skill-Selective Immigration Policies: Welfare States and the Commodification of Labour Immigrants." *Journal of European Social Policy* 29 (4): 478–97.

Koning, Edward Anthony. 2019. *Immigration and the Politics of Welfare Exclusion: Selective Solidarity in Western Democracies*. Toronto: University of Toronto Press.

Kootstra, Anouk. 2016. "Deserving and Undeserving Welfare Claimants in Britain and the Netherlands: Examining the Role of Ethnicity and Migration Status Using a Vignette Experiment." *European Sociological Review* 32 (3): 325–38.

Koslowski, Rey. 2014. "Selective Migration Policy Models and Changing Realities of Implementation." *International Migration* 52 (3): 26–39.

Kosterman, Rick, and Seymour Feshbach. 1989. "Toward a Measure of Patriotic and Nationalistic Attitudes." *Political Psychology* 10: 257–74.

Kramer, Gerald H. 1983. "The Ecological Fallacy Revisited: Aggregate- Versus Individual-Level Findings on Economics and Elections, and Sociotropic Voting." *American Political Science Reivew* 77 (1): 92–111.

Kropko, Jonathan, and Robert Kubinec. 2020. "Interpretation and Identification of Within-Unit and Cross-Sectional Variation in Panel Data Models." *PLOS One* 15 (4): 1–22.

Kukathas, Chandran. 2021. *Immigration and Freedom*. Princeton, NJ: Princeton University Press.

Kunovich, Robert M. 2009. "The Sources and Consequences of National Identification." *American Sociological Review* 74: 573–93.

Kustov, Alexander. 2017. "How Ethnic Structure Affects Civil Conflict: A Model of Endogenous Grievance." *Conflict Management and Peace Science* 34 (6): 660–79.

——. 2019a. "Borders of Compassion: International Migration and the Politics of Parochial Altruism." PhD diss., Princeton University.

——. 2019b. "Is There a Backlash Against Immigration from Richer Countries? International Hierarchy and the Limits of Group Threat." *Political Psychology* 40 (5): 973–1000.

——. 2021. "Borders of Compassion: Immigration Preferences and Parochial Altruism." *Comparative Political Studies* 54 (3–4): 445–81.

——. 2022a. "Immigration Opponents Are Far More Passionate Than Supporters." *Washington Post*, July 14.

——. 2022b. *Reproduction of "Changing Tides: Public Attitudes on Climate Migration."* Technical report. Charlottesville, VA: Center for Open Science.

——. 2022c. " 'Bloom Where You're Planted': Explaining Public Opposition to (E) migration." *Journal of Ethnic and Migration Studies* 48 (5): 1113–32.

——. 2023a. "Do Anti-immigration Voters Care More? Documenting the Issue Importance Asymmetry of Immigration Attitudes." *British Journal of Political Science* 53 (2): 796–805.

——. 2023b. "Testing the Backlash Argument: Voter Responses to (Pro-)immigration Reforms." *Journal of European Public Policy* 30 (6): 1183–1203.

——. 2024a. "Beyond Changing Minds: Raising the Issue Importance of Expanding Legal Immigration." *Perspectives on Politics*, ahead of print, June 14, https://doi.org/10.31219/osf.io/meujy.

——. 2024b. "Why Some Countries Are Less Welcoming to International Students." *Good Authority*, May 20. https://goodauthority.org/news/new-restrictions-on -international-students/.

——. 2024c. "Why Americans have reversed their thinking on immigration." *Good Authority*, July 25. https://goodauthority.org/news/why-americans-have -reversed-their-thinking-on-immigration/.

Kustov, Alexander, Dillon Laaker, and Cassidy Reller. 2021. "The Stability of Immigration Attitudes: Evidence and Implications." *Journal of Politics* 83 (4): 1478–94.

Kustov, Alexander, and Michelangelo Landgrave. 2023. "Immigration Is Difficult?! Informing Voters About Immigration Policy Fosters Pro-immigration Views." OSF Preprints. https://doi.org/10.31219/osf.io/mu4j5.

Kustov, Alexander, and Giuliana Pardelli. 2018. "Ethnoracial Homogeneity and Public Outcomes: The (Non)effects of Diversity." *American Political Science Review* 112 (4): 1096–1103.

——. 2024. "Beyond Diversity: The Role of State Capacity in Fostering Social Cohesion in Brazil." *World Development* 180: 106625.

Kustov, Alexander, and Marcel Roman. 2024. "No Backlash: Reassessing Public Responses to High-Profile Immigration Reforms." Working Paper.

Lacetera, Nicola, Mario Macis, and Robert Slonim. 2012. "Will There Be Blood? Incentives and Displacement Effects in Pro-social Behavior." *American Economic Journal: Economic Policy* 4 (1): 186–223.

Landgrave, Michelangelo. 2020. "Constructing a U.S.-Canadian Bilateral Labor Agreement." In *12 New Immigration Ideas for the 21st Century*, ed. Alex Nowrasteh and David J. Bier, 15–19. Washington, DC: Cato Institute.

Larsen, Erik Gahner. 2019. "Policy Feedback Effects on Mass Publics: A Quantitative Review." *Policy Studies Journal* 47 (2): 372–94.

Lee, Soyoung. 2023. "Domestic Distributional Roots of National Interest." *American Political Science Review*, 1–16, https://doi.org/10.1017/S0003055423001284.

Lee, Taeku. 2008. "Race, Immigration, and the Identity-to-Politics Link." *Annual Review of Political Science* 11: 457–78.

Leeper, Thomas J., Sara B. Hobolt, and James Tilley. 2020. "Measuring Subgroup Preferences in Conjoint Experiments." *Political Analysis* 28 (2): 207–21.

Legrain, Philippe. 2007. *Immigrants: Your Country Needs Them.* Princeton, NJ: Princeton University Press.

——. 2020. *Them and Us: How Immigrants and Locals Can Thrive Together.* London: Oneworld.

Lengauer, Günther, Frank Esser, and Rosa Berganza. 2012. "Negativity in Political News: A Review of Concepts, Operationalizations and Key Findings." *Journalism* 13 (2): 179–202.

Lenz, Gabriel S. 2012. *Follow the Leader: How Voters Respond to Politicians' Policies and Performance.* Chicago: University of Chicago Press.

Lettieri, John, and Connor O'Brien. 2024. "EIG Poll: Voters in Both Parties Want More High-Skilled Immigration." Economic Innovation Group, June 4. https://eig.org/hsi-voter-survey/.

Levy, Morris, Matthew Wright, and Jack Citrin. 2016. "Mass Opinion and Immigration Policy in the United States: Re-assessing Clientelist and Elitist Perspectives." *Perspectives on Politics* 14 (3): 660–80.

Lewin, Leif. 1991. *Self-Interest and Public Interest in Western Politics.* New York: Oxford University Press.

Liao, Steven, Neil Malhotra, and Benjamin J. Newman. 2020. "Local Economic Benefits Increase Positivity Toward Foreigners." *Nature Human Behaviour* 4 (5): 481–88.

Linde, Jonas, and Yvette Peters. 2020. "Responsiveness, Support, and Responsibility: How Democratic Responsiveness Facilitates Responsible Government." *Party Politics* 26 (3): 291–304.

Littman, Rebecca, Alexandra Scacco, and Chagai Weiss. 2023. "Reducing Prejudice Through Intergroup Contact Interventions." In *Psychological Intergroup Interventions*, ed. Eran Halperin, Boaz Hameiri, and Rebecca Littman, 3–16. London: Routledge.

Lu, Yao, and Feng Hou. 2020. "Immigration System, Labor Market Structures, and Overeducation of High-Skilled Immigrants in the United States and Canada." *International Migration Review* 54 (4): 1072–1103.

Lutz, Philipp. 2019. "Variation in Policy Success: Radical Right Populism and Migration Policy." *West European Politics* 42 (3): 517–44.

——. 2024. "Between Common Responsibility and National Interest: When do Europeans Support a Common European Migration Policy?" *European Union Politics* 25 (2): 313–32.

Lutz, Philipp, and Marco Bitschnau. 2023. "Misperceptions About Immigration: Reviewing Their Nature, Motivations and Determinants." *British Journal of Political Science* 53 (2): 674–89.

Macaluso, Mariele. 2022. "The Influence of Skill-Based Policies on the Immigrant Selection Process." *Economia Politica* 39 (2): 595–621.

Macaskill, William, Krister Bykvist, and Toby Ord. 2020. *Moral Uncertainty.* Oxford: Oxford University Press.

Magni, Gabriele. 2021. "Economic Inequality, Immigrants and Selective Solidarity: From Perceived Lack of Opportunity to In-Group Favoritism." *British Journal of Political Science* 51 (4): 1357–80.

——. 2024. "Boundaries of Solidarity: Immigrants, Economic Contributions, and Welfare Attitudes." *American Journal of Political Science* 68 (1): 72–92.

Mair, Peter. 2009. "Representative Versus Responsible Government." MPIfG Working Paper 09/8. Max Planck Institute for the Study of Societies, Cologne.

Malhotra, Neil, Yotam Margalit, and Cecilia Hyunjung Mo. 2013. "Economic Explanations for Opposition to Immigration: Distinguishing Between Prevalence and Conditional Impact." *American Journal of Political Science* 57 (2): 391–410.

Manski, Charles F. 2004. "Measuring Expectations." *Econometrica* 72 (5): 1329–76.

Marbach, Moritz, Jens Hainmueller, and Dominik Hangartner. 2018. "The Long-Term Impact of Employment Bans on the Econo.mic Integration of Refugees." *Science Advances* 4 (9): 1–6.

Marchand, Jean. 1966. *White Paper on Immigration.* Ottawa: Queen's Printer for Ontario.

Margalit, Yotam, and Omer Solodoch. 2022. "Against the Flow: Differentiating Between Public Opposition to the Immigration Stock and Flow." *British Journal of Political Science* 52 (3): 1055–75.

Marie, Olivier, and Paolo Pinotti. 2024. "Immigration and Crime: An International Perspective." *Journal of Economic Perspectives* 38 (1): 181–200.

Markowitz, Peter L. 2020. *A New Paradigm for Humane and Effective Immigration Enforcement.* Washington, DC: Center for American Progress. https://www .americanprogress.org/article/new-paradigm-humane-effective-immigration -enforcement/.

Marsh, Abigail A., Sarah A. Stoycos, Kristin M. Brethel-Haurwitz, Paul Robinson, John W. VanMeter, and Elise M. Cardinale. 2014. "Neural and Cognitive Characteristics of Extraordinary Altruists." *Proceedings of the National Academy of Sciences* 111 (42): 15036–41.

Martin, Philip, and Martin Ruhs. 2011. "Labor Shortages and U.S. Immigration Reform: Promises and Perils of an Independent Commission." *International Migration Review* 45 (1): 174–87.

Martino, Daniel Di. 2022. *Improving U.S. Immigration: Employment-Based Visas Should Attract the World's Best, Not Repel Them.* New York: Manhattan Institute.

Martinsson, Johan, and Ulrika Andersson. 2021. *Swedish Trends 1986–2021.* Gothenberg: SOM Institute.

Marwell, Gerald. 1982. "Altruism and the Problem of Collective Action." In *Cooperation and Helping Behavior: Theories and Research*, ed. Valerian J. Derlega and Janusz Grzelak, 207–26. New York: Academic.

Massey, Douglas S., Jorge Durand, and Karen A. Pren. 2016. "Why Border Enforcement Backfired." *American Journal of Sociology* 121 (5): 1557–1600.

Maxwell, Rahsaan. 2019. "Cosmopolitan Immigration Attitudes in Large European Cities: Contextual or Compositional Effects?" *American Political Science Review* 113 (2): 456–74.

Mayda, Anna Maria, Giovanni Peri, and Walter Steingress. 2016. "Immigration to the U.S.: A Problem for the Republicans or the Democrats?" NBER Working Paper 21941. National Bureau of Economic Research.

Mazzolari, Francesca, and David Neumark. 2012. "Immigration and Product Diversity." *Journal of Population Economics* 25 (3): 1107–37.

McCarthy, Nolan. 2019. *Polarization: What Everyone Needs to Know*. Oxford: Oxford University Press.

McConnell, Allan. 2010. "Policy Success, Policy Failure and Grey Areas In-Between." *Journal of Public Policy* 30 (3): 345–62.

McCrone, David. 2002. "Who Do You Say You Are? Making Sense of National Identities in Modern Britain." *Ethnicities* 2 (3): 301–20.

McHugh, Margie. 2018. *In the Age of Trump: Populist Backlash and Progressive Resistance Create Divergent State Immigrant Integration Contexts*. Washington, DC: Migration Policy Institute.

Mercer, J. Jonathan. 2005. "Prospect Theory and Political Science." *Annual Review of Political Science* 8 (1): 1.

Mercier, Hugo. 2020. *Not Born Yesterday: The Science of Who We Trust and What We Believe*. Princeton, NJ: Princeton University Press.

Micklewright, John, and Anna Wright. 2004. "Private Donations for International Development." In *New Sources of Development Finance*, ed. A. B. Atkinson, 132–55. Oxford: Oxford University Press.

MIPEX. 2020. "Migration Integration Policy Index 2020: Main Findings." https://www.mipex.eu/key-findings.

Milanovic, Branko. 2015. "Global Inequality of Opportunity: How Much of Our Income Is Determined by Where We Live?" *Review of Economics and Statistics* 97 (2): 452–60.

Miller, Dale T. 1999. "The Norm of Self-Interest." *American Psychologist* 54 (12): 1053–60.

Miller, David. 2016. *Strangers in Our Midst: The Political Philosophy of Immigration*. Cambridge, MA: Harvard University Press.

Miller, David, and Sundas Ali. 2014. "Testing the National Identity Argument." *European Political Science Review* 6 (2): 237–59.

Mironova, Vera, and Sam Whitt. 2021. "Conflict and Parochialism Among Combatants and Civilians: Evidence from Ukraine." *Journal of Economic Psychology* 86: 102425.

Molloy, Raven, Christopher L. Smith, and Abigail Wozniak. 2011. "Internal Migration in the United States." *Journal of Economic Perspectives* 25 (3): 173–96.

Monroe, Kristen Renwick. 1998. *The Heart of Altruism Perceptions of a Common Humanity*. Princeton, NJ: Princeton University Press.

Mortimore, Roger. 2017. "Half of Public Support More Immigration by Highly Skilled Workers." Ipsos, April 18. https://www.ipsos.com/en-uk/half-public -support-more-immigration-highly-skilled-workers.

Munobwa, Jimmy Stephen, Fereshteh Ahmadi, and Mehrdad Darvishpour. 2021. "Diversity Barometer 2020: Attitudes Towards Immigration and Ethnic Diversity in Sweden." *Social Sciences* 10 (10): 401.

Muste, Christopher P. 2013. "The Dynamics of Immigration Opinion in the United States, 1992–2012." *Public Opinion Quarterly* 77 (1): 398–416.

Mutz, Diana C. 2018. "Status Threat, Not Economic Hardship, Explains the 2016 Presidential Vote." *Proceedings of the National Academy of Sciences* 115 (19): E4330–39.

Mutz, Diana C., and Eunji Kim. 2017. "The Impact of In-Group Favoritism on Trade Preferences." *International Organization* 71 (4): 827–50.

Mutz, Diana C., and Jeffery J. Mondak. 1997. "Dimensions of Sociotropic Behavior: Group-Based Judgments of Fairness and Well-Being." *American Journal of Political Science* 41 (1): 284–308.

Mylonas, Harris, and Maya Tudor. 2023. *Varieties of Nationalism: Communities, Narratives, Identities*. New York: Cambridge University Press.

National Academies of Sciences, Engineering, and Medicine. 2022. *Protecting U.S. Technological Advantage*. Washington, DC: National Academies Press.

Naumann, Elias, and Lukas F. Stoetzer. 2018. "Immigration and Support for Redistribution: Survey Experiments in Three European Countries." *West European Politics* 41 (1): 80–101.

Naumann, Elias, Lukas F. Stoetzer, and Giuseppe Pietrantuono. 2018. "Attitudes Towards Highly Skilled and Low-Skilled Immigration in Europe: A Survey Experiment in 15 European Countries." *European Journal of Political Research* 57 (4): 1009–30.

Newman, Benjamin J. 2013. "Acculturating Contexts and Anglo Opposition to Immigration in the United States." *American Journal of Political Science* 57 (2): 374–90.

Newman, Benjamin J., Todd K. Hartman, Patrick L. Lown, and Stanley Feldman. 2013. "Easing the Heavy Hand: Humanitarian Concern, Empathy, and Opinion on Immigration." *British Journal of Political Science* 45 (3): 1–25.

Newman, Benjamin J., and Neil Malhotra. 2019. "Economic Reasoning with a Racial Hue: Is the Immigration Consensus Purely Race Neutral?" *Journal of Politics* 81 (1): 153–66.

Norris, Pippa. 2023. *In Praise of Skepticism: Trust but Verify*. Oxford: Oxford University Press.

Norris, Pippa, and Ronald Inglehart. 2019. *Cultural Backlash: Trump, Brexit, and Authoritarian Populism*. New York: Cambridge University Press.

Nowrasteh, Alex. 2022. "Border Chaos and the Catch-22 of Immigration Reform." Cato at Liberty (blog), August 10. https://www.cato.org/blog/border-chaos-catch-22-immigration-reform.

Nowrasteh, Alex, Sarah Eckhardt, and Michael Howard. 2023. *The Fiscal Impact of Immigration in the United States*. Washington, DC: Cato Institute.

Nowrasteh, Alex, and Benjamin Powell. 2020. *Wretched Refuse? The Political Economy of Immigration and Institutions*. New York: Cambridge University Press.

Nowrasteh, Alex, and Ilya Somin. 2024. "The Case Against Nationalism." *National Affairs* 58. https://www.nationalaffairs.com/publications/detail/the-case-against-nationalism.

OECD. 2019a. "How Do OECD Countries Compare in Their Attractiveness for Talented Migrants?" *Migration Policy Debates* 19: 1–8.

——. 2019b. *Recruiting Immigrant Workers: Canada 2019*. Paris: OECD.

——. 2020. *International Migration Outlook 2020*. Paris: OECD.

——. 2021. *International Migration Outlook 2021*. Paris: OECD.

O'Grady, Tom, and Tarik Abou-Chadi. 2019. "Not So Responsive After All: European Parties Do Not Respond to Public Opinion Shifts Across Multiple Issue Dimensions." *Research and Politics* 6 (4): 1–17.

Oliner, Samuel P., and Pearl M. Oliner. 1988. *The Altruistic Personality: Rescuers of Jews in Nazi Europe*. New York: Free Press.

Oliver, J. Eric, and Tali Mendelberg. 2000. "Reconsidering the Environmental Determinants of White Racial Attitudes." *American Journal of Political Science* 44 (3): 574–89.

Ollerenshaw, Trent, and Ashley Jardina. 2023. "The Asymmetric Polarization of Immigration Opinion in the United States." *Public Opinion Quarterly* 87 (4): 1038–53.

Ortega, Francesc, and Giovanni Peri. 2013. "The Effect of Income and Immigration Policies on International Migration." *Migration Studies* 1 (1): 47–74.

Ozimek, Adam, Kenan Fikri, and John Lettieri. 2019. *From Managing Decline to Building the Future: Could a Heartland Visa Help Struggling Regions?* Washington, DC: Economic Innovation Group.

Paluck, Elizabeth Levy, Roni Porat, Chelsey S. Clark, and Donald P. Green. 2021. "Prejudice Reduction: Progress and Challenges." *Annual Review of Psychology* 72: 533–60.

Papademetriou, Demetrious, and Madeleine Sumption. 2011. *Rethinking Points Systems and Employer-Selected Immigration*. Washington, DC: Migration Policy Institute.

Paquet, Mireille. 2021. "Researching, Monitoring, and Managing: Immigration Policy Work in Canada." *American Review of Canadian Studies* 51 (1): 62–77.

Pardelli, Giuliana, and Alexander Kustov. 2022. "When Coethnicity Fails." *World Politics* 74 (2): 249–84.

Park, Alison, E. Clery, J. Curtice, M. Phillips, and D. Utting. 2012. *British Social Attitudes: The 29th Report*. London: NatCen Social Research.

Parusel, Bernd. 2015. "Lessons from Sweden." In *A Fair Deal on Talent—Fostering Just Migration Governance*, 145–52. Gütersloh: Verlag Bertelsmann Stiftung.

——. 2016. "Sweden's U-Turn on Asylum." *Forced Migration Review* 52: 89–90.

Patashnik, Eric M. 2023. *Countermobilization: Policy Feedback and Backlash in a Polarized Age*. Chicago: University of Chicago Press.

Pelling, Lisa. 2020. *Opening Doors to Labour Immigration: Lessons from Sweden*. Brussels: Foundation for European Progressive Studies.

Penner, Louis A., John F. Dovidio, Jane Allyn Piliavin, and David A. Schroeder. 2005. "Prosocial Behaviour: Multilevel Perspectives." *Annual Review of Psychology* 56 (1): 365–92.

Pereira, Cícero, Jorge Vala, and Rui Costa-Lopes. 2010. "From Prejudice to Discrimination: The Legitimizing Role of Perceived Threat in Discrimination Against Immigrants." *European Journal of Social Psychology* 40: 625–34.

Pérez, Efrén O. 2010. "Explicit Evidence on the Import of Implicit Attitudes: The IAT and Immigration Policy Judgments." *Political Behavior* 32: 517–45.

Peters, Margaret E. 2017. *Trading Barriers: Immigration and the Remaking of Globalization*. Princeton, NJ: Princeton University Press.

——. 2022. "Immigration in Historical Political Economy." In *The Oxford Handbook of Historical Political Economy*, ed. Jeffery A. Jenkins and Jared Rubin, 787–806. Oxford: Oxford University Press.

Pevnick, Ryan. 2024. "Immigration, Backlash, and Democracy." *American Political Science Review* 118 (1): 332–44.

Picot, Garnett, and Arthur Sweetman. 2011. "Canadian Immigration Policy and Immigrant Economic Outcomes: Why the Differences in Outcomes Between Sweden and Canada?" (translated). *Kanadamodellen. Där invandring leder till jobb* 25: 67–111.

Pierson, Paul. 1993. "When Effect Becomes Cause: Policy Feedback and Political Change." *World Politics* 45 (4): 595–628.

Pisor, Anne C., and Cody T. Ross. 2024. "Parochial Altruism: What It Is and Why It Varies." *Evolution and Human Behavior* 45 (1): 2–12.

Porter, Ethan, and Thomas J. Wood. 2019. *False Alarm: The Truth About Political Mistruths in the Trump Era*. New York: Cambridge University Press.

Pottie-Sherman, Yolande, and Rima Wilkes. 2017. "Does Size Really Matter? On the Relationship Between Immigrant Group Size and Anti-immigrant Prejudice." *International Migration Review* 51 (1): 218–50.

Poushter, Jacob, Janell Fetterolf, and Christine Tamir. 2019. *A Changing World: Global Views on Diversity, Gender Equality, Family Life and the Importance of Religion*. Washington, DC: Pew Research Center.

Powell, Benjamin. 2015. "Conclusion: Alternative Policy Perspectives." In *The Economics of Immigration: Market-Based Approaches, Social Science, and Public Policy*, ed. Benjamin Powell, 210–30. New York: Oxford University Press.

Pratto, Felicia, and Demis E. Glasford. 2008. "Ethnocentrism and the Value of a Human Life." *Journal of Personality and Social Psychology* 95: 1411–28.

Pritchett, Lant. 2006. *Let Their People Come: Breaking the Gridlock on Global Labor Mobility*. Washington, DC: Center for Global Development.

——. 2018. *Alleviating Global Poverty: Labor Mobility, Direct Assistance, and Economic Growth*. Washington, DC: Center for Global Development.

Prokop, Andrew. 2016. "What Hillary Clinton Told Wall Street Bankers in Private, According to Leaked Emails." *Vox*, October 7. https://www.vox.com/2016/10 /7/13206882/hillary-clinton-wikileaks-speeches-goldman.

Quillian, Lincoln. 1995. "Prejudice as a Response to Perceived Group Threat: Population Composition and Anti-immigrant and Racial Prejudice in Europe." *American Sociological Review* 60 (4): 586–611.

Radford, Jynnah, and Phillip Connor. 2019. "Canada Now Leads the World in Refugee Resettlement, Surpassing the U.S." Pew Research Center, June 19. https://www.pewresearch.org/short-reads/2019/06/19/canada-now-leads -the-world-in-refugee-resettlement-surpassing-the-u-s/.

Ramón, Cristobal, and Angelina Downs. 2020. *Immigration Systems in Transition*. Washington, DC: Bipartisan Policy Center.

Reitz, Jeffrey G. 2011. *Pro-immigration Canada: Social and Economic Roots of Popular Views*. IRPP Study No. 20. Montreal: Institute for Research on Public Policy.

Reny, Tyler T., Loren Collingwood, and Ali A. Valenzuela. 2019. "Vote Switching in the 2016 Election: Racial and Immigration Attitudes, Not Economics, Explains Shifts in White Voting." *Public Opinion Quarterly* 83 (1): 91–113.

Reny, Tyler, and Justin Gest. 2023. "Viewers Like You: The Effect of Elite Co-identity Reinforcement on U.S. Immigration Attitudes." *Politics, Groups, and Identities*, 1–17, https://doi.org/10.1080/21565503.2023.2265906.

Riek, Blake M., Eric W. Mania, and Samuel L. Gaertner. 2006. "Intergroup Threat and Outgroup Attitudes: A Meta-analytic Review." *Personality and Social Psychology Review* 10: 336–53.

Robalo, Pedro, Arthur Schram, and Joep Sonnemans. 2017. "Other-Regarding Preferences, In-Group Bias and Political Participation: An Experiment." *Journal of Economic Psychology* 62: 130–54.

Robinson, Lee, and Anita Käppeli. 2018. "Policies, Outcomes, and Populism: The Integration of Migrants in Sweden." Center for Global Development, November 15. https://www.cgdev.org/blog/policies-outcomes-and-populism -integration-migrants-sweden.

Rodriguez, Joshua. 2022. "Learning from the Best: What the World's Most Successful Immigrant Integration Countries Can Teach the U.S." Niskanen Center, March 28. https://www.niskanencenter.org/learning-from-the-best-what-the -worlds-most-successful-immigrant-integration-countries-can-teach-the-u-s/.

Rogers, Jonathan. 2014. "A Communotropic Theory of Economic Voting." *Electoral Studies* 36: 107–16.

Romano, Angelo, Daniel Balliet, Toshio Yamagishi, and James H. Liu. 2017. "Parochial Trust and Cooperation Across 17 Societies." *Proceedings of the National Academy of Sciences* 114 (44): 1–27.

Rooduijn, Matthijs, Stijn Van Kessel, Caterina Froio, Andrea Pirro, Sarah De Lange, Daphne Halikiopoulou, Paul Lewis, Cas Mudde, and Paul Taggart. 2019. "The PopuList: An Overview of Populist, Far Right, Far Left and Eurosceptic Parties in Europe." https://popu-list.org/

Rosenberg, Andrew S. 2022. *Undesirable Immigrants: Why Racism Persists in International Migration*. Princeton, NJ: Princeton University Press.

Rosenberg, János E. X. 2020. The German Skilled Immigration Act 2019 ('Fachkräfteeinwanderungsgesetz, FEG'). Master's thesis, Dalarna University.

Rosenbluth, Frances McCall, and Ian Shapiro. 2018. *Responsible Parties: Saving Democracy from Itself*. New Haven, CT: Yale University Press.

Rotemberg, Julio J. 2014. "Models of Caring, or Acting as if One Cared, About the Welfare of Others." *Annual Review of Economics* 6: 129–54.

Rothmund, Tobias, Laurits Bromme, and Flávio Azevedo. 2020. "Justice for the People? How Justice Sensitivity Can Foster and Impair Support for Populist Radical-Right Parties and Politicians in the United States and in Germany." *Political Psychology* 41 (3): 479–97.

Rothstein, B. 1998. *Just Institutions Matter: The Moral and Political Logic of the Universal Welfare State*. Cambridge: Cambridge University Press.

Rueda, David. 2017. "Food Comes First, Then Morals: Redistribution Preferences, Parochial Altruism and Immigration in Western Europe." *Journal of Politics* 80 (1): 225–39.

Ruedin, Didier. 2015. "Increasing Validity by Recombining Existing Indices: MIPEX as a Measure of Citizenship Models." *Social Science Quarterly* 96 (2): 629–38.

Ruhs, Martin. 2013. *The Price of Rights: Regulating International Labor Migration*. Princeton, NJ: Princeton University Press.

——. 2022. "Who Cares What the People Think? Public Attitudes and Refugee Protection in Europe." *Politics, Philosophy & Economics* 21 (3): 313–44.

Ruist, Joakim. 2015. "The Fiscal Cost of Refugee Immigration: The Example of Sweden." *Population and Development Review* 41 (4): 567–81.

Rusch, Hannes, Robert Böhm, and Benedikt Hermann. 2016. "Parochial Altruism: Pitfalls and Prospects." *Frontiers in Psychology* 7: 1004.

Ryan, Timothy J., and Hamilton Hall. 2019. "Actions Versus Consequences in Political Arguments: Insights from Moral Psychology." *Journal of Politics* 81 (2): 426–40.

Rydgren, Jens. 2008. "Immigration Sceptics, Xenophobes or Racists? Radical Right-Wing Voting in Six West European Countries." *European Journal of Political Research* 47: 737–65.

Saad, Lydia. 2023. "Americans Showing Increased Concern About Immigration." Gallup, February 13. https://news.gallup.com/poll/470426/americans-showing -increased-concern-immigration.aspx.

Salam, Reihan. 2018. *Melting Pot or Civil War? A Son of Immigrants Makes the Case Against Open Borders*. New York: Sentinel.

Sanandaji, Tino. 2020. *Mass Challenge: The Socioeconomic Impact of Migration to a Scandinavian Welfare State*. London: Palgrave Macmillan.

Schaffer, Lena Maria, and Gabriele Spilker. 2019. "Self-interest Versus Sociotropic Considerations: An Information-Based Perspective to Understanding Individuals' Trade Preferences." *Review of International Political Economy* 26 (6): 1266–92.

Schemitsch, Laura. 2022. "No More Excuses for Our Immigration Backlog." *CBA National*, February 4. https://nationalmagazine.ca/en-ca/articles/law/opinion/2022/no-more-excuses-for-our-immigration-backlog.

Schildkraut, Deborah J. 2011. "National Identity in the United States." In *Handbook of Identity Theory and Research*, vol. 2, ed. Seth J. Schwartz, Koen Luyckx, and Vivian L. Vignoles, 845–65. New York: Springer.

——. 2014. "Boundaries of American Identity: Evolving Understandings of 'Us.'" *Annual Review of Political Science* 17: 441–60.

Schnellenbach, Jan, and Christian Schubert. 2015. "Behavioral Political Economy: A Survey." *European Journal of Political Economy* 40: 395–417.

Schueth, Sam, and John O'Loughlin. 2008. "Belonging to the World: Cosmopolitanism in Geographic Contexts." *Geoforum* 39 (2): 926–41.

Schwartz, Cassilde, Miranda Simon, David Hudson, and Jennifer Van-Heerde-Hudson. 2021. "A Populist Paradox? How Brexit Softened Anti-immigrant Attitudes." *British Journal of Political Science* 51 (3): 1160–80.

Schwartz, Shalom H. 2007. "Universalism Values and the Inclusiveness of Our Moral Universe." *Journal of Cross-Cultural Psychology* 38 (6): 711–28.

Schwartz-Shea, Peregrine, and Randy T. Simmons. 1991. "Egoism, Parochialism, and Universalism: Experimental Evidence from the Layered Prisoners' Dilemma." *Rationality and Society* 3 (1): 106–32.

Sears, David O., and Carolyn L. Funk. 1990. "The Limited Effect of Economic Self-Interest on the Political Attitudes of the Mass Public." *Journal of Behavioral Economics* 19 (3): 247–71.

——. 1991. "The Role of Self-Interest in Social and Political Attitudes." *Advances in Experimental Social Psychology* 24: 1–91.

Sen, Amartya. 1977. "Rational Fools: A Critique of the Behavioral Foundations of Economic Theory." *Philosophy & Public Affairs* 6 (4): 317–44.

Shayo, Moses. 2009. "A Model of Social Identity with an Application to Political Economy: Nation, Class, and Redistribution." *American Political Science Review* 103 (2): 147–74.

Shulman, Stephen. 2002. "Challenging the Civic/Ethnic and West/East Dichotomies in the Study of Nationalism." *Comparative Political Studies* 35 (5): 554–85.

Sides, John, Michael Tesler, and Lynn Vavreck. 2018. *Identity Crisis: The 2016 Presidential Campaign and the Battle for the Meaning of America*. Princeton, NJ: Princeton University Press.

Simler, Kevin, and Robin Hanson. 2018. *The Elephant in the Brain: Hidden Motives in Everyday Life*. New York: Oxford University Press.

Simmons, Alan B., and Kieran Keohane. 1992. "Canadian Immigration Policy: State Strategies and the Quest for Legitimacy." *Canadian Review of Sociology* 29 (4): 421–52.

Singer, Peter. 2015. *The Most Good You Can Do: How Effective Altruism Is Changing Ideas About Living Ethically.* New Haven, CT: Yale University Press.

Skinner, Gideon, and Glenn Gottfried. 2017. *Global Views on Immigration and the Refugee Crisis.* Paris: Ipsos. https://www.ipsos.com/sites/default/files/ct/news/documents/2017-09/Global_Advisor_Immigration.pdf.

Slothuus, Rune, and Martin Bisgaard. 2021. "How Political Parties Shape Public Opinion in the Real World." *American Journal of Political Science* 65 (4): 896–911.

Smith, Rogers M. 2004. "Identities, Interests, and the Future of Political Science." *Perspectives on Politics* 2 (2): 301–12.

Smith, Tom W. 2009. "Loving and Caring in the United States: Trends and Correlates of Empathy, Altruism, and Related Constructs." In *The Science of Compassionate Love: Theory, Research, and Applications*, ed. Beverley Fehr, Susan Sprecher, and Lynn G. Underwood, 81–119. New York: Wiley-Blackwell.

Sniderman, Paul M., and Sean M. Theriault. 2004. "The Structure of Political Argument and the Logic of Issue Framing." In *Studies in Public Opinion: Attitudes, Nonattitudes, Measurement Error, and Change*, vol. 3, ed. Willem E. Saris and Paul M. Sniderman, 133–65. Princeton, NJ: Princeton University Press.

Sobolewska, Maria, and Robert Ford. 2020. *Brexitland.* Cambridge: Cambridge University Press.

Sobolewska, Maria, Silvia Galandini, and Laurence Lessard-Phillips. 2017. "The Public View of Immigrant Integration: Multidimensional and Consensual. Evidence from Survey Experiments in the UK and the Netherlands." *Journal of Ethnic and Migration Studies* 43 (1): 58–79.

Solodoch, Omer. 2021. "Regaining Control? The Political Impact of Policy Responses to Refugee Crises." *International Organization* 75 (3): 735–68.

Somin, Ilya. 2015. "The Ongoing Debate Over Political Ignorance: Reply to My Critics." *Critical Review* 27 (3–4): 380–414.

Sommer, Udi, Or Rappel-Kroyzer, Amy Adamczyk, Lindsay Lerner, and Anna Weiner. 2023. "The Political Ramifications of Judicial Institutions: Establishing a Link Between Dobbs and Gender Disparities in the 2022 Midterms." *Socius* 9, https://doi.org/10.1177/23780231231177157.

Song, Sarah. 2018. "Political Theories of Migration." *Annual Review of Political Science* 21 (1): 385–402.

Soroka, Stuart, Patrick Fournier, and Lilach Nir. 2019. "Cross-National Evidence of a Negativity Bias in Psychophysiological Reactions to News." *Proceedings of the National Academy of Sciences of the United States of America* 116 (38): 18888–92.

Spinner-Halev, Jeff, and Elizabeth Theiss-Morse. 2003. "National Identity and Self-Esteem." *Perspectives on Politics* 1 (3): 515–32.

Stapp, Alec, and Jeremy Neufeld. 2022. *The Case for High-Skilled Immigration Reform (and How to Make It Happen).* Washington, DC: Institute for Progress.

Stenner, Karen. 2005. *The Authoritarian Dynamic*. New York: Cambridge University Press.

Stephan, Walter G., Oscar Ybarra, and Kimberly Rios Morrison. 2009. "Intergroup Threat Theory." In *Handbook of Prejudice Stereotyping and Discrimination*, ed. Todd D. Nelson, 43–59. New York: Psychology.

Stolcke, Verena. 1995. "Talking Culture: New Rhetorics, New Boundaries of Exclusion in Europe." *Current Anthropology* 36: 1–24.

Straume, Sivert, and Magnus Odèen. 2010. "International and Domestic Altruism: A Study Among the Adult Population in Norway." *Journal of Applied Social Psychology* 40 (3): 618–35.

Stryker, Sheldon, and Richard T. Serpe. 1994. "Identity Salience and Psychological Centrality: Equivalent, Overlapping, or Complementary Concepts?" *Social Psychology Quarterly* 57 (1): 16.

Sumption, Madeleine, and Peter William Walsh. 2022. "The Points System Is Dead. Long Live the Points System! Why Immigration Policymakers in the UK Are Never Quite Happy with Their Points Systems." *Journal of Immigrant & Refugee Studies* 21 (1): 89–103.

Tajfel, Henry, and John C. Turner. 1986. "The Social Identity Theory of Intergroup Behavior." In *Psychology of Intergroup Relations*, ed. William G. Austin and Stephen Worchel, 7–24. Chicago: Nelson-Hall.

Talaska, Cara A., Susan T. Fiske, and Shelly Chaiken. 2008. "Legitimating Racial Discrimination: Emotions, Not Beliefs, Best Predict Discrimination in a Meta-analysis." *Social Justice Research* 21 (2008): 263–96.

Tamir, Yael. 2020. *Why Nationalism*. Princeton, NJ: Princeton University Press.

Tankard, Margaret E., and Elizabeth Levy Paluck. 2016. "Norm Perception as a Vehicle for Social Change." *Social Issues and Policy Review* 10 (1): 181–211.

Taylor, Zack. 2021. "The Political Geography of Immigration: Party Competition for Immigrants' Votes in Canada, 1997–2019." *American Review of Canadian Studies* 51 (1): 18–40.

Tetlock, Philip E. 2003. "Thinking the Unthinkable: Sacred Values and Taboo Cognitions." *Trends in Cognitive Sciences* 7 (7): 320–24.

Theiss-Morse, Elizabeth. 2009. *Who Counts as an American? The Boundaries of National Identity*. Cambridge: Cambridge University Press.

Thomas, Sue. 2008. " 'Backlash' and Its Utility to Political Scientists." *Politics and Gender* 4 (4): 615–23.

Thomsen, Lotte, Eva G. T. Green, and Jim Sidanius. 2008. "We Will Hunt Them Down: How Social Dominance Orientation and Right-Wing Authoritarianism Fuel Ethnic Persecution of Immigrants in Fundamentally Different Ways." *Journal of Experimental Social Psychology* 44: 1455–64.

Thorson, Emily. 2024. *The Invented State: Policy Misperceptions in the American Public*. New York: Oxford University Press.

Thorson, Emily, and Lamis Abdelaaty. 2023. "Misperceptions About Refugee Policy." *American Political Science Review* 117 (3): 1123–29.

Titmuss, Richard Morris. 1997. *The Gift Relationship from Human Blood to Social Policy.* New York: New Press.

Transue, John E. 2007. "Identity Salience, Identity Acceptance, and Racial Policy Attitudes: American National Identity as a Uniting Force." *American Journal of Political Science* 51 (1): 78–91.

Triadafilopoulos, Triadafilos. 2013. "Dismantling White Canada: Race, Rights, and the Origins of the Points System." In *Wanted and Welcome? Policies for Highly Skilled Immigrants in Comparative Perspective*, ed. Triadafilos Triadafilopoulos, 15–37. New York: Springer.

——. 2021. "The Foundations, Limits, and Consequences of Immigration Exceptionalism in Canada." *American Review of Canadian Studies* 51 (1): 3–17.

——. 2022. "Good and Lucky: Explaining Canada's Successful Immigration Policies." In *Policy Success in Canada: Cases, Lessons, Challenges*, ed. Evert Lindquist, Michael Howlett, Grace Skogstad, and Geneviève Tellier, 161–82. Oxford: Oxford University Press.

Triandafyllidou, Anna. 2001. *Immigrants and National Identity in Europe.* London: Routledge.

Troper, Harold. 1993. "Canada's Immigration Policy Since 1945." *International Journal* 48 (2): 255.

Ugland, Trygve. 2014. "Canada as an Inspirational Model: Reforming Scandinavian Immigration and Integration Policies." *Nordic Journal of Migration Research* 4 (3): 144.

Uhlmann, Eric Luis, David A. Pizarro, David Tannenbaum, and Peter H. Ditto. 2009. "The Motivated Use of Moral Principles." *Judgment and Decision Making* 4 (6): 476–91.

United Nations. 2018. *World Migration Report 2018.* Geneva: International Organization for Migration.

Ura, Joseph Daniel. 2014. "Backlash and Legitimation: Macro Political Responses to Supreme Court Decisions." *American Journal of Political Science* 58 (1): 110–26.

Vala, Jorge, Cícero Pereira, and Rui Costa-Lopes. 2009. "Is the Attribution of Cultural Differences to Minorities an Expression of Racial Prejudice?" *International Journal of Psychology* 44 (1): 20–28.

van de Beek, Jan H., Hans Roodenburg, Joop Hartog, and Gerrit W. Kreffer. 2023. *Borderless Welfare State: The Consequences of Immigration for Public Finances.* Zeist, Netherlands: Demo-Demo.

van de Wardt, Marc, Catherine E. De Vries, and Sara B. Hobolt. 2014. "Exploiting the Cracks: Wedge Issues in Multiparty Competition." *Journal of Politics* 76 (4): 986–99.

van der Duin, David, Francesco Nicoli, and Brian Burgoon. 2023. "Towards a Theory of Genuine Sociotropic Concern: The Three Dimensions of Caring About the Collective Interest. A Theory Building Exercise and Systematic Literature Review." Amsterdam Centre for European Studies Research Paper No. 3. Amsterdam Centre for European Studies.

Van Hauwaert, Steven M. 2023. "Immigration as a Thermostat? Public Opinion and Immigration Policy Across Western Europe (1980–2017)." *Journal of European Public Policy* 30 (12): 2665–91.

van Lange, Paul, Daniel P. Balliet, Craig D. Parks, and Mark Vugt. 2014. *Social Dilemmas: Understanding Human Cooperation*. New York: Oxford University Press.

Vasilopoulou, Sofia, and Liisa Talving. 2019. "Opportunity or Threat? Public Attitudes Towards EU Freedom of Movement." *Journal of European Public Policy* 26 (6): 805–23.

Visintin, Stefano, Kea Tijdens, and Maarten van Klaveren. 2015. "Skill Mismatch Among Migrant Workers: Evidence from a Large Multi-country Dataset." *IZA Journal of Migration* 4: 14.

vom Hau, Matthias, Marc Helbling, Maya Tudor, Andreas Wimmer, and Daphne Halikiopoulou. 2023. "The Consequences of Nationalism: A Scholarly Exchange." *Nations and Nationalism* 29 (3): 810–30.

Voss, Kim, Fabiana Silva, and Irene Bloemraad. 2020. "The Limits of Rights: Claims-Making on Behalf of Immigrants." *Journal of Ethnic and Migration Studies* 46 (4): 791–819.

Vrânceanu, Alina, and Romain Lachat. 2021. "Do Parties Influence Public Opinion on Immigration? Evidence from Europe." *Journal of Elections, Public Opinion and Parties* 31 (1): 1–21.

Wagner, Ulrich, Julia C. Becker, Oliver Christ, Thomas F. Pettigrew, and Peter Schmidt. 2012. "A Longitudinal Test of the Relation Between German Nationalism, Patriotism, and Outgroup Derogation." *European Sociological Review* 28: 319–32.

Wallace, Rebecca, Erin Tolley, and Madison Vonk. 2021. *Multiculturalism Policy Index: Immigrant Minority Policies*, 3rd ed. Kingston, ON: Queen's University School of Policy Studies.

Weeden, Jason, and Robert Kurzban. 2017. "Self-Interest Is Often a Major Determinant of Issue Attitudes." *Political Psychology* 38: 67–90.

Weiner, Rachel. 2013. "How Immigration Reform Failed, Over and Over." *Washington Post*, January 30. https://www.washingtonpost.com/news/the-fix/wp/2013/01/30/how-immigration-reform-failed-over-and-over/.

Weldon, Steven A. 2006. "The Institutional Context of Tolerance for Ethnic Minorities: A Comparative, Multilevel Analysis of Western Europe." *American Journal of Political Science* 50 (2): 331–49.

Westin, Charles. 2006. *Sweden: Restrictive Immigration Policy and Multiculturalism*. Washington, DC: Migration Policy Institute.

Wiesbrock, Anja. 2011. "The Integration of Immigrants in Sweden: A Model for the European Union?" *International Migration* 49 (4): 48–66.

Williamson, Scott, Claire L. Adida, Adeline Lo, Melina R. Platas, Lauren Prather, and Seth H. Werfel. 2021. "Family Matters: How Immigrant Histories Can Promote Inclusion." *American Political Science Review* 115 (2): 686–93.

Wimmer, Andreas. 1997. "Explaining Xenophobia and Racism: A Critical Review of Current Research Approaches." *Ethnic and Racial Studies* 20: 17–41.

———. 2018. *Nation Building: Why Some Countries Come Together While Others Fall Apart*. Princeton, NJ: Princeton University Press.

Wimmer, Andreas, and Nina Glick Schiller. 2003. "Methodological Nationalism, the Social Sciences, and the Study of Migration: An Essay in Historical Epistemology." *International Migration Review* 37 (3): 576–610.

Wintour, Patrick. 2018. "Hillary Clinton: Europe Must Curb Immigration to Stop Rightwing Populists." *Guardian*, November 22. https://www.theguardian.com/world/2018/nov/22/hillary-clinton-europe-must-curb-immigration-stop-populists-trump-brexit.

Wit, Arjaan P., and Norbert L. Kerr. 2002. " 'Me Versus Just Us Versus Us All' Categorization and Cooperation in Nested Social Dilemmas." *Journal of Personality and Social Psychology* 83 (3): 616–37.

Wlezien, Christopher. 1995. "The Public as Thermostat: Dynamics of Preferences for Spending." *American Journal of Political Science* 39 (4): 981.

Wlezien, Christopher, and Stuart N. Soroka. 2016. "Public Opinion and Public Policy." *Oxford Research Encyclopedia of Politics*. https://oxfordre.com/politics/display/10.1093/acrefore/9780190228637.001.0001/acrefore-9780190228637-e-74.

Wong, Cara. 2010. *Boundaries of Obligation in American Politics: Geographic, National, and Racial Communities*. New York: Cambridge University Press.

Wooldridge, Adrian. 2022. "Sweden Is Rethinking What Makes It Great." *Bloomberg*, November 22. https://www.bloomberg.com/opinion/articles/2022-11-22/sweden-is-rethinking-what-makes-it-great.

Wright, Matthew, Jack Citrin, and Jonathan Wand. 2012. "Alternative Measures of American National Identity: Implications for the Civic-Ethnic Distinction." *Political Psychology* 33: 469–82.

Wright, Matthew, Richard Johnston, Jack Citrin, and Stuart Soroka. 2017. "Multiculturalism and Muslim Accommodation: Policy and Predisposition Across Three Political Contexts." *Comparative Political Studies* 50 (1): 102–32.

Wright, Matthew, and Morris Levy. 2020a. "American Public Opinion on Immigration: Nativist, Polarized, or Ambivalent?" *International Migration* 58 (6): 77–95.

———. 2020b. *Immigration and the American Ethos*. Cambridge: Cambridge University Press.

Yale-Loehr, Stephen, and Mackenzie Eason. 2020. *Recruiting for the Future: A Realistic Road to a Points-Tested Visa Program in the United States*. Technical report. Ithaca, NY: Cornell University Law School.

Yamagishi, Toshio, and Nobuhiro Mifune. 2008. "Does Shared Group Membership Promote Altruism? Fear, Greed, and Reputation." *Rationality and Society* 20 (1): 5–30.

Yglesias, Matthew. 2020. *One Billion Americans: The Case for Thinking Bigger*. New York: Portfolio.

Yogeeswaran, Kumar, and Nilanjana Dasgupta. 2014. "Conceptions of National Identity in a Globalised World: Antecedents and Consequences." *European Review of Social Psychology* 25 (1): 189–227.

Yukich, Grace. 2013. "New Sanctuary Movement Constructing the Model Immigrant: Movement Strategy and Immigrant Deservingness in the New Sanctuary Movement." *Social Problems* 60 (3): 302–20.

Zavodny, Madeline. 2023. "Should Countries Auction Immigrant Visas? Selling the Right to Immigrate to the Highest Bidders Would Allocate Visas Efficiently but Might Raise Ethical Concerns." Article No. 202. IZA World of Labor.

Zhou, Yang-Yang, and Jason Lyall. 2024. "Prolonged Contact Does Not Reshape Locals' Attitudes Toward Migrants in Wartime Settings: Experimental Evidence from Afghanistan." *American Journal of Political Science*, ahead of print, April 24, https://doi.org/10.1111/ajps.12862.

INDEX

Abbott, Tony, 15
AfD. *See* Alternative für Deutschland
age, impact in national interest
   randomized study, 99–100
Alternative für Deutschland (AfD),
   Germany, 136
altruism, 2, 3; Abbott on
   immigration support and
   misplaced, 15; bounded,
   17; compatriots priority in
   public policy and, 16–17, 70;
   dilemma of open immigration
   and nationalism, 15–17, 203;
   effective and extraordinary, 36;
   freer immigration opposition
   from voters with, 17, 66–67,
   98; Gallup World Poll data
   on nonrelationship with
   immigration attitudes, 22, 58,
   61, 62; GSS on public opinion
   connection to, 58; national
   favoritism and immigration, 57,
   58, 66; pro-immigration attitudes
by, 66–67, 67; pro-immigration
   policies appeal to, 15; selfishness
   weakness and power of, 35–37, 52;
   self-report surveys on preferences
   of, 57–58; voters pro-immigration
   or anti-immigration stance on
   compatriots, 22, 105–6. *See also*
   humanitarian altruism
altruism hypothesis, 45
altruism in politics: cross-national
   surveys on political preferences,
   57; global patterns of, 58–61, 60,
   62; political participation in OECD
   countries relationship to, 59, 60;
   political science and behavioral/
   attitudinal outcomes, 15, 246
altruist dilemma hypothesis, 45;
   in-group intrinsic bias, 44;
   national favoritism interaction
   with altruism, 44; on nationalism
   and open immigration policies,
   15–17, 203
altruistic cosmopolitanism, 65

economic development, migration as
form of, xii–xiii, 7–8
economic game, for preference
revelation design: altruistic
nationalism prevalence in, 72–74,
73, 75; charity donations in, 71–72;
on egoist, parochial altruism,
humanitarian altruism types,
71–72; incentivized participants
with raffle money, 48, 71–74, *73,
75*. *See also* incentivized economic
game
economic immigration, 261n14;
Sweden restriction of, 187, 189
economic-oriented immigration
flows, of high-income countries,
171–72
economic selection, of Canada, 174
"Economies and Emigration"
(Clemens), ix
effective altruism, 36
"Efficiency Gain from Elimination
of International Barriers
(Percent of World GDP)"
(Clemens), xii
egoism, 40, *41*; advancement of
own well-being, 41, 42; charity
donations absence in, 23,
72–74, *73*
employment bans, for refugees and
asylum seekers, 125
Employment Permits Act (2006),
Ireland, 241
endogeneity concerns, 22
enlightened national interest
approach, 208–9
ethics, immigration restrictions
and, 7
ethnocentrism, 117, 261n14
Europe: cross-sectional data-set
on pro-immigration policies

backlash with countries of,
135–42, *138, 139, 140, 141*; growing
acceptance of immigration in, 11;
immigration policy data on, 48;
increase in populist voting and
immigration policy openness, 137,
138; pro-immigration conservative
reforms in, 151; public opinion
preference for white immigrants
from, 31
European refugee crisis
(2015–2016), 111
European Union (EU): as desirable
immigration destination, 5; on
immigration challenges, 1; UKIP
and Leave campaign withdrawal of
UK from, 47
existing immigrant population,
citizen opinions about, 6
extraordinary altruism, 36

Fachkräfteeinwanderungsgesetz (FEG)
(Skilled Immigration Act) (2020),
Germany, 153–55, 213
family migration: populist voters and,
24; voters support of immediate
relatives immigration, 158; work-
related immigration to high-
income countries and, 128–29
family reunification, xvii, 7, 19;
Sweden policies of, 187
favoritism: in-group, xiii, 38, *41*, 42,
44, 53; national, *41*, 55, 57, 58, 63,
65, 233
FEG. See *Fachkräfteeinwanderungsgesetz*
foreigners: chauvinism denigration
of, 38; compatriots benefits at
expense of well-being of, 29, 51,
113; DB policymaking principle on
help in need, 224; discounted value
of lives of, 52

parochial altruism (*continued*)
case selection, 46; Gallup World
Poll use in, 46; GSS use in, 46;
incentivized charity game on
prosocial motivations, 48, 71–74,
73, 75; individual variation of,
45; International Social Survey
Programme use, 46; national
parochial altruism hypothesis,
45, 101; nonimmigration
political attitudes questions
for comparison, 48; original
population-based survey in, 47;
parochial altruism hypothesis,
45; political behavior explained
from, 205, *247*; scope conditions
and case selection, 45–46;
support of policies benefiting
their nation, 52, 205; UK and
U.S. surveys on immigration
attitudes and policy choice,
47–48; value of foreigner lives
discounted, 52
parochial altruism hypothesis, 45
patriotism, 17, 210; commitments to
compatriots by, 38
persuasion: DB immigration policies
study on factors for, 159–62,
161; durable in DB immigration
policies, 107–9; efforts for pro-
immigration policies, 25, 48, 108–9;
immigration popularity efforts
and failure of common, 109–14;
through policymaking, 24, 109,
118–20, 204–7
persuasion by policy design, 204, 206;
altruistic nationalism and, 23–24
place-based visas, 218, 219
point-based system: of Canada,
25, 174, 178, 179, 199, 213, 214;
immigration popularity beyond

skills and consideration for,
214–20; UK difficulty with, 216
policy choice experiment, on
parochial altruism, 3, 23, 30
policymaking: Canada challenges
in immigration, 184–85; DB,
120–26, 209–10, 222–26; delegation
to independent agencies, 119;
persuasion through, 24, 109,
118–20, 204–7; public opinion and,
25, 48, 204–7, 213; responsible
and responsive, 109, 206. *See also*
demonstrably beneficial (DB)
policymaking
political attitudes: altruistic
nationalism as determinant of,
67–68, *68*; altruistic nationalism
data and, 75–77, *76, 77*; parochial
altruism and nonimmigration, 48
political behavior: national identity
predictor of, 50; parochial altruism
explanation for, 205, *247*
political decision-making, 96, 207;
nationalism guiding of, 30; voters
value on well-being of others in, 83
political participation: across OECD
countries, altruism and, 59, *60*;
prosocial motivations for, 35
political preferences, cross-national
surveys on altruism and, 57
political surveys, incentivized
economic games in, 47
political tragedy, of international
migration, 4–8
politicians: immigration
misinformation from, xiii; pro-
immigration commitments for
existing immigrants, 8–9
politics: dysfunctional of illegal
immigration across border,
19; nationalism as parochial

social identity theory, self-interest and, 52

societal locus of control, nationalism as parochial altruism on, 54–56

sociotropic perceptions: public opinion determined by, 125; public opinion on immigration and, 105

sociotropic politics, 256n83; high-skilled immigrants social benefit, 54; immigration public attitudes from, 105; nationalism as parochial altruism, 54–56

South Korea, as desirable immigration destination, 5

stability and longevity, of immigration attitudes, 110–11, 114

statistical discrimination, nationalism as parochial altruism on, 53–54

Stenergard, Maria Malmer, 190

stereotypes: on demographic change, 261n14; immigrants inaccurate, 156–57

student migration, xvii; Malengo movement of students from low-income to high-income countries, 218–19; popularity of, 157–58

Sweden, x; absence of skilled immigration priority, 186, 189; Canada comparison to, 3, 24–25, 48, 174–76, 175, 195–99; CDI category of migration first ranking, 186–87; Center for Global Development on immigration policies of, 195; cosmopolitan opposition to freer immigration, 193–95, 194; Democrats new immigration restrictions, 190, 192; as desirable immigration destination, 174; family reunification policies, 187; foreign professionals and immigration policies of, xii; Green

Party alliance with, 189; historical evolution of immigration politics in, 109; humanitarian approach to freer immigration, 48, 174, 175, 186; immigration integration and, 186, 187, 191, 194; immigration policies design in, xii, 109, 173–76, 185–95, 204; immigration reforms in 2008, 190; labor immigration policies in, 189, 190; as moral superpower, 174, 185–89; multiculturalism commitment of, 174, 177, 187–88; open immigration suppression by right-wing government, 21, 189–93; populism rise and end of openness, 189–93; refugee and asylum seekers permanent immigration in, 174, 186, 187, 188, 189, 192–93; restricted economic immigration by, 187, 189; restricted immigration admissions, 5, 109, 194; universalist immigration approach in, 25, 174

Swedish Migration Agency, 186; on humanitarian goals of immigration, 112

Switzerland, freer immigration and, 5

Thatcher, Margaret, 15

threat: chaos theory on immigration perceived as, 55; group, 34, 54–56, 131–32; racial prejudice and arguments on, 31

Timbro Authoritarian Populism Index, 136

trade-offs, in immigration policies, 19

Trump, Donald, 127, 206; attack on U.S. Capitol on January 6, 2021, 128; DACA program ending by, 148–49; election 2016 of, 111; negative immigration attitudes, 47

GPSR Authorized Representative: Easy Access System Europe, Mustamäe tee 50, 10621 Tallinn, Estonia, gpsr.requests@easproject.com